A history of water in modern England and Wales

MANCHESTER
UNIVERSITY PRESS

A history of water in modern England and Wales

John Hassan

Manchester University Press
Manchester and New York

distributed exclusively in the USA by St. Martin's Press

Published by Manchester University Press
Oxford Road, Manchester M13 9NR, UK
and Room 400, 175 Fifth Avenue, New York, NY 10010, USA

Distributed exclusively in the USA by
St. Martin's Press, Inc., 175 Fifth Avenue, New York,
NY 10010, USA

Distributed exclusively in Canada by
UBC Press, University of British Columbia, 6344 Memorial Road,
Vancouver, BC, Canada V6T 1Z2

British Library Cataloguing-in-Publication Data
A catalogue record for this book is available from the British Library

Library of Congress Cataloging-in-Publication Data applied for

ISBN 0 7190 4308 5 *hardback*

First published 1998

02 01 00 99 98   10 9 8 7 6 5 4 3 2 1

Typeset by Servis Filmsetting Ltd, Manchester
Printed in Great Britain
by Bookcraft (Bath) Ltd, Midsomer Norton

Contents

Tables

Preface

Many people have contributed to the making of this book. I express my gratitude to my family, Elizabeth, Matthew and David, for their toleration, optimism and faith. In the Department of Economics and Economic History at the Manchester Metropolitan University, my thanks are due to many people who have assisted me in my endeavours. While it is impractical to mention at least a dozen colleagues, and to therefore worry about exclusions from the roll-call, I would nevertheless particularly wish to refer to Alan Fowler, Paul Nunn and Professor Derek Aldcroft, who in different ways have provided invaluable support. My thanks are due to Dr Peter Taylor, while a Research Fellow in the Department, for directing me to some relevant material. Thanks are due to Helen Dawson for preparing the final manuscript. I also acknowledge with gratitude the encouragement and help provided by Bob Millward, Professor of Economic History at Manchester University, Dr Christopher Hamlin of the University of Notre Dame, and Professor Bill Luckin of Bolton Institute.

Much of the material used in the book was collected over the years at public libraries, and gratitude is due to the staff at Manchester Central Library, the John Rylands Library at Manchester University and All Saints Library of the Manchester Metropolitan University. Perusal of material held at the Public Record Office, Kew, is invaluable for grasping the Westminster and Whitehall perspectives on public policy issues. A selective understanding of events at a local or regional level is obtained through consulting the material held at many local history libraries or collections, including Bristol Central Library, Bristol Record Office, Bolton Central Library, Bury Reference Library, the Lancashire Record Office, and the West Riding of Yorkshire Record Office. The remarkable patience shown and assistance provided by staff who work in these institutions have been indispensable for this work – my thanks are due to them all. Information and material has also been provided by the Water Services Association, the National Rivers Authority, and North West Water; and gratitude is expressed to these organisations and their staff. A final word of thanks to Tony Wakefield is due; chairman of the Coastal Anti-Pollution League for some thirty years, he has been instrumental in making their records available to researchers.

John Hassan

Abbreviations

ACW	Advisory Committee on Water
AMP	asset management plan
AWE	Association of Waterworks Engineers
BA	Bolton Archives and Local Studies Library
BOD	British oxygen demand
BRL	Bury Reference Library
BRO	Bristol Record Office
BWA	British Waterworks Association
CACW	Central Advisory Committee on Water
CCTV	closed-circuit television
CEGB	Central Electricity Generating Board
CMP	catchment management planning
COPA	Control of Pollution Act
CWPU	Central Water Policy Unit
DoE	Department of the Environment
DSIR	Department of Scientific and Industrial Research
DVWB	Derwent Valley Water Board
DWI	Drinking Water Inspectorate
EAP	Environmental Action Programme
EC	European Community
EPA	Environmental Protection Agency
EQO	environmental quality objective
FBI	Federation of British Industry
ghd	gallons per head per day
gpd	gallons per day
HL	House of Lords
HMIP	Her Majesty's Inspectorate of Pollution
IPC	integrated pollution control
JCWR	Joint Committee on Water Resources
LGB	Local Government Board
LRO	Lancashire Record Office

MAF   Ministry of Agriculture and Fisheries
MHLG   Ministry of Housing and Local Government
MWB   Metropolitan Water Board
MYB   *Municipal Year Book*
NRA   National Rivers Authority
NWC   National Water Council
NWWA   North West Water Authority
Ofwat   Office of Water Services
PCB   polychlorinated biphenyl
PPP   polluter pays principle
PRO   Public Record Office (Kew)
RA   River Authority
RB   West Riding of Yorkshire River Board Records
RCEP   Royal Commission on Environmental Pollution
RWA   Regional Water Authority
SC   Select Committee
SCORP   Standing Committee on Rivers Pollution
STW   sewage treatment works
SWQO   statutory water quality objective
TWE   *Transactions of the British Association of Waterworks Engineers*, later
              Transactions of the Association of Water Engineers, later *Transactions of
              the Institute of Water Engineers*
UES   uniform emission standards
WB   Water Board
WOC   water supply-only company
WPRL   Water Pollution Research Laboratory
WRB   Water Resources Board
WRO   West Riding of Yorkshire Record Office
WSA   Water Services Association
WSC   water service company
WWE   *Water and Water Engineering*

1

Introduction

Aims

Water has, until recently, been a fairly neglected area of historical investigation. Useful introductory material could be found in the studies by Porter (1978), Parker and Penning-Rowsell (1980) and Smith (1972). The historical treatment in these books was, however, subsidiary to the authors' contemporary, policy-orientated concerns. An important theme to emerge in them was the centrality of physical concepts, particularly the water cycle and the watershed basin, in any study of water.

There is a large literature of often commissioned or commemorative histories, which traces the development of water supplies to particular towns. While some (for example, Rennison 1979) constitute fine municipal or business histories, many are limited in scope, with an emphasis upon administrative responses to the growing urban demand for water.

The historiography of water has improved considerably since the mid-1980s. Barty-King (1992) provides a very good survey of the organisational and technological history of the water supply and sewage treatment sectors since about 1800, although with a tendency to rather uncritically celebrate the industry's development. In his studies of 1988 and 1994 Kinnersley offers a searching, if broad-brush, investigation of the interactions between hydrological imperatives, environmental threats, the struggles among water users and policy and political outcomes. The most extensive scholarly treatment of the history of water is contained in John Sheail's prolific work. He has not only studied the history of environmental movements, but he has also examined the interrelationships between water resource development, local and central government, the planning and policy-making processes and the activities of pressure groups. One disadvantage is that his work is dispersed across a large number of case-studies and publications, which obviously reduces its accessibility for the student.

If Sheail and Kinnersley have contributed to the political history of the water industry, the economic historiography of water is less well developed. Shifts in ownership patterns have been discussed by Millward (1989) and Hassan (1985) (see also Foreman-Peck and Millward 1995). These studies utilise concepts drawn from microeconomic theory in an attempt to explain the development of the water supply industry. Emphasis is placed upon its natural monopoly characteristics, externalities, and the regulatory framework. The value of integrating economic concepts into a history of water is indicated below.

Over the last twenty-five years environmental history as a discrete sub-discipline has begun to attract the interest of scholars. Despite the common interest in industrialisation, however, it is only very recently that economic history in Britain has engaged with this field. A number of factors account for the comparative neglect. First, the environment as a historical theme is relatively under-developed in this country in comparison with, for example, France, where the interdisciplinary methodologies favoured by historians have frequently led to the exploration of the interactions between humanity and nature, or the United States, where the wilderness, the frontier and conservation have loomed large. Second, environmental history is thematically diffuse, characterised by a variety of approaches which do not readily lend themselves to synthesis. The broad temporal and spatial perspectives of some environmental historians, many of whom are based in the natural sciences, may also be unfamiliar to some economic historians. Finally, American historians have recognised that 'efforts to control and master nature, in particular water, were a fundamental aspect of industrial change' (Steinberg 1990: 25; see also Goubert 1986 for France); but much economic history assumes – if it does not celebrate – humanity's conquest over nature, and in its anthropocentrism contrasts with environmental history's core concern over the over-exploitation of natural resources caused by industrialisation (Warren and Goldsmith 1983; Massa 1993; Bowler 1993).

Thus there is much that distinguishes the two disciplines. The environmental historians' interest in reconstructing ecosystems in the past, in investigating the history of environmental literature or movements, and their concern over the conservation of landscapes, wildlife or habitats, are not the natural province of economic history. There is, however, one issue of considerable common interest – the causes and impact of unclear air, water and soil. Economic history is, moreover, extremely well equipped to make an important contribution to a better understanding of severe pollution as a historical phenomenon, particularly through a recognition of the multiple-use characteristics and externality problems associated with the deployment of natural resources, as well as the social and political conflicts that might be generated by the manner of their exploitation in human society. It is quite apparent from a number of studies that the methods of economic history can shed invaluable insights on such problems (MacLeod 1967; Jones 1979; Flick 1980; Dingle 1982; Bartrip 1985; Clapp 1994). The significant change in the nature of environmental pollution brought about by nineteenth-century industrialisation was recognised by contributors to a collection edited by Bilsky (1980). This represented an original attempt to investigate historically the interactions between the natural environment and economic and social life. In the volume, Glick studied

London's 'Great Stink' of 1858, for example, and argued that industrialisation created fundamentally unsound urban ecologies in which, due to 'species packing', natural processes were incapable of absorbing and purifying the growing volume of human-generated wastes (Glick 1980).

Some of the above scholars would not describe themselves as economic historians and, despite its enormous topicality and importance, economic history has only recently developed an interest in the environmental consequences of industrialisation. On the other hand, social historians of public health and medicine have engaged much more actively with such issues. The works of Smith (1979), Wohl (1983), Luckin (1986) and Hamlin (1982, 1985a, 1985b, 1987, 1988, 1990, 1994) have progressively broken new ground. By incorporating findings from urban and sociomedical history, Smith's and Wohl's books achieved a refreshingly novel approach to the history of public health. Wohl, moreover, undertook a pioneering study of river pollution and management in the Victorian period. Luckin acknowledged his debt to these historians in his social history of the River Thames in the nineteenth century, which examined the interrelationships between sociopolitical processes, class ideologies and environmental change. An issue which Luckin touched upon was the uneven social impact of environmental deterioration. His own work on the social and spatial context of disease was taken further by Hardy (1993), and by economic historians such as Lee (1991). There is now a considerable literature on health inequalities. However, even works, like that of Chevalier (1973) and Kearns (1991a,1991b), which originally seek to investigate 'biological' social inequalities, focus less on the degradation of the natural environment as it affected the urban poor. Rather, they stress the under-provision of housing, health and other services, as revealed in indicators such as mortality and crime rates.

Separate mention must be made of Hamlin. His work underlines the complexities of the interrelationships between water, public health, science, ideology, the social climate and the pursuit of vested interests. It would be impossible to do justice to his scholarship in this introduction. Hamlin's approach to the political and social factors determining, and provoked by, the development of water resources may diverge somewhat from that favoured by the present author. For example, he tends to approach the means adopted for exploiting water resources as a reflection of issues 'broader' than the environmental, for instance as to how they reflect Victorian anxieties about relationships between humanity, nature and God (1985a), the function of science (1990), or urban stability (1994: 332). This writer places environmental degradation in a more central place in the analysis, as both an important cause and effect in economic and political relationships or activities. Consequently a possibly more censorious interpretation of the causes of the political and market failures which punctuate the history of water is adopted. Such differences of emphasis are surely justifiable in their own right, and the indebtedness of all writers in these fields to Hamlin's imaginative research must be acknowledged.

Returning to social inequalities, historical geographers have produced findings in this area through the application of multivariate analysis to a host of variables, including socio-economic indicators and spatial structures. This research enables a clearer picture to emerge of nineteenth-century urban ecologies. Robson (1971), Taylor (1976) and Pooley and Pooley (1984) produced valuable findings on the spatial and social distribution of poor living conditions, over-crowding, access to amenities like water supply and sewerage, and ill health. While the statistical techniques used to investigate spatial expressions of social inequalities were very sophisticated, the nature of causalities remained less well understood. Again, this research investigates social inequalities in the provision of amenities, rather than how environmental deterioration may have impacted upon the different social classes.

This is a challenging theme which, in fact, will barely be touched upon in this study. One justification for this omission is that to outline the basic history of water in England and Wales since the industrial revolution is a sufficient undertaking in itself. The topics covered in this book include the development of water supply and sewage treatment industries, questions of river conservation, environmental protection and misuse, the impact of the increasingly water-intensive patterns of activity in the home and the economy as a whole, struggles among interest groups to gain privileged access to water, and interrelationships between the water sectors, lobbies and the State. There is a danger that being drawn into so many fields will produce incoherence. While not claiming methodological innovation, one of the book's unifying themes may be indicated at this stage. As noted above, economic analysis has highlighted the problem of externalities – the tensions existing between the profitable business of supplying water, and the social benefits and costs associated with its use. This distinction clarifies why the essentially uncommercial task of environmental protection has tended to receive less attention than the development of water supplies. The analysis is facilitated by acknowledging water's multiple-use characteristics and also by recognising the relationship with natural cycles. Water has been described as a common and restless resource in the open environment (Kinnersley 1985: 10); and the river as 'an organic system characterised by physical linkages and interdependencies which translate into economic ones' (Parker and Derrick Sewell 1988: 754). The physical characteristics of hydrological systems, therefore, partly account for economic externalities.

It is these interdependencies which lead to vexed conflicts and policy dilemmas being generated by the exploitation of the water environment. The difficulty of developing policies which efficiently and fairly satisfy most interests may be illustrated by the problems relating to the ownership structure of the water supply industry. It is even more clearly demonstrated over the question of pollution prevention, where the problem was exacerbated by the lack of viable technologies. Inadequate environmental protection strategies have tended to characterise British policy. Time and again, the central and local authorities have given greater consideration to private-industrial interests than to the wider, social costs of pollution. Consequently, attempts to reform and improve waste management were invariably incomplete, if not harmful, in impact; they had the effect of physically, and often temporally, displacing the core problem of pollution, rather than addressing it at source. Only when the resultant pollution costs became unendurable, which was perceived at a national level only in the last twenty-five years or so, was society prepared to undertake the by now enormous expenditure to remedy past neglect, to raise water quality and to thereby ensure the sustainable use of the water environment.

I have not imposed a uniform structure on each chapter, which sequentially examine the unfurling of these problems since the industrial revolution. Themes are handled in ways which illuminate the historical issues of each period. Chapter 2 covers the Victorian and Edwardian years. In this era water services were virtually developed from scratch. Priority was given to the delivery of reasonably clean water to the domestic consumer and pollution control, for example, was neglected. The impact of such choices will be explored in this chapter.

The period up to 1914 witnessed, to all intents and purposes, the emergence of the modern water industry. Due to the unregulated and unplanned way in which water resources were developed, discrete interests and lobbies proliferated. By 1914 these structures had crystallised. Vested interests in aspects of the status quo had developed. Chapter 3, covering the inter-war and post-war years, focuses on the way that effective reform was hindered by the manner in which special interests interacted and collided with one another and with government.

Eventually, the need to reform water management in line with the requirements of a modern society and a growing economy became a more central issue. Some reforms were legislated for in the 1940s, but they were only initial steps. The institutional framework inherited from the nineteenth century remained substantially intact. In the relevant literature in the 1950s the concept of integrated water management, based on river basins, represented the reformer's ideal. Chapter 4, which studies the period from 1951 to 1973, focuses on the dominating theme of the period, the pursuit of integrated management.

This goal appeared to have been reached in 1973. Provision for 'source-to-mouth' management of all stages of the water cycle was made with the creation of the Regional Water Authorities (RWAs). Chapter 5 covers the period when the RWAs operated, from 1973 to 1989. The 1973 reform was a sweeping achievement and promised much. The eventual failure of the RWAs to satisfy expectations was partly due to faults in the RWAs and deficiencies in the 1973 reform itself. But the principal responsibility for the RWAs' failure to deliver required service standards lay with government. The harmful impact of government interventions, motivated by expediency and short-term considerations, is stressed in Chapter 5.

A further reform was carried out in 1989. The final chapter evaluates the record of the first five years of the privatised water industry. The effectiveness of the regulatory solutions, and the impact and implications of the means adopted to finance the modernisation of the industry and raise water quality, are among the issues explored in Chapter 6.

The uses of water

Some observers are bemused when the modern water companies spend millions of pounds on surveys which ask water consumers: 'What do you want?' In fact, water is far from being a homogeneous product, performing many functions besides quenching people's thirst. There has indeed been a proliferation of water-using habits and devices in recent decades. The growing customs of regularly watering or cleansing body, vehicle and garden have contributed to the emergence of a water-intensive lifestyle, which was inconceivable a century ago.

About 1970 total domestic consumption of water was almost 30 million cubic metres a day in England and Wales, out of a total use of about 150 million cubic metres daily. What accounts for the remainder? First, a distinction has to be made between public water supplies delivered from the mains, and direct, frequently private, abstractions made from sources. Most discussions about water use, includ-ing those in this book, are about public water supplies. In fact, direct abstractions are on a far greater scale. Most direct abstractions are for industrial purposes, where potability is not required. Whereas industry and trade currently consume approximately one-third of the public water supply in the UK, its share of total consumption, including cooling purposes, is about two-thirds of the total (Lanz 1995: 119). A survey of industrial users indicated that in 1969 cooling plant accounted for up to seventy per cent of all water used in manufacturing, compared to fourteen per cent employed for process purposes and four per cent for steam production (Smith 1972: 152). Cooling water is taken directly from rivers. Although some of this evaporates, much is returned and is used by successive riverside installations. In addition many big works, like British Steel (BSC), had massive reserves of their own in private reservoirs, and the majority of breweries had their own boreholes (Barber 1983).

But a wide range of industries also draw on the public mains, partly because of their quality requirements. Industry consumed some 14 million cubic metres from the public supplies in 1970. For the chemical industry water was described as an 'essential raw material . . . of equal importance to coal and oil' (Cooper and Smith 1960: 1). In soap manufacture, paper-making and textile-finishing large quantities of water were used, and, furthermore, for these sectors the water had to be soft and clean. For example, a Leicester firm used 4 million gallons of piped supplies a week, for the dyeing and finishing of knitwear supplied to Marks & Spencer. The specialised needs of other industries also led them to draw on mains water, including pharmaceutical enterprises such as Boots, the electricity supply industry for the very pure water used to drive turbines, and even heavy chemical manufacturers. Imperial Chemical Industries (ICI) at Billingham, consuming 40 million gallons daily in the early 1980s, did have its own sources for lower-grade purposes, but it also drew significant quantities from the public town supplies (Barber 1983).

Access to water has been a decisive influence upon industrial location. The consumption of filtered water for process purposes in leading Lancashire paper-making firms in the mid-Victorian period was at least equivalent to that of a medium-sized town. Bleachers' requirements were every bit as demanding. The choice of location by leading firms to sites north of Bolton was significantly influenced by access to sources of water, which were 'clean pure excellent in quality' (BA 1871: 3–7). Agricultural water consumption is important in some parts of the country, salad growers in eastern England using vast quantities for irrigation. It is also used for watering stock, enterprises like chicken breeders requiring large volumes of uninterrupted supplies.

The use of water for public services became significant from the Victorian period, especially with the introduction of the water-carriage method of waste disposal. In 1882 in forty-eight leading provincial towns, 60.3 per cent of piped supplies was delivered to domestic households, 33.4 per cent was consumed by industry and trade, and 6.3 per cent was used for sanitary and other public purposes (Hassan 1985: 542). The distribution pattern of public supplies remained remarkably constant long after that time.

Much of the water used in the home and elsewhere, which passes through sewage treatment works (STWs) will, like cooling-tower water, be returned to the cycle and be available for subsequent users. Over and above obvious use as a consumption or intermediate good, there are many other demands upon water, including its employment as a recreational or aesthetic amenity, its employment in canals and its application for power generation and irrigation purposes, and its use in inland fisheries, as well as for the transport and dilution of municipal and industrial effluent.

The volume of water falling as precipitation on Britain is well in excess of normal requirements – in 1970 only about one-sixth of the total volume of water available through precipitation was actually abstracted. But half was lost through evaporation, transpiration by plants or run-off to the sea (Jeger Report 1970: 3). Furthermore, there are also well-known regional imbalances, the relatively dry, water-intensive economy and society of the South-East, standing in contrast to the rainy and, in places, relatively unpopulated North-West. There are three main sources of water, and each contributed about one-third to total national consumption in 1970, again with regional variations. The industrial North depends heavily upon impounded upland rivers. Underground sources are important in the West Midlands and the Home Counties, while river abstractions are very significant in London itself.

The management of water resources is a complex task for many reasons.

First, the water industry supplies consumers with water. Second, it treats and disposes of domestic and industrial wastes through sewerage and sewage treatment. Third, there are the tasks of water conservation, river management, flood control and land drainage. There are also environmental services, notably pollution prevention, which are probably best regarded as a fourth separate set of responsibilities. All these functions are carried out within the unity of the water cycle. This is initiated for present purposes when rain replenishes upland gathering-grounds and temporarily finishes when river water reaches the sea, only to be repeated through the evaporation of seawater into cloud cover, with precipitation restarting the cycle. One function within the cycle inevitably influences the others: sewage disposal will pollute sources used for domestic consumption; abstraction of water influences a river's capacity to dilute and carry effluent, and affects the interests of many other river users such as fisheries and navigation undertakings.

These interdependencies operate within the physical parameters of the river basin. Illustrative of the complexities are the conflicts which emerge among the users of a salmon river. Macleod (1967: 116) identified five separate groups – sportspeople and anglers interested in protecting spawning salmon; downstream proprietors, netting much of the salmon, but less interested in replenishing stocks; tidal fisheries, which were inclined to catch salmon before they entered fresh water; and mill- and factory-owners whose operations dammed or polluted the river. The almost incompatible nature of water users' interests created a major problem. To overcome it, recommendations were made for the adoption of the integrated management of all functions within the hydrological unity of the river basin. The first conscious conceptualisation of the watershed as the framework appropriate to the human management of water resources was Phillippe's recommendation of this solution to the French Academy of Sciences in 1752 (Smith 1969: 101). Since Chadwick the ideal of integrated river management has been repeatedly advocated as a solution to the problems inherent in water use.

For economists the task of recommending organisational solutions is particularly complex because of water's divergent economic characteristics. The delivery of water as a private good, a good which, once consumed by one consumer, cannot then be consumed by another, may on grounds of efficiency be organised by firms operating in a competitive market environment. However, falling long-run average costs occur within the water supply and sewage sectors, which are related to their natural monopoly characteristics: under such conditions, it is technically inefficient for enterprises to duplicate networks in an attempt to competitively supply these services. As noted, externalities also occur, such as excessive pollution when effluent is inadequately treated. Where the water environment supports wildlife, amenities and aesthetic values, it functions as a public good, where – like externalities – consumers are unwilling to pay for the good because of the problem of free-riders. In certain circumstances, especially in the case of the sea, water is a common property resource, one of whose chief characteristics is that no one is excluded from using it – whether for pleasure or dumping sewage.

Natural monopolies, externalities, public goods and the common property resource indicate to economists situations where there is market failure – meaning inefficiency in the delivery of a product, or resource over-use leading to excessive pollution; this analysis attributes such failures to imperfect property rights. As Tomkins (1996) has stressed, market failure and imperfect, or even non-existent, property rights systems are endemic in the provision of water services. Property rights do, of course, exist, especially those enjoyed by riparian interests. But they are imperfect, and exclusion of others from using the resource is incomplete. In fact, given its fluid nature, absolute exclusion is difficult to conceive.

Water's multiple characteristics create almost unique problems in devising appropriate market and regulatory structures to govern the delivery of water services. The search for an acceptable solution to these problems is a central theme running through the history of water since the industrial revolution.

2

The Victorian and Edwardian periods

The consumption, provision and disposal of water

The consumption of water

Water has been described as the '*sine qua non* of the city . . . whether for sustenance, sanitation, fire-fighting or industrial use, water was the original public utility and historically the first urban problem' (Lampard, cited in Hassan 1985: 531). As in France, the nineteenth-century drive to address these needs has been interpreted as the outcome of the recognition that water was a matter of collective, not simply private, concern. Public health anxieties, in particular, were paramount (Hardy 1984: 250; Dupuy 1982: 244–6). Yet the concern of medical and sanitary experts was almost exclusively directed at the moment of human consumption. What animated them, above all, were the adequacy and the safety of drinking water supplies. Human ingenuity in developing this industry concentrated initially on the task of bringing water to the individual consumer. Wider public issues, such as the management of the water cycle on a regionally equitable or environmentally sound basis, received understandably little attention for the time being.

Society, especially middle-class society, according to Hardy (1984: 272), craved greatly improved access to water, for reasons of personal health, convenience, ease and enjoyment. She has stressed the cultural importance of water to the English, in its use in washing, cooking and making beverages: 'Water was also used to make tea – that great British consolation, a luxury which even the very poor deemed essential to everyday life.' In addition, reformers were tireless in their advice to the working-classes to employ water and soap more regularly in order to stave off the threat of disease: 'Among the poor in London there will always be filth, putrefaction, and all the essences of plague and pestilence . . . . To display clean things to a dirty man is to throw pearls to swine, who will certainly trample them in the filth of their stye', it was stated in 1871 (*The Field*, 3 June 1871, quoted in Taylor 1946: 30). But this was not a typical attitude. Much more so was the Royal Sanitary Commission's opinion of that year, that one of the first priorities of a 'civilised social life' was 'the supply of wholesome and sufficient water for drinking and washing' (cited in Hassan 1985: 543).

The main impediment to acting on reformers' good advice was the state of water supplies in the early nineteenth century. Water was so scarce in Liverpool that begging for it was common and, with barely enough for cooking or drinking, it was scarcely surprising that little was used for personal hygiene (Taylor 1976: 145). The local authority provided water free of charge to the poor in Bolton, but it was 'of a nasty green colour', the source polluted by farmland, and generally fit only for street-cleansing (Hassan and Taylor 1996: 13). Well-water was popular with Londoners because of its flavour, but scientific assessment from the 1860s revealed the extent to which it was contaminated by cesspool soakage (Hardy 1993: 158). In Bristol in 1845, 73,443 persons relied wholly on wells which were also liable to cesspool contamination, water from which was delivered by water-carriers to the poor in many parts of the city at expensive rates (BRO, 40619/A/2/b, 1845). The modernisation of the water industry from the 1840s brought better piped supplies to many, but social inequalities remained. The proportion of homes in Manchester with access to water fittings increased from about 50 per cent in 1846 to almost complete coverage by the 1870s, and the proportion with an internal supply increased from 23.4 per cent in 1846 to 79.4 per cent in 1879. Poorer districts were less well provided for, and here reliance on standpipes persisted into the 1870s (Hassan 1984: 35). So inadequate was provision that the first fountain erected by a new philanthropic society in London to supply free, filtered water attracted over 7,000 people daily, after it was opened at St Sepulchre's in 1859 (Davies 1989: 14). Octavia Hill, who managed tenement homes for the poor with the intention of promoting higher domestic standards, provided only cold water to her houses, piped to a communal tap on each floor; this was better than what it replaced, namely a single source for many storeys. Until the 1890s in London, many private homes were without a piped supply of water at all (Hardy 1984: 273). As late as 1913, there were still 43,000 houses in Birmingham without internal fittings, where all water had to be fetched from outside (Reynolds 1943: 99).

Thus, in nineteenth-century England domestic consumption of water was held back by the lack of appropriate installations. In early nineteenth-century America, according to popular sentiment, those who bathed risked dissipation and ill health, but significantly, once waterworks were built demand for water quickly outstripped supply (Wilkie 1986: 649). It is revealing that historians of water-using amenities such as baths and water-closets, often emphasise the behaviour of royalty – a reflection of social imbalances in this area.

The aristocracy and monarchy may have been fashion pace-setters, but there was consumer resistance to the use of water for cleansing, 'dry cleaning' through rubbing down and powdering being preferred, at least up to the seventeenth century, in the belief that washing could provoke all manners of ailments, or even prove lethal (Lanz 1995: 45). French monarchs in the eighteenth century might, on coming to the throne, inherit fabulous *appartements de bains* in their royal palaces, only for the facilities to be demolished or converted to other uses due to indifference. Louis XIII, in the early eighteenth century, made do with a wooden tub for bathing (Wright 1960: 8). When Victoria became Queen in 1837 Buckingham Palace lacked a bathroom (Allen 1976: 30). Similarly, even though the aristocracy pioneered their use, 'rather rare and rude' water-closets were a novelty in great English houses of the eighteenth century (Wright 1960: 103). Nevertheless, innovation in this area of personal hygiene was concentrated in the upper classes. In the eighteenth century, Hepplewhite encased washstands made an appearance, although there was Anglo-Saxon resistance to *bidification*, with its 'aura of Continental impropriety', even in Georgian England (Wright 1960: 115).

Nineteenth-century exhortations to wash as an aid to good health formed a connection with an older hydropathic tradition associating health with regular bathing. Perhaps making a virtue out of a necessity given the virtual absence of hot water, the benefits of the cold bath were extolled in Victorian England (at a time, nevertheless, when the immersion of invalids in winter seas was becoming less fashionable as a cure). Icy-cold plunges were believed to be particularly good for the young. According to Wright (1960: 165): 'Until the end of the century a healthy young man who took his bath hot was thought effeminate.' There was a widespread view in both England and America in the middle decades of the century, justified by spurious pseudo-science, that warm bathing could cause numerous skin or other maladies. Nor, surprisingly, was the use of soap unanimously encouraged. Thus, according to much mid-century advice, 'the typical bath consisted of a cold plunge or sponge unencumbered by the use of soap and taken solely as a prescription for health' (Wilkie 1986: 652). In time the fascination with cold immersions abated and the pleasures of hot bathing were discovered. Attempts to employ gas for these purposes, such as heating cast-iron baths directly by a gas-burner, sometimes had disastrous results for the bather. Subsequently techniques slowly improved.

The main influences upon the spread of bathing and other water-based activities were the availability of piped supplies, the quality of available appliances, arrangements for heating water, the state of plumbing and trends in living standards. Americans apparently obtained fixtures in order of perceived usefulness: sinks, washtubs and water-closets all preceding fixed bathtubs and hot-water heaters. Plumbing shortcomings and production difficulties ensured that fixed bathtubs remained a rare bourgeois luxury (Wilkie 1986: 649). A similar chronology undoubtedly prevailed in Britain, although this was considerably delayed, especially among the poor.

The inadequacy of piped supplies restrained the spread of water-closets. But these formed only part of the 'total water system'. The full system included networks for piping water to more than one room in the house for use in sinks, bathtubs and showers, and provision for its disposal after use. Even in more advanced America, such complete systems were widely diffused only from the middle of the twentieth century (Cowan 1983: 87). In Britain, although spare bedrooms were converted increasingly into bathrooms from the 1860s, they were, as yet, rarely purpose-built, baths and washbasins being typically portable affairs. According to Wright (1960: 258–60), it was only from the 1920s that bathrooms began to be built routinely in new middle-class homes, although Allen (1976: 34) traces this trend to an earlier period.

The difficulties in heating water restricted its use for personal hygiene or for food preparation. Gas cooking had been demonstrated at the Great Exhibition of 1851, and gas heating of water for kitchen and bathroom use did gradually expand thereafter. But gas in the home was used mainly for lighting and, despite aggressive marketing by gas suppliers in the 1880s to promote the use of gas for other household purposes, the penetration of gas appliances into the domestic market was limited well into the twentieth century. Where gas ranges had been installed they were expected only to cook, with a hot-water cylinder as an optional extra. In fact, for a long time, gas ranges failed to displace the traditional coal range (Ravetz 1968: 455–8).

However, the adverse effects of this may be exaggerated. The traditional coal-fired range displayed many merits, so that even in the 1930s these were almost as numerous as gas cookers. Their multiple functions made them the most acceptable and economical kitchen stove, 'serving all the needs of the kitchen', including cooking, heating water and space heating; the hot water might be piped to a scullery or upstairs bath (Ravetz: 437). While the grandest ranges were in bourgeois homes, an artisan's kitchen in the mid-Victorian period might have a coal range and possibly a sink, although indoor sanitation and piped water would be lacking (Yarwood 1981: 28). Coal-fired central heating, by piping hot water or steam through the house, had even made an appearance. In truth, however, even in the United States, central heating was an expensive luxury enjoyed by comparatively few until after the First World War (Cowan 1983: 94). On a more mundane level, washing, particularly of clothes, was affected by technical developments. The manufacture of soap and detergent had been improved after 1800, and the later repeal of the tax on soap helped it to become cheaper and more plentiful. The laundering of the clothes of the members of the Victorian household remained, however, a huge operation. For the time being attempts to develop washing-machines did not lead to any reduction in the heavy dependence upon human effort and hand power for carrying out this task (Yarwood 1981: 129–49).

An outcome of the restricted spread of water fittings in working-class districts before 1900 was the municipal or philanthropic promotion of public bath- and wash-houses. The movement emerged in the 1840s, reflecting the fact that the poor, having to make do with communal fountains or standpipes, lacked the means and privacy for the ablutions which they were repeatedly exhorted to undertake. Public bath-houses were promoted in Liverpool from 1842, for example, to compensate for this want (Allen 1976: 31). Anxieties about cholera were among the factors leading London's Lord Mayor to launch a fund for the building of cheap public bath- and wash-houses, the first of several Public Baths- and Wash-Houses

Acts being passed in 1846. However, demand constantly outstripped supply. Even in 1908 there was only one 'municipal tub' for every 2,000 Londoners (Wright 1960: 151). Provision, nevertheless, improved hugely in some provincial towns. By 1879 every district in Liverpool boasted a public bath- and wash-house (Liverpool 1903: 233–4). In Manchester their number grew from two to twenty-five and the annual number of customers from some 50,000 to over 1 million in the half century up to 1904/5 (Hassan 1984: 36).

One of the most significant areas of change within the home was the spread of the water-closet. Efficient, large-scale carriage of human wastes became possible with Bramah's introduction of the improved version in the 1770s. Joseph Bramah, cabinet-maker, patented his water-closet, incorporating an improved flush-control valve, in 1778. For all its noisy and unpredictable deficiencies, the Bramah closet was the accepted design up to 1870, when it was supplanted by improved valve-closets. By 1797 Bramah had made 6,000 closets, and by the 1830s they were widely used in London (Wright 1960). Up to the 1870s the closet used by the majority of the London poor had no water laid on, but had to be flushed through the use of the hand-pail, creating serious bacteriological and health risks. Thereafter, the 'hopper' or valve-closet gradually replaced the pan in working-class housing, but still suffered from objectionable drawbacks, providing often only a dribble of water to wet the basin. It was only from the 1890s that 'the modern type of closet, with basin and trap all one piece, finally emerged in a cheap and reliable form' (Hardy 1993: 163). Meanwhile the shortcomings of water supply and sewer networks restricted the spread of the water-closet to principally middle-class neighbourhoods until the late nineteenth century (Wohl 1983). Nevertheless, use of internal water fittings, taps, basins, baths and toilets undoubtedly grew over the course of the century. The impact of the reform and professionalisation of plumbing should not be overlooked (Hardy 1993: 169–72). Encouraging the growth in demand for pure water and appropriate fittings was the clearer recognition of the relationship between per- sonal hygiene and health. Understanding typhoid as an independent disease with a specific cause, as opposed to infection generally arising from miasmatic emanations and, more broadly, the growing influence of the germ theory of disease, contrib- uted to shifts in attitude (Hardy 1993: 151; Wilkie 1986: 655). By the end of the century standards of hand-washing and food preparation had so improved for Hardy (1993: 164) to recognise their contribution to the decline of disease.

By 1914 most urban areas benefited from piped supplies, only twenty-nine boroughs or urban districts out of over 1,100 in England and Wales being without this service, although there were still sixty-seven urban areas without a piped supply to over fifty per cent of their houses, and 320 lacking supplies to over five per cent of houses, with provision also being especially poor in many rural districts (*Return of water undertakings* 1914: xxxvii).

An important cause of increased water demand was industrial expansion, especially in the textile belt, where the softness and purity of the new supplies developed from the 1840s was particularly beneficial to bleaching, soap, silk-man-ufacturing and dyeing firms (Hassan 1985: 541). The scale of the consumption of an individual firm could be prodigious. Manchester's total piped supplies in the 1850s of barely 9 million gallons per day (gpd) can be compared to the consump-tion of 5 million gpd by Cromptons, paper manufacturers of Farnworth (*Bolton Chronicle*, 15 April 1854). Not taking into account compensation supplies reserved for riparian owners, it appears that industry and trade took about one-third of the water undertakings' net output in the second half of the nineteenth century, although for individual towns it could be much higher, such as sixty per cent for Leeds in 1884. More typically the ratio of domestic to industrial consumption was in the proportion roughly 2: 1, as in Glasgow and Liverpool just before the First World War, although there were considerable variations (Wegmann 1918: 4–8).

Urban water-consumption levels were influenced by a number of factors, such as supply conditions, water charges, economic structures and civic policies. Although what comparative evidence there is should be treated with care, some generalisations can nevertheless be made. In the 1830s average consumption in England was about 4 imperial gallons per head per day (ghd), rising by the 1910s to approximately six times this very low level, and moving on to about ten times that amount by 1970 (Parker 1913: 604; Smith 1972: 137). Internationally, a strong contrast was emerging between North America, where urban consumption levels in the 1910s of between 50 and 90 ghd lay well in excess of British consumption of 15 to 50 ghd, contrasting, in turn, with consumption of some 8 to 10 ghd in Indian cities. When the European poor were still having to share a communal tap among several households in the early twentieth century, many American homes had acquired a second bath. Parker (1913: 601) felt that 'there is no doubt that the population [in America] does use more water for legitimate purposes than in sim-ilarly situated European populations', adding that among Americans the daily bath was 'a widely spread habit' (Parker 1913: 603). Estimates cited by Parker show how evolving social trends led to increased water consumption (Table 2.1).

Although England and Wales did not approach American consumption pat-terns, there was nevertheless a transformation during the reign of Victoria. Average consumption per head increased quite dramatically in industrial cities with the progressive modernisation of the water industry after 1850. This led to many benefits: water was delivered from purer sources under high pressure on a constant basis, replacing previous intermittent, low-pressure systems. The new supplies were often of soft water, bringing advantages to householders, such as less wear and tear on clothes and savings in the use of soap. Water consumption increased rapidly. The growth in annual consumption per head varied from 0.3 per cent in the London region from 1825 to 1913/14, to 2.4 per cent for Newcastle and Gateshead in the second half of the century, with Manchester, Leeds and Liverpool perhaps with more typical increases in this period of between 1.5 per cent and 1.9 per cent (see Table 3.3).

Table 2.1 *The impact of additional fittings upon household water consumption (estimates based upon an American family of five, 1913)*

	ghd	ghd
One kitchen tap	5.5	5.5
Additional tap	1.1	6.6
One water-closet	5.0	11.6
Additional water-closet	2.2	13.8
One bath	4.1	17.9
Additional bath	0.8	18.7

Source: Parker 1913: 603.

The provision of water: the development of supplies and the treatment of water

Such rates of growth, sustained over a long period, were made possible because the water supply industry effectively emerged as a modern business in this period. The initial impetus to transform the supply of water, however, arose out of a situation of crisis in the early Victorian years.

As noted above, up to the industrial revolution many communities relied on rough and ready means of obtaining water from local streams or wells, supplemented perhaps by a public fountain or conduit. Few towns received piped supplies. These arrangements came under growing strain as urban and economic expansion led not only to increased water demand, but also to the destruction or pollution of many traditional sources: slaughterhouses and bleachworks appeared on riverbanks, building activity obliterated springs, and underground sources were degraded.

When, in the 1840s, the beginnings of water-borne waste disposal were added to these conditions, the result was a public health crisis and the circumstances which contributed to the growth of those two classic water-borne diseases, cholera and typhoid. It became imperative to improve water supplies. Although a number of larger boroughs were beginning to assume responsibility for waterworks, it was private enterprise which accounted for the mid-century growth of the industry. The proportion of a sample of larger provincial towns served by joint stock enterprise increased from twenty-six per cent in 1831 to fifty-four per cent in 1851 (Hassan 1985: 536). Following the decay of the communal administration of water supplies in the eighteenth century, the authorisation of private companies, able to raise capital by issuing shares to the public, appeared to offer the best prospect of improving water supplies. Direct competition between undertakers was very rarely authorised by Parliament, however, and given *de facto* monopolies, it also took steps to protect the public interest. This was done through general and local Acts of Parliament and has been described as arms-length regulation

(Millward 1989: 201–4). The Waterworks Acts of 1847 and 1863, and significant modifications incorporated in local legislation, provided a code of practice governing undertakers' operations, including financial controls and technical provisions governing, for example, the laying of mains. Dividend payments were restricted to ten per cent, undertakers being required to invest surplus profits in government stock. Companies were obliged to provide fire-plugs on the mains, and to make a supply available to all houses in a street where a main was laid.

Mid-Victorian arms-length regulation was largely a failure. Even the consumers who did have access to a supply, either from internal fittings or from company standpipes, received an intermittent, poor-quality service. Before mid-century, consumers who enjoyed even this patchy provision were a fortunate minority. Nor was the advent of company control always a cause for undiluted joy. The trustees of Bolton's public fountains, for example, became shareholders in a company authorised in 1824, whereupon 'It became their interest to neglect the spring and public pumps, for the supply of the poor inhabitants, free of charge, and to force upon the payment of a high rate of charges' (*Bolton Free Press*, 13 May 1843). Over the next few decades the service offered by private companies improved, but there were still numerous instances where it remained very poor indeed.

Their lamentable performance was the outcome, Millward explains, of prevailing economic conditions, which, for example, encouraged 'skimping'. The Manchester and Salford Water Company and the Devonport Water Company in the 1840s both preferred 'ingenious expedients' or 'unscrupulous ploys' to solve the problem of meeting growing demand, such as abstracting water from polluted canals. The Manchester company consciously decided in the 1830s and 1840s to deny a supply to expanding neighbourhoods until more houses were built. Powers were obtained by Halifax in 1848 to acquire the waterworks because private enterprise regarded it as unprofitable to adequately supply this expanding town (Spencer 1911: 267). Before the supply was modernised, only some 5,000 in Bristol, 'constituting the most wealthy inhabitants', out of a population of 130,000 received piped well-water in the mid-1840s (Chattock 1926: 231). Nor did the promoters of a statutory company see the merit in correcting this social imbalance: the Merchant Venturers' Water Works only intended 'to supply Clifton and the more wealthy parts of Bristol, and would have left the densely populated and poorer part of the city wholly unprovided for' (Jones 1946: 16).

One reason for the private companies being less willing to develop sales, relative to the subsequent efforts of municipal enterprise, is the threat of competition which, under conditions of falling long-run costs, would render such expansions unprofitable (Millward 1989: 198; Foreman-Peck and Millward 1995: 35–9). A possible source of competition for company customers were local wells, springs and streams. It was, however, their very degradation, rendering them unfit even for industrial use, which led increasingly from the 1840s to the promotion of schemes to tap more distant, purer sources (*Bolton Chronicle*, 2 February 1854; BA 1854: 36–40). Nor was the competitive threat from other companies very great. Only two towns in the 1840s were served by more than one company and the supply of towns tended to be 'districted' (Millward 1989: 196). Acts of 1799 and 1822, for example, had authorised two companies to competitively supply Liverpool, and both laid pipes in the same streets. This proved 'ruinous', leading them to define areas of supply so that each 'should have a monopoly' in their own areas (Liverpool 1903: 186–7). Parliament considered each proposal on its merits, yet was disposed to confirm in its legislation, as later in the case of Liverpool, the natural monopoly characteristics of water supply. Private companies submitted rival schemes for the supply of Bristol in the 1840s, for instance, but Parliament viewed such competition as untenable and decided that only one company should serve the city (Jones 1946: 16–18).

Whatever the causes, the evidently unsatisfactory nature of company supplies led to a re-evaluation of the preferred means of organising the industry. The crucial period for the Victorian decision to opt for a municipal solution was located between 1861 and 1881, when the proportion of the larger provincial towns supplied municipally doubled from 40.8 per cent to 80.2 per cent, reaching 90.1 per cent in 1901 (Hassan 1985).

A number of factors account for the municipalisation of water supplies in an age of *laissez-faire*. Legislation in the 1840s made it easier for local authorities to set up their own waterworks, but this was fenced in with safeguards for existing private companies. Crucially, under the Public Health Act of 1875 sanitary authorities were required to ensure that water supplies were adequate in their areas, if necessary by acquiring private waterworks. While this legislation facilitated municipalisation, it did not guarantee it. Parliament did not inevitably concede local government applications for compulsory acquisition of private waterworks, there being several instances of refusal in the 1890s and 1900s (Millward 1989). Also, there were a number of instances of companies successfully resisting repeated attempts at municipal takeover, for example the Newcastle and Gateshead Water Company, which survived as an independent enterprise until acquired by Lyonnaise des Eaux in 1988.

In economic terms, Millward (1989: 197) summarises succinctly the difficulties which were, nevertheless, faced by private enterprise in this industry: water provision enjoyed some economies of scale and its social values exceeded its private value. In combination with the natural monopoly characteristics of water supply, the externality problem tended to favour some form of public control over the provision of supplies. Furthermore, the municipal water enterprises soon appeared to be responding to their communities' needs better than most private companies had ever done. By 1881 water supply per head in sixty-six publicly managed waterworks was a full fifty per cent higher than was the case for the fourteen provincial towns still supplied by the larger private companies (Hassan 1985: 533).

In comparison with municipal enterprise, private companies operated as if acting on the basis of limited time-horizons, limited knowledge and limited resources. In this period the advantages in obtaining cheap sources of finance lay with local government rather than private companies (Priestly 1905: 16–19). The repayment of loans was frequently up to 100 years and at least in one case for 200 years. This kept down the cost of borrowing and may even have encouraged a municipal overdevelopment of sources (Barber 1982: 6; BRL 1889a). Over the period from 1848 to 1872 local authorities borrowed only £11 million from central government for sanitary purposes. In the years 1872 to 1880 the Local Government Board (LGB) sanctioned over £22 million for such loans, and a further £66 million between 1880 and 1897. Borrowing without LGB sanction, but under the provision of local Acts, also occurred on a large scale. While it was not the only factor, the municipalisation of the water industry was helped by easy funding arrangements (Szreter 1992; Clifford 1887). These conditions helped municipal enterprises to operate with extended time-horizons and to be concerned with covering only long-run costs.

Contemporaries certainly regarded the hallmark of municipal enterprise as the readiness to plan for *future* urban requirements (Priestly 1905: 116–17). The unsatisfactory outcome of arms-length regulation in the mid-Victorian period encouraged the authorities to prefer the use of public agencies for the subsequent development of water resources. By the late nineteenth century there was a tendency for Parliament to accede to applications for the transfer of ownership to local authorities on the grounds that where there had been some neglect of duty, water as a necessity of life should be provided at the least possible cost ('Water supply', *WWE*, 20 July 1932: 344).

A further dimension to the evolving ownership structure of the Victorian water industry was that it was, by and large, a non-ideological, and at the national level, a non-party political issue. The achievements of Glasgow, Liverpool, Birmingham and Manchester, 'in providing themselves with a full supply of water from distant sources, free from the risk of contamination', were greatly admired. It was evident to Priestly, a past President of the British Association of Waterworks Engineers speaking in 1905, that private companies lacked the resources to contemplate works on the scale of those executed by municipal management. There was an exceptionally prolonged and complex debate over the organisation of London's water supplies, revolving around the competence of private companies to deliver safe water (Clifford 1887; Luckin 1986). Elsewhere, however, the local authorities and private sector often co-operated satisfactorily on matters of common concern. A constructive working relationship between the water company and the Corporation of Bristol generally prevailed, especially on public health matters, for example ('Water enterprises', *British Medical Journal*, 29 October 1898: 1351). The question of the form of ownership was regarded as 'academical' ('Water supply', *WWE*, 20 July 1932: 344).

Local disputes over water were often quite bitter, but conflicts derived less from ideological conviction, and had more to do with short-term political advantage or even personal gain. While developments were sometimes held back as a result, it is the pragmatism of actions taken which is often striking. In Bolton, for example, after years of the Liberals trying to improve supplies, it was under Tory control that the private waterworks were transferred into municipal ownership in 1847. A key factor was that many of the councillors were also shareholders and stood to gain substantially on the agreed purchase price, estimated to be almost one-third above its true value (Hassan and Taylor 1996). There were incentives for private shareholders to sell out. Purchase terms were usually agreed before application to Parliament, or through arbitration, on terms favourable to companies, including a substantial addition for goodwill (Falkus 1977: 152). A failed municipal bid for the Bristol water company in the 1870s is instructive. The company phlegmatically recognised the current trend and the legislature's favourable attitude to municipalisation, and engaged in prolonged negotiations with the Corporation. The deal fell through simply because insufficiently enticing terms could be agreed. As the directors commented: 'The Board, though they saw no cause for desiring to part with your property, would have been willing to recommend your acceptance of fair and reasonable terms.' The company's successors have survived up to the present day (BRO, 40619/A/2/b, 30 March 1878). In Bradford in the 1850s, there were political disputes over water, but leading Liberals were among the most vociferous supporters both for and against municipalisation. In the view of one commentator, it was of little concern to the public whether 'the limpid fluid is conveyed in municipal or the company's pipes' (quoted Elliott 1982: 120).

There was some confidence among the late Victorians, nevertheless, that municipal management would deliver desired results (Clifford 1887: 502). 'Civic pride' doubtless encouraged local authorities to improve public utilities. More precisely, the propertied and commercial classes supported the municipalisation of water supplies, in contributing to reduced fire risks, the enhancement of property values, a healthier workforce, and lower industrial costs. The supply of water to manufacturing industry was often extremely poor, only one-fifth of all commercial and industrial enterprises in Manchester, for example, being customers of the local company in 1845. Often river water grew so polluted as to become 'utterly unsuitable' for manufacturing purposes. The deteriorating quality of local supplies led industrialists and others to support municipalisation. In Bolton, for example, local sources had become so contaminated by seepage from 'cesspools and other filth' from the town that the Corporation moved quickly, after assuming responsibility for supplies in 1847, to secure pure water on favourable terms from Pennine catchments, well adapted to the needs of paper and other manufacturers (BA 1848; *Bolton Chronicle*, 1853–54, *passim*).

The municipal effort to improve water supply was also closely linked to public health concerns. Local authorities wished to accelerate the installation of water-closets and water-carriage sewerage, but by the 1860s only London enjoyed the benefits of an integrated sewer system. One of the major disadvantages of water companies' supplies was that typically they were provided only for a few hours a day at low pressure. This severely restricted the degree to which modern waste-removal systems could be introduced. There had been a view that the continuous water-supply system would be too expensive, likely to cause serious leakages and wear and tear of plant, until Nottingham's experience proved otherwise (Binnie 1981: 130–1; Fabry 1991: 87–8).

Abandoning dry conservancy for water-closets was impractical until water supplies had been improved. Liverpool adopted a policy of converting to water-closets in 1854, but only from 1863, with the advent of a satisfactory water supply, could the conversion proceed in earnest. The Leeds Water Company flushed sewers once a month, and refused to supply water for water-closets unless a domestic supply was laid on (Wohl 1983). The improvement of water supplies from the 1880s enabled sewer systems to function more effectively and allowed the conversion to water-closets to be accelerated. However, this generalisation held true only for the larger cities. Because of infrastructural inadequacies, for middling towns, let alone villages, conversion from privy middens and ashpits to water-closets was delayed well into the twentieth century (LRO, PHM/2, 23 July 1908; PWM/2, 14 September 1931).

To meet their expanding needs the large industrial towns built new waterworks during the second half of the nineteenth century. The impounding of valleys and the building of long-distance aqueducts involved overcoming unanticipated obstacles (such as sliding dams due to unstable foundations), and embodied many detailed innovations in hydraulic engineering over and above the grand concept of bringing water some distance by gravitation from upland gathering-grounds. Although there were one or two minor gravitation works built before 1848, the first large-scale application of the principle was the Longdendale scheme. Serving Manchester, it was built in stages between 1848 and 1877 and for a time constituted probably the largest system of artificial lakes in the world. The aqueduct's length was eighteen miles. At about the same time Liverpool was developing the Rivington works on a similar scale. In 1853 it was proposed that Glasgow should be supplied by water collected in Loch Katrine and brought to the city by an aqueduct thirty-five miles long. 'The proposal was at first startling by its magnitude, but after much discussion it was sanctioned and carried out' by 1859 (*Royal Commission on Water Supply 1867–69*: 19–20).

Subsequently even more ambitious schemes were developed. Between 1879 and 1904 Manchester, Liverpool and Birmingham had developed long-distance gravitation works, bringing into use sources respectively 106, 68 and 74 miles distant from the area supplied. The Vyrnwy scheme, delivering water to Liverpool by 1891, incorporated the biggest artificial dam yet, the first in Britain where a high masonry embankment was employed. This method of responding to growing water demand, by tapping distant sources in upland gathering-grounds, persisted into the next century. Later, these fixed-site works were regarded as a costly and inflexible method of exploiting water resources. But under contemporary conditions they were an effective response to the expanding urban demand for water.

The achievements of the water industry before 1914 should not be belittled. The innovation of constant, high-pressure and pure piped supplies was introduced in many localities, the needs of industrial and domestic consumers were more adequately met, and gains in private convenience and health were achieved. In some cases the new municipal supplies made a striking impact. Average consumption increased from 8.1 ghd in 1851 to 20.5 ghd in 1871 in Leeds following their introduction, and from 4.8 ghd in 1841 to 32.6 ghd in 1875 in Manchester (Hassan 1985: 538). By 1914, of 1,130 boroughs and other urban districts outside London, there were only twenty-nine without piped supplies.

As well as quantitative growth, qualitative achievements were also sought of the Victorian water industry. At the beginning of the century drinking water was 'little better than dilute sewage', which led to 'repeated invasions of cholera and typhoid' (Hamlin 1990: 3). However, in mid-century, professional chemists lacked the scientific knowledge to validate what was little more than a common-sense hunch that filthy water was bad for health (Hamlin 1990: 119–20). As Luckin (1986: 94–5) stated: 'Pure water was desirable but it was emphatically not conceived as an essential ... precondition for exemption against cholera.' This reflected the lingering influence of the miasma theory of infection. In the 1860s, even after the publication of Snow's epidemiological findings associating high incidence of disease to the area served by the Broad Street pump, there was outright disagreement among the most eminent sanitarians and scientists over causality. Armed with hindsight, Snow's demonstration often seemed more significant to later observers. Chadwick dismissed the 'notion of water-borne disease' (Hamlin 1990: 180–1). However, the cumulative trauma of cholera in 1848–49, 1853–54 and 1866 led sanitarians and the medical profession to abandon their reservations regarding the link between filthy water and infection.

Notwithstanding new gravitation works, river water was still heavily relied upon. In London sixty per cent of supplies came from the Thames in 1913 and twenty per cent from the Lee, sewage effluent figuring prominently in the dry-weather flow of these rivers (Houston 1913: 2). With the growing recognition of the appalling epidemic potential of rivers (Luckin 1986: 95), undertakers gave greater attention to improving water quality.

Nevertheless, by and large, the chief line of defence in the struggle to ensure pure supplies was 'in the selection of as pure a source as possible' (Taylor 1946: 26–7) – distant upland rather than increasingly polluted local river water was preferred whenever possible. Confidence in the purity of upland sources was reflected in Manchester's decision to send Longdendale water, arriving from the Pennines from 1851, unfiltered into the city. The only precautions initially taken were the building of deep reservoirs to inhibit the growth of vegetation and the straining of water through fine wire gauze before admitting it into inhabitants' houses (Hassan and Wilson 1979: 109–11). In similar circumstances, water authorities strove to protect gathering grounds from contamination by sheep, and to generally restrict human activity there.

River water was a different matter. Over much of the nineteenth century reliance was placed upon treatment by 'slow sand filters', which began to be introduced in the 1820s. The earliest filtration beds included those built by the Chelsea Company from 1825 to 1834 and the Lambeth Company in 1841. They incorporated a deep filtering medium of up to eight feet of gravel and sand, through which water was passed before distribution to consumers. Legislation of 1852 required that water taken from parts of the Thames and Lee within five miles of St Paul's be stored and filtered by the companies before being delivered to the public (Luckin 1986: 36–7). This led to manifest improvements in the quality of supplies (Hamlin 1982: 59). Where water was brought by gravitation from purer sources the construction of filter beds proceeded much later, often after 1880, as in the North and Bristol.

Snow had demonstrated in 1854 that polluted water could spread disease. But the science of water treatment and water analysis was uncertain. Influential figures like Edward Frankland recognised the limitations of prevailing chemical-analytical techniques, even including its inability to distinguish safe from polluted water (Hamlin 1982: 59). Frankland, in the 1860s and 1870s, through his semi-official position as London's water analyst made, however, important contributions to water quality, for example in his practical stress on the fact that while putrefy-ing matter was not always virulent, a link did exist between putrefaction and morbidity. Gradually the credibility of bacteriological, as opposed to chemical, modes of water analysis increased. The publication of Koch's methods of bacterio-logical study in the 1880s facilitated this process.

In the 1890s two developments in water treatment promised further advances in water purification. First, there was the application of chlorine to water supplies, first carried out at Maidstone in 1897; second, in the mid-1890s, experi-mental work undertaken in America led to the development of the rapid sand filter (Taylor 1946). Chlorination would become the basis of the scientific purification of water supplies in England and Wales, being widely used by the 1940s. At first, however, there was consumer resistance to the introduction of chemicals into public water supplies. Chlorination was available from 1912 and extensively diffused only after 1920.

The human consumption of water was a particularly sensitive moment in the water cycle, and attention and resources were devoted to improving drinking-water quality. Scientific understanding was quite incomplete, water analysis being no better at detecting dangerous contamination in 1900 as it had been in 1850 (Hamlin

1990: 299) Fortunately, local authorities and water companies did not wait to act until the question of what constituted safe water was beyond controversy. In London the closure of private wells, improved drainage which helped to reduce the contamination of soil and underground sources of drinking water, the removal of water company intakes from the lower Thames in the 1850s, the spread of resting and filtration practices, and the introduction of official monitoring of water quality in the 1870s, all contributed to improvements (Hardy 1993: 158, 175–7). Subsequently slow sand filtration appeared to offer the most promising path forward, being, by the 1890s, regarded as an essential part of good waterworks practice (Luckin 1986: 48). Nevertheless, aberrations and scares still occurred. Intermittent, 'inexplicable' typhoid outbreaks struck middle-class as well as poorer districts, and the breakthroughs in bacteriological analysis in the 1880s did little, in fact, to ease fears. Bacteriological analysis of Thames and Lee water in 1885–88 produced findings which astonished contemporaries – it was found that the apparently physical method of purification through filtration could, because biological processes were involved, remove ninety-five per cent and more of the micro-organisms present in the water (Hardy 1984: 272; Luckin 1986: 48). Many were still very concerned about those remaining and were not convinced that London water, treated in this way, was safe for human consumption.

Nevertheless, as a result of steps taken to treat supplies and to tap purer sources, drinking water in the early twentieth century was much safer than it had been some fifty years earlier. Cholera mortality became virtually unknown by the end of the period. Typhoid and gastrointestinal disorders, admittedly provoked by a number of causes other than polluted water, declined significantly from the late nineteenth century. Luckin (1986: 179) comes to generally optimistic conclusions about the state of the water drunk by Londoners: sanitary measures 'contributed to the creation of a river greatly less polluted in 1900 than it had been during the years of crisis between 1830 and 1860'. Thames water even attracted enthusiastic exponents, Houston (1913: 103; 1917: 70) claiming that purification processes reduced the densities of undesirable microbes 1,000 times, thereby producing typhoid levels even lower than in North American cities. By 1921 London's water supplies had improved so much that it was considered safe for the Board of Trade to abolish the post of Metropolitan Water Examiner (Hardy 1984: 282).

Faced with expanding requirements, Victorian Britain strove to develop an institutional and regulatory regime to facilitate the emergence of a modern water supply industry. The solutions chosen placed much of the onus for achieving this upon local, municipal enterprise. The regulatory intervention by the State to guide the industry's development was very limited. The advantages of this approach in effectively harnessing the energy and resources of local self-interest have been described in this section. But disadvantages also arose from employing this permissive regime, such as inefficient patterns of resource development and environmental costs. These will be discussed later in the chapter. Yet the Victorians and

Edwardians achieved important goals – the development of industry and trade was not threatened by inadequate supplies and increasingly potable water of acceptable quality was delivered to the home.

The removal of wastes

So far humanity's intervention in the earlier stages of the water cycle has been traced. Once investment in water had helped to satisfy private consumption needs and to generate some public health benefits, less success was achieved in addressing the problems of disposal after use.

Up to the late eighteenth century the management of household and industrial wastes was not considered an issue of major importance. Household filth, human excrement and horse manure accumulated in the streets. By the early nineteenth century little advance was made in the removal of human waste. Each dwelling or group of dwellings was supposed to dispose of its own refuse. In Liverpool, for example, this meant periodic excavation of midden pits, into which sewage had soaked (Taylor 1976: 137–8). Dunghills were being replaced by cesspools – progress of a sort. The reason for the growing resort to cesspools in the early nineteenth century was the increasing popularity of the water-closet. Shallow trenches or pits, some made more permanent through lining with brick or stone, were dug to receive human excrement (Barty-King 1992: 105). While the spread of water-closets was a major cause for the increasing use of cesspools, it was also the reason for their growing inadequacy. They became choked, with adjoining land saturated and nearby wells contaminated. Liquid wastes overflowed into yards and adjoining streams. An intolerable situation was developing, and a public health crisis, previously alluded to, was threatening to engulf the early nineteenth-century city.

One way of alleviating the crisis was to improve sewerage. Sewer commissions were ancient institutions, but their main concern was the drainage of surface water. In fact, while some foul matter may have been thrown into sewers, it was a penal offence to do so until early in the nineteenth century (Spencer 1911: 242–5). From the late eighteenth-century improvement commissioners were active sewer-builders, but their constructions were inadequate in several respects, for example, no legislation before 1835, according to Spencer, compelled the drainage of houses into public sewers. The public health importance of underground drainage was as yet unrecognised (Webb and Webb 1922: 104). Nevertheless, the more effective removal of household waste from residential neighbourhoods was clearly a factor behind increased sewer building. Some sewers were little more than culverted watercourses, as in Bolton in 1858, the paving over of the Croall being the solution to the 'loitering of wastes' in the town centre. Waste removal was thereby expedited to a mill lodge, which became a settling tank for the whole of the town's sewage (Walklett 1993: 175–6).

Sewers of a recognisably modern type, however, were beginning to be built, two to three miles of them dating from between 1792 and 1828 still being in use in Manchester in the 1970s (Read 1979: 1–2). Sidwick and Murray (1976 I: 66) indicate that from 1847 it became compulsory to drain houses into sewers, and certainly more local legislation required this. A primitive version of the 'combined system' was resorted to, that is, sewers removing surface wastes received domestic effluent as well. By 1870, in preference to whole or partial reliance on cesspools, 146 out of 178 towns in England and Wales had household wastes removed by sewers, in 13 towns there were no sewers, with cesspools still being relied upon, and a combination of methods was utilised in the remainder. Sewage was treated before disposal into watercourses, however, in only 46 out of the 178 towns (Barty-King 1992: 107).

Trends in urban waste-disposal in the second half of the nineteenth century were confused. Concerns over river pollution did lead to delays in the adoption of water-closets in some boroughs. Consequently, the water-closet remained the preserve of the well-to-do in many parts of the country until the twentieth century. In Manchester in 1868, of 67,000 dwelling houses, only about 10,000 had water-closets connected to the sewers, and there were approximately 36,000 with ash-pits (Read 1979: 6). The improvement of domestic waste-disposal initially consisted of draining cesspools, making them watertight and self-contained. The introduction of dry-conservancy in the homes of the poor was the next step forward. Manchester replaced 40,000 middens replaced by the pail and midden system by 1877, and converted 60,000 privies to dry conservancy by 1881. Other cities, such as Edinburgh and Leeds, also remained committed to labour-intensive, dry conservancy down to the 1880s, restraining factors being cost and the as yet insufficient capacity of water supply networks (Wohl 1983: 95–101).

Nevertheless, the expansion of water-closets and town sewers after 1850 was inexorable and so the volume of municipal effluent increased. It is, therefore, helpful to try to identify the main trends in urban waste-disposal practice.

First, from the early nineteenth century up to the 1850s urban authorities increasingly felt it was essential to remove wastes from the immediate vicinity of residential neighbourhoods by a system of underground pipes. During the drought of 1864 sewage disposal was impeded by the water shortage, and the *London Daily News* (2 September 1864, cited in BRO, 40619/A/2/b) reported that 'The medical men are anxiously looking for a flow of water, to stop the poisoning of the air' caused by blocked drains. No consideration was given, as yet, to the fate or impacts of discharges beyond the point of outfall. Some municipalities displayed ingenuity in keeping down the cost of sewer works by introducing gravitation or steam-pumping in the 1850s to expedite the removal of sewage.

Second, from the mid-1850s attention began to be paid to the question of treating sewage before discharge. While some towns responded to the growing problem of river pollution by developing dry-conservancy, in general the introduction of water-closets and sewers continued. Bristol, Cardiff and Carlisle followed

London's lead and constructed integrated sewer systems in the 1860s. According to Richards (1982: 1.13), smaller municipalities with a population less than 9,000 and a low rateable value could avail themselves of loans more freely sanctioned after 1863 through the Public Loans Commissioners. This led to much building but only of intercepting sewers, which hastened the transfer of raw wastes into rivers.

There were, however, growing worries about sewage pollution. In the search for an effective method of disposing of sewage 'for beneficial and profitable uses', and even for the 'relief of local taxation', its application to land came to be regarded as a superior solution in many situations. Although the sewage farm often disappointed as a commercial venture, this conclusion emerged as a persistent theme in the sequence of Sanitary and Rivers Pollution Commission reports published between 1858 and the late 1870s. As Goddard (1995) suggests, filth would be transformed into food, although anticipated public health and environmental benefits also attracted the Victorians to land irrigation. By 1890 many towns had adopted it. It predominated in urban Lancashire, where the proportion of the population which had its sewage treated increased from 11.4 per cent to 49.6 per cent between 1863 and 1893 (Richards 1982: 3.23). In Nottingham the sewage farm attracted foreign visitors, some 60 horses, 400 cows, 320 sheep and 70 pigs grazing there (Wohl 1983: 110).

For Wohl (1983: 101) the final phase in the development of sanitation started in the 1890s. The quarter-century leading up to the First World War witnessed not only the replacement of older systems in the major towns and cities of Britain by water-borne sewage and modern filtration and treatment plants, but also a search for 'scientific' alternatives to sewage farming. Some historians observe that exponents of land irrigation were almost incapable of recognising its limitations, suggesting that land receiving town sewage was apt to become weed-ridden, a waterlogged mess in winter or contaminated by heavy metals or parasites, eventually to become 'sewage sick' without the capacity to purify (Sheail 1983; Goddard 1995). Hamlin (1985a, 1987), however, is more tolerant of local authorities' commitment to sewage farming which persisted, in fact, until the 1930s. Well-run sewage farms did not display the alleged deficiencies, sewage did have utility as a fertiliser and, perhaps most significantly of all, a viable alternative to the technique was not available. The heavy-metal problem excited later observers more than the Victorians, although a consulting engineer did advise that on account of the presence of metals in sewage: 'A farmer would really be better off if he declined to accept it as a gift' (WRO, WA, 13 December 1897). Public health anxieties over the technique did increase. The Royal Commission on Sewage Disposal (1904: 169–73) exhibited considerable concern that water supplies could be contaminated by effluent discharged from sewage farms.

A further difficulty for local authorities was the scarcity and cost of suitable land. Often vast tracts were required, such as an additional acre of land per week for a proposal put forward by Birmingham in the 1890s. Towns like Bolton faced with a shortage of appropriate farmland were in a very difficult position and were forced, ahead of developments in scientific understanding, to commit themselves to largely untried technologies ('Bolton's sanitary crusade', *Municipal Journal*, 21 February 1902: 151).

For some time the adoption of alternatives to land irrigation had been inhibited by the attitude of the LGB, which authorised loans to local authorities including those used for new STWs, by strongly favouring sewage farming, while the authorities were becoming more anxious to build 'artificial' systems. The ensuing conflict led to the appointment of the Royal Commission on Sewage Disposal in 1898, which was asked to investigate sewage treatment, identify appropriate methods and make recommendations. By its Fourth Report (1904: 173), it recognised grounds for reappraising sewage farming: things had changed 'greatly' over recent decades, including population growth, pressure on land, increased use of water and water-closets, and the retention of harmful microbes in sewage-farm soil 'in great abundance'. The Royal Commission became supportive of artificial methods and the LGB amended its stance. Paving the way for a change in policy were developments in scientific methods, the viability of biological sewage treatment having been demonstrated by Dibdin by the 1890s. By the end of the following decade several English towns had adopted the new technique (Hamlin 1985b).

Hamlin (1988: 82–3) has rightly taken issue with criticisms of Victorian slovenliness in promoting improvements in sewage treatment. He emphasises that the Victorian councils were pioneers, struggling to find solutions to novel sewage-disposal problems. Uncertainty about the best methods of effluent purification, and the high cost of making mistakes recommended a cautious approach. In 1874 alone there were thirty-two patents out for sewage treatment. Without condemning, however, it is appropriate to explore the impact of the chosen sanitary policies upon the natural environment in this period.

Some environmentalist writing is wont to attribute a plundering and exploitative approach to the use of natural resources as the standard characteristic of industrial civilisation (Massa 1993; Bowler 1993). This is too simplistic. The Victorians did not want to ravage the environment. In fact their very attraction to sewage farming, for example, was due to the way it appeared to maintain natural cycles, avoided the loss of valuable nutrients, and promised to offer a 'technology which so uniquely resolved their anxieties about humanity's place in Nature' (Hamlin 1985a: 396). But there was a headlong decline in river quality in the Victorian period, which has to be accounted for.

Policy and institutional shortcomings will be described in the following section. In the context of the present discussion, however, it was the failure to achieve a balanced development of water supply and wastewater services which led directly to the deterioration of Victorian rivers. Heavy expenditure on, and the modernisation of, urban waterworks, proceeded decades ahead of comparable action on sewage. In Manchester almost spectacular achievements in water supply can be contrasted with a history of civic failure in sewage treatment (Hassan 1984; Richards 1982: chs.9–10). Officially authorised loans were by no means the only source of capital for waterworks, self-finance and departmental transfers possibly being even bigger sources of funds. But it is significant that waterworks contributed easily the most to local authority debt between 1868 and 1898, accounting for 18.3 per cent of the total, compared to 10.4 per cent for sewerage (Fowler 1900: 384–7). In London water supply had been prioritised since the Middle Ages (Glick 1980: 128). Waste management lagged. From the early nineteenth century, London experienced the spread of water-closets, the ending of dry conservancy, the emptying of house drains in sewers and thence into the Thames, the commercial expansion of the metropolitan water companies, and a marked deterioration in the river's condition (Hardy 1993: 157). By 1853 about ten per cent of London's homes were discharging raw wastes into the river. Its resultant plight eventually shattered complacency in Father Thames's self-purifying powers. The unbalanced development of water services led to ecological imbalance. During the 'Great Stink' of 1858 noxious odours infiltrated the House of Commons, forcing Gladstone to 'beat an ignominious retreat from [the] committee-room, handkerchief to the nose' (Glick 1980: 123). The partiality of the response further illustrates underlying themes in the history of water. Reforms did follow, specifically Bazalgette's famous sewerage scheme, completed between 1858 and 1865. Two great intercepting sewers were built. They simply relocated pollution downstream, aggravating the public health of estuarine towns.

The difficulties which arose from the unbalanced development of water and sewage services lay partly with the faulty science which informed sanitary policies. Chadwick's influential attachment to the common filth hypothesis and the subsequent, more sophisticated zymotic theory of infection, led to the greatest emphasis being paid, from the 1840s, to the swift removal of decomposing matter (Hamlin 1985a). The resultant vast networks of pipes and sewers built by the Victorians has been seen as a great achievement: 'The purpose – and great accomplishment – of sanitarian rhetoric was to effect environmental change' (Hamlin 1985a: 410). Unfortunately, the change was not wholesome. The spread of water-closets and water-carriage sewage disposal, together with a neglect of sewage treatment, were pushed ahead of a full appreciation of the environmental consequences of such actions.

However, it is too easy for the modern environmentalist to dismiss the conversion to water-carriage and the abandonment of dry-conservancy as a disaster (Lanz 1995). More than the cost and administrative inconvenience involved in servicing dry closets, it is quite evident why most progressive-minded councils made the conversion to water-closets and water-carriage sewage disposal. Compared to towns relying on older forms of conservancy, those which made the transition to 'modern' methods in the late nineteenth century achieved significant reductions in typhoid mortality. The introduction of water-closets, water-carriage disposal, and constant water supplies made considerable improvements in domestic hygiene possible, thereby considerably reducing the threat of infection by the bacterial population within the home (Hardy 1993: 160–2).

It would be foolish to suggest other than that many Victorians searched agonisingly for sanitary solutions which were environmentally benign. Yet it is striking how, once the unprofitability of the once-favoured technique of sewage farming was grasped, cheap and simple methods of sewage disposal were embraced. From the 1870s sanitarians were attracted to 'pouring sewage into the sea ... [as] the simplest way of getting rid of it' (Hamlin 1985a: 409). While their predecessors were attracted to sewage farming as offering an environmentally suitable system of waste disposal, when its lack of viability became apparent the instinct of the late Victorians was simply to 'throw away' the difficulty (Sheail 1996).

River pollution and management

River pollution

As Kearns comments (1991b: 94), 'The concentration of an increasing population in towns altered the relation between society and nature.' Nineteenth-century industrialisation, and the municipal triumph of bringing water supplies from afar by gravitation, led to unprecedented volume of liquid wastes being discharged into small local catchments. Consequently, for the first time ecosystems were overwhelmed, and the natural processes of purification could no longer be performed (Glick 1980; Kinnersley 1988). This section seeks to explain the considerable decline in the quality of the country's inland waters before 1914. Emphasis is placed upon an apparent lack of political will to commit sufficient resources to environmental protection, which itself derives from factors outlined in Chapter 1. To Hamlin the deterioration was due primarily to the lack of a viable technology for the treatment of effluent. The two approaches are not mutually exclusive, although the former can be more readily extended to account for the continuing plight of the rivers throughout most of the twentieth century.

It is unnecessary to dwell on the increase in river pollution which has been graphically described in many sources. In some areas the decline may have started with a growth in the effluent from factories, slaughterhouses, tanneries and bleachworks. People falling into rivers risked death through poisoning, not drowning. The conversion to water-carriage waste disposal meant that municipal sewage also became a serious source of pollution. Smith (1979: 219) and Hamlin (1987: 15) differ on the relative contribution of industrial and municipal pollution, but it would be unwise to minimise the impact of either. Moreover, in many areas noisome discharges from sinks and gullies, including urine and slops, found their way into watercourses, ensuring that town sewage was a serious cause of pollution, long before the conversion to water-carriage, let alone water-closeting (Royal Commission on Rivers Pollution 1870: 7–30; BRL 1900: 7–10).

The deteriorating state of the rivers had serious implications for inland fisheries. Municipal effluent incorporated a large mass of bacteria, which absorbed much oxygen. The low oxygen content of the water drove away fish, killed insect life and damaged weed growth. The progressive death of the English rivers was reflected in declining fish catches. In the 1870s six leading English rivers together produced about 185,000 salmon yearly. By the Second World War their combined yield was less than 50,000 annually (Netbuoy 1968: 175, 210). The salmon catch on the Tyne fell from 130,000 in 1870 to less than 6,000 in 1915. That on the Tees fell from 10,000 in 1867 to 130 in 1930. The disappearance of the species from notable salmon rivers was bound up with estuarine pollution. A considerable mortality of adult fish attempting to pass through the tidal stretches to the spawning grounds occurred. The pollutants discharged into the Tees estuary included crude sewage, coke-oven effluent, and 'spent pickle liquors, arising from the cleansing of steel … in hydrochloric acid'. After discharge these materials contributed to a belt of partially deoxygenated water, forming in the central part of the estuary and moving to and fro under tidal action ('Water pollution', *WWE*, 20 October 1932: 497).

A selective reading of the secondary literature may lead to the conclusion that Victorian society was relatively unconcerned about environmental issues, certainly in comparison with today, and felt that river pollution, for example, was a price worth paying for industrial progress. Moreover, researchers have been struck by the lack of interest of the labour movement in the environment, apart from momentary back-to-nature responses like the Chartist Land Company, Keir Hardie's advocacy of reforestation, and localised and episodic manifestations of working-class interest. In the North-West, a region much more badly affected than most by river pollution, Richards (1982) and Walklett (1993) were both impressed by the muted public concern and scant newspaper coverage of the problem. Kearns (1991a: 27) states that there is little evidence of interest in public health reform among the working class in the 1830s and 1840s: 'instead working-class activity wanted a thoroughgoing reform and renewal of political institutions'.

On the other hand, the history of political thought contains numerous examples of anti-capitalist utopianism (Wall 1994), and the Victorian literature includes many instances of a search for ecological harmony (Hamlin 1985a). Sanitarians, doctors and other professional groups were vexed about the damage done to health or industry by environmental pollution. Parliamentary inquiries exhaustively deliberated the best means of curtailing river pollution. Shifting the perspective, the roots of modern environmentalism might be traced to this period. Animated by a sense of the vulnerability of wildlife, many nature conservation societies were formed in the early and mid-Victorian years, and in due course important

legislation for species protection was obtained. However, the numbers involved in
the nature conservation movement were very small. As late as the 1950s the relevant organisations counted only a few thousand members, compared to several
hundred thousand two decades later (Lowe 1983). The emergence of mass political environmentalism was certainly a late twentieth-century phenomenon (Pepper
1984; Weale 1992).

Furthermore, Victorian interest-group lobbying against the effects of
unclear air or water did not typically stem from a sense that the manner of society's
use of these resources was unsustainable. In cases where the lobbying led to legislative action it often derived from more immediate worries over the economic
damage caused by pollution. The inland fisheries movement of the 1870s, for
example, did not see itself as an environmental pressure group and did not even
regard river pollution as a national problem as such; it was principally concerned
with securing measures to protect fish stocks (Bartrip 1985: 293). The origins of
an 'exceptional' case of intervention, the Alkali Act of 1876 which imposed some
controls over atmospheric discharges from chemical plants, were landowners concerned about the decline in rental income and the capital value of agricultural land
caused by chemical pollution (Dingle 1982: 533–48). Endeavours to arrest the
worsening pollution of the waters within the Mersey–Irwell catchment area can be
traced to the efforts of the Mersey and Irwell Navigation Company; this secured
the Mersey and Irwell Navigation and Protection Act of 1862. It was not concern
over threatened ecosystems which animated the promoters of this measure. Their
concern was the annual discharge of 35,000 tons of industrial refuse into the Irwell,
which was raising its beds and threatening navigation (Broome 1971: 26). Similar
problems led the Mersey Docks and Harbour Board to unsuccessfully press for the
control of sewage discharges into the Mersey estuary in the late nineteenth century
(PRO 1930).

At the level of town politics, disputes apparently over environmental policy
often originated from narrow clashes of interest among different property-owning
groups affected by the proposed changes (Kearns 1991b). For instance, the controversy over proposals for addressing Edinburgh's sewage disposal problem in
1839–40 derived less from worries about the impact upon the environment,
reflected more such 'broader issues' as religious schism and urban crisis, but was
at bottom 'a rather sordid private squabble about land and money' (Hamlin 1994:
312).

The complaints by parties injured by water pollution did become sufficiently
intense for legislation to follow. The need for reform became clear as the victims of
pollution discovered that the principal procedures for seeking redress – either
through the common-law courts or by filing a bill in Chancery – were extremely
ponderous, costly and uncertain of outcome. From the 1850s landowners and
inland fisheries were involved in a campaign seeking protection for rivers against
pollution. They secured the Salmon Fisheries Acts of 1861 and 1865. The latter

provided for a system of inspection, pollution prevention measures and the establishment of Fisheries Boards for entire groups of rivers. Netbuoy (1968: 188) stated that, though weak, the Acts did help to arrest the decline of salmon fisheries, although this seems to be contradicted by the catch figures he quotes. Macleod does not believe that the legislation achieved its aims. The powers actually conferred on the Fisheries Boards were very limited, and the salmon fisheries administration declined after a promising start. Large river areas were uninspected and poaching was a flourishing pastime in the last quarter of the century. Macleod (1967: 147) believes that the evidence shows that public enthusiasm for a broad policy of natural resource conservation was still lacking in the 1900s.

The mid-century concerns about the damage to fisheries had, nevertheless, raised awareness of river pollution. This was reflected by the appointment of a Royal Commission to inquire into the problem. A sanitarian and environmental campaign eventually succeeded in extracting from Parliament the Rivers Pollution Prevention Act of 1876. To Luckin (1986: 158), however, the environmental lobby was confronted by more powerful and influential industrial interests. Attempts to develop adequate rivers protection legislation were fatally weakened by the growing influence of the Alkali Association. Manufacturing spokespersons insisted that universal standards, advocated by environmentalists, were unfair and unworkable and that emphasis should be placed on the specific condition of individual rivers. Influential politicians, like Lord Salisbury, were persuaded by the manufacturers' case (Luckin 1986: 156–7).

Consequently, the Act of 1876, though a pioneering measure in placing an absolute prohibition on polluting discharges and the cornerstone of national rivers pollution law until the 1950s, emerged from Parliament fatally weakened. Numerous 'safeguards' protected polluters, especially the provision that manufacturers, who could show that they had employed the 'best practicable and available means' for treating emissions, could not be prosecuted under the Act. Works which had been, or were being, built at the time of the Act, were also immune. Only with the LGB's permission could sanitary authorities pursue pollution complaints (Wohl 1983). The prevailing view is that the 1876 Act failed as a pollution prevention measure. It was also a 'fundamental mistake' to entrust to local authorities the responsibility for enforcing the legislation (Smith 1972: 25). As major polluters their role in this respect was compromised. This defect was soon recognised (BRL 1885a: 4), but nothing was done to remedy it. Ten years after it was passed only fifty-six legal actions to enforce its provisions had been initiated and only twenty-six had succeeded.

Moreover, the 1876 measure nullified clauses in the Public Health Act of 1875, which appeared to require local authorities to provide sewers for draining industrial discharges. As long as 'practicable' sewage disposal methods had been used, the 1876 Act provided immunity from prosecution; the right was also given to sanitary authorities to refuse to take trade effluent into sewers on a variety of grounds, such as insufficient capacity or public health risks (Sheail 1993b: 151). With such inadequate and rarely employed legal remedies against municipal or industrial polluters, it is not surprising that river quality did not improve before 1900.

The period from 1870 to 1914 witnessed some progress in pollution control. Improvements in sewage treatment have been noted. Institutional innovations will be considered below. However, endeavours to minimise the social costs arising from the intensified use of rivers lacked conviction. The steps taken were often partial in effect, which failed to overcome pollution and frequently transferred it to another part of the environment.

As Wohl (1983: 254–5) observed, river pollution continued to worsen until the turn of the century, when 'the unimaginable had come to pass and ocean waters were becoming polluted'. This was partly due to the discharge of raw, untreated sewage from coastal towns into the sea – the prevalent practice along the length of the British coastline. It was also the result of the flow of contamination along polluted rivers into the sea. In some cases this was the result of the efforts of inland bodies, such as the Thames Conservancy, in seeking to protect waters under their jurisdiction, which had the effect of expediting the movement of urban refuse downstream (Sheail 1986a: 287). The tendency of much Victorian sanitary improvement to lead to the shifting of wastes around the natural environment, as opposed to reducing pollution at source, is graphically illustrated by the case of Bristol. The difficulties here started with the emptying of the city's raw sewage into stretches of urban river and harbour, leading to a growing problem of faecal contamination. Throughout the period, improvised solutions to these noisome accumulations were introduced, which involved accelerating their dispatch to the Avon, thence, through tidal action, to the sea. Bolder solutions aspired to the transport of the problem to the sea by a long-distance sewer. Sewage *treatment* was not considered expedient. The vision of a trunk sewer to the coast, however, was not realised until the 1960s (Green 1848; Ashmend 1879; Bristol 1898; Gray 1986).

Such strategies were commonplace. As well as threatening the late Victorian seaside holiday trade, the pollution of coastal waters had a damaging impact upon the prosperity of offshore fisheries particularly, for example, the North Kent oyster fishery, easily the most important centre of oyster cultivation in the country. The Royal Commission on Sewage Disposal devoted volumes to examining the worsening pollution of tidal waters, without suggesting any significant policy changes (see *Royal Commission on Sewage Disposal* 1904, *Fourth Report*; 1915 *Final Report*: 1–10). In the 1900s a significant proportion of typhoid cases were traced back to contaminated shellfish – one-third of all cases in Brighton were attributed to this cause. Three people died of the fever and many were taken ill after eating oysters at a mayoral banquet in Whitstable. Bacteriological analysis showed that many oyster fisheries were sewage polluted (Sheail 1986a: 284–5). As Wohl (1983: 254–5) put it: 'Apparently England's moat against the "envy of less happy lands" had fallen victim to pollution.'

Returning to inland waters, the creation of County Councils under the Local Government Act of 1888 appeared to significantly improve the prospects for pollution control. The new Councils' responsibilities included application of the 1876 Rivers Pollution Prevention Act. As Sheail (1986b: 54–5) says, their extent, strength in terms of rental income and the fact that, unlike urban boroughs, they had no direct responsibility for water supply and sewage, appeared to place them in a better position to adopt a more detached view of river management. In the industrial North swift moves to take advantage of the reform were indeed taken in the early 1890s. Lancashire, Cheshire and neighbouring boroughs took steps to create river-basin-based committees covering the Mersey and Irwell, and the Ribble. The powers of the new rivers committees were greater than any previous pollution prevention body: the clause requiring economic interests to be taken into account was even omitted in the Mersey and Irwell Act of 1892, and potential sanctions against polluters were much greater than under the 1876 Act (PRO 1927a).

Similarly, the West Riding of Yorkshire Rivers Board and a joint committee for the Tame, a tributary of the Trent, were also established in 1894. The activities of the four new rivers bodies have often been favourably assessed. For Wohl (1983: 254) they represented 'an important advance'. Richards (1982: 11.2) and Walklett (1993: 340–1) both stress the significance of the size, cohesiveness and authority of the two north-west committees. Their success is attributed to their persuasive techniques and ability to collaborate with local authorities and achieve collective solutions with limited resort to legal actions. Broome (1971: 33) attributes the improving quality of the Irwell between 1880 and 1904 to the efforts of the joint committee – plant life along its banks was returning, and manufacturers who had previously found its waters so polluted as to be unusable were now employing it again.

From a longer-term perspective these appraisals of the joint committees may be too positive. Richards (1982: 8.27) admits that municipal sewage in the North-West remained largely out of control. A major cause of the deteriorating state of inland waters, in this region and elsewhere, were unconstrained industrial discharges. The Mersey and Irwell joint committee had less success in tackling industrial pollution, because the 'best practicable means' clause was construed as applying merely to the settlement of solid material. Thus the discharge of grossly contaminating, high-oxygen-absorbing effluent was difficult to stop (Walklett 1993: 340–1). The West Riding River Board even had considerable difficulty in persuading the county justices of the legal substance of their attempts to prosecute manufacturers who threw sand, gravel and solid refuse into rivers (WRO, RB minutes 1897–98). But a principal reason for the failure to reduce the industrial pollution of rivers was the reluctance of local authorities to admit trade effluent into their sewers and STWs which, under prevailing technical conditions, was the only way a higher standard of effluent could have been achieved (*Royal Commission* 1915; Sheail 1993b: 151).

The ambivalence of the municipal position on river pollution was illustrated by a case brought by the Irwell joint committee against Bury. It transpired that an Act of 1846, providing for the connection of sewers to a public watercourse, was effectively a 'charter of the town of Bury to pour sewage into the rivers ... Parliament had in express terms authorised and enjoined the town of Bury to discharge its sewerage into the rivers'. In the borough's view, subsequent national legislation of 1875, 1876 and even that establishing the joint committee in 1892 had not altered that 'right' (BRL 1900: 7–10). Later, the county boroughs of the West Riding of Yorkshire successfully opposed attempts by the River Board to acquire greater powers to control trade effluent. They argued that the River Board was conceived as merely a superintending body, and that the imposition of controls should remain in their hands. Thus there remained no jurisdiction in the land, other than Parliament, concluded Sheail (1986b: 54–5), with the power to reconcile and adjust the interests of different users of water; and even Parliament would only intervene on an *ad hoc* basis in response to whatever scheme was being promoted by individual undertakers. By the early twentieth century there were only a small number of cases where local legislation required trade effluent to be received into municipal sewers, such as Halifax in 1905 and Salford in 1920 (Sheail 1993b: 152).

Many manufacturers continued to discharge grossly contaminating wastes into watercourses, knowing that they would thereby face negligible legal retribution. Though charged with the responsibility, the local authorities, as owners of polluting STWs, were embarrassed to instigate legal action against fellow polluters. Moreover, under the 1876 and later legislation, the economic consequences of forcing polluters to install abatement methods had to be taken into account. The LGB was statutorily required not to sanction river protection measures by any local authority unless it was satisfied that it would cause 'no material' injury to industrial interests. Wohl (1983: 242) insists upon the pre-eminence of industrial over environmental considerations in Victorian Britain. Victorian society was not ready to bear the burden of pollution prevention measures, or contemplate the local economic dislocations, which significant steps to abate pollution might cause (Richards 1982: 11.3). Even contemporaries interpreted the 'safeguard', protecting dischargers employing the 'best practical means' from prosecution, as virtually a licence to pollute (Wohl 1983: 248).

Luckin stresses that until the end of the century, if not beyond, any suggestion that the law against pollution should be revised was countered by an insistence that such legislation would cause irreparable damage to the economy. Effective national legislation against river pollution 'would have trespassed in an unthinkable manner on the rights of property and the rights of capital'. All this was reiterated 'with little subtlety or apology by those, mainly from the manufacturing districts of Lancashire who derided scientific standards and dictated terms to Disraeli's government' (Luckin 1986: 173). At the local level too, industrial interests strongly opposed attempts to control the 'festering pollution' caused by their effluent (BRL 1885b: 89). An impressive coalition of trade and manufacturing interests supported the municipal faction in denying river authorities the power to require local authorities to take trade wastes into public sewers (WRO, RB minutes 1903–05).

Positive assessments, therefore, of the impact of the joint committees established in the industrial North in the 1890s require some qualification. Richards (1982: 10.4–9) notes a loss of earlier gains in water quality after 1914, because of wartime and post-war economies in sewage treatment, the real recovery in water quality being postponed until after 1934. Furthermore, river pollution remained an exceptionally acute problem in the North-West decades later. Nor were the four bodies established from 1892 to 1894 prototypes for pollution protection agencies. They covered relatively small, heavily industrialised regions, and bodies with similar powers and responsibilities were not created for another half-century or more.

It is, therefore, useful to recognise the limited progress made before 1914 in developing water conservation policies in England and Wales, as it is to acknowledge the particular factors which led Parliament to concede the establishment of stronger regional river protection bodies. The relatively exceptional authority and impact of the Joint Committees arose out of exceptional circumstances. In these intensively industrialised districts, the mounting social costs of severe river pollution finally became intolerable for influential local interests. Among these in the North-West were: medical and public health groups, ever more anxious about the connections between filth and disease; the fishing lobby, in the shape of the conservators of the River Ribble, who were active in promoting the Ribble Joint Committee; some firms who required a supply of clean water for manufacturing purposes; resentment of Salford's self-appointed role as conservator of the Irwell, and therefore a general readiness to accept a single regulator for the whole watershed; the Manchester Ship Canal Co., who lobbied influentially for more efficient river-basin management, concerned that river pollution might have the effect of turning the waterway, with its locks and slow movement of water, into a succession of stagnant ponds; and civic interests in Cheshire, who feared that a polluted ship canal would assist the swift communication of epidemics from Manchester and Salford to their county (Walklett 1993).

The various regional interests favouring a strengthening of water-quality management now coalesced in the newly-formed county councils. For once they represented a stronger, more cohesive and articulate lobby than the relatively fragmented industrial opposition to reform. But conditions in the Ribble, Mersey and Irwell basins were not representative of the country as a whole. Overall, as Wohl (1983: 256) concludes: 'The pollution of rivers called for a degree of administrative centralisation and professionalisation that the nation was not yet ready to accept.'

River management

Moreover, water-quality protection is only one aspect of river management. Ideally, river authorities should have responsibility for managing all tasks within catchments, thereby reducing the conflicts inherent in water use. River-basin management would seek to: maintain channel flows for the needs of fisheries, railways, canals and agriculture; maintain supplies for industrial and domestic consumers and for the performance of public health tasks; keep land well drained and prevent flooding; and maintain channel flows so as to transport, dilute and purify domestic and industrial effluent.

In the 1840s Edwin Chadwick had advocated the integrated management of drainage, sewage, and water supplies under single watershed authorities. Similar proposals were reiterated in later reports, as in the recommendations made by the Rivers Pollution Commission in the 1860s and, perhaps as forcibly as anywhere, in the Royal Commission on Sewage Disposal in the Fifth (1908) and Final (1915) Reports. The sequence of official recommendations continued after the First World War, when the concept of a national approach to water resource development even attracted interest. The developing expert consensus made virtually no practical impact on official policy before the 1930s.

Because of the tendency of the low-lying clay lands of eastern England to flooding, land drainage has been important for settlement and farming patterns and has had a long history (Newson 1992a: 252–3). The earliest drainage authority was probably that for Romney Marsh, whose origin is found in a commission in the reign of Henry II. Many Sewer Commissions were established under the Bill of Sewers of 1531 and later legislation. In addition, many drainage authorities were created in the low-lying areas like the Fens and Somerset levels. Almost all were established by special Acts, with considerable variations in their powers and procedures.

The Land Drainage Act of 1861 introduced another variety of drainage authority. It provided for elective Boards, with all the powers of Commissions of Sewers and more precisely defined boundaries of jurisdiction. A considerable number were set up, but were generally very small (*Royal Commission on Land Drainage* 1927: 8–11). In fact, none of the petty Commissions of Sewers, Drainage Boards or local Act authorities were in charge of even the greater part of a single main river and none had sufficient resources to discharge such a function (*MYB 1939*: 657). Illustrative of the fragmented state of land drainage in the late nineteenth century, the River Within and its tributaries were under the jurisdiction of forty separate authorities. The River Nene was managed by fourteen bodies on its thirty-mile passage from Peterborough to the sea. Such authorities, far from being able to reconcile the interests of river users (agriculturalists, navigators and fisheries all desired different flow levels), were unable to discharge even the most basic of functions, such as protecting riverbanks against damage (De Rance 1897: 56).

Wohl (1983: 251) described the Thames and Lee Conservancy Boards as prototype river boards. They acquired powers well beyond those assigned to earlier drainage authorities. The Thames Conservancy was reconstituted by Act of Parliament in 1857, and entrusted with a wide range of river-management duties, in particular the navigation and improvement of the river between Staines and the sea. The Lee Conservancy Board was established by local Act in 1868. Its powers were similar to those of the Thames Conservancy. Contrary to the impression created by Wohl (1983: 151), the London conservancies did strive quite effectively in the face of physical and political difficulties to reduce river pollution (Clifford 1887; Luckin 1986).

The two Boards established a model for a multifunctional river authority which, however, was not really imitated. The creation of the four aforementioned river-basin joint committees in the 1890s was a step forward, but their range of responsibilities was very limited, being restricted to pollution prevention. No other attempt was made to create river-basin management agencies before the First World War, with the exception of special legislation obtained by Middlesex County Council in 1898, which designated the county as the competent drainage authority within its boundaries. But its powers related more to urban health problems rather than wider conservation tasks.

This segmented approach to river management created an increasingly confused situation institutionally. New initiatives added further layers to the system. The resultant confusion promised little for the more effective reconciliation of interests. Even the realisation of mundane objectives such as preventing land from becoming waterlogged, and keeping channels clear was being put at risk by the early twentieth century.

The scramble for sources and the solidification of interests

The legal framework

Consistent principles to guide the development of the nation's water resources in a socially fair and hydrologically effective manner were not incorporated into the legislative framework or official policy before 1914. The impact of the waterworks code, as embodied in the general Acts of 1847 and 1863 and a host of local amending measures, was restricted to technical and financial controls over undertakings' operations.

Statutory water-supply undertakings were obliged by the terms of their authorisations to provide water for consumers, and growing demand forced them to carry out ever more distant source developments as local sources became increasingly inadequate due to pollution or decay. Each riparian owner had equal rights to use water in a stream, provided the use did not prejudice other owners' interests. If a water undertaker wished to impound, or abstract water from, a stream, this could be achieved only if all the riparian owners agreed. In practice, this was almost never. The exercise of riparian owners' rights complicated attempts by water-supply undertakers to tap sources. One owner out of twenty-five prevented a rural district from obtaining a much-needed supply (*Return of water undertakings* 1914: xxvi). In another case, the House of Lords decided that while it was reasonable for a canal company to use a stream to supply their canal, it was not reasonable for a waterworks company, as a riparian owner, to impound the stream for a town's supply (*Joint Select Committee* 1910: 2).

Because of the need to obtain the virtually unobtainable unanimous agreement of riparian owners to abstract water from a channel, local authorities and companies had to obtain special legislation to acquire the powers to develop new sources. Parliament took account of the particular situation of each case and legislated accordingly. The result was that the waterworks code governing source developments, including technical and other requirements, came to display great variety – or 'a bit of a jumble' as it was subsequently described (PRO 1929b). A great disunity of practice emerged, 'not infrequently the results of "Parliamentary bargains" between the water undertakings and their opponents, rather than any settled course of policy' (Ministry of Health 1943–44: 14). For Parliament to judge each case on its merits seemed superficially reasonable, but it was a parochial approach which led to the emergence of atomistic structures in the water services field.

The lack of regional co-ordination

The incoherence of the waterworks code was paralleled by similar difficulties over source developments. Effectively, water sources could only be developed by undertakings buying land and thereby the exclusive rights pertaining to aquifers, lakes and rivers. The result was a competitive scramble by undertakers to obtain the right to develop sources in order to satisfy growing demand and to meet their statutory obligations. This led to a hydrologically uncoordinated and wasteful pattern of provision.

Conflicts arose between local authorities in their attempts to secure control over sources, disputing the definition of watersheds, for example, in the areas which supplied their towns (Sheail 1986b: 48–9). Disputes also occurred between water undertakings and other owners of water rights for both underground and surface water. For example, although the New River and East London Companies obtained over eighty per cent of their supplies from underground sources in Hertfordshire and supplied 2.6 million people living in the London area, hardly any water was supplied to Hertfordshire, which had to draw on alternative sources (Sheail 1982: 396).

It was in the competitive rush to develop upland surface supplies, however, where the failure to plan the development of catchments produced some of the worst ill-effects. Towns claimed sources but failed to use them to their full capacity. Other, smaller towns were denied use of convenient sources. Some in Lancashire and Yorkshire were particularly hard hit. Those in the upper Irwell valley, for instance, were denied adequate supplies, despite being close to gathering-grounds, whence water was taken by mains to big brother downstream, Bury. Even in 1894 only just one-third of Rossendale was supplied with piped water, the majority of the population having to rely on springs and wells (Hoyle 1987; BRL 1889b: 92–3). The lack of relationship between gathering-grounds and consuming areas was shown in the way trunk mains crossed and recrossed one another in the north of England (Sheail 1986b: 48–9).

Proposals made from the 1860s for the creation of Watershed Boards reflected recognition that smaller towns had lost out in the rush by more financially powerful cities to secure control over sources. The Royal Commission on Water Supply (1867–69: cxxviii) had recommended that cities should not be allowed 'to appropriate a source of supply which naturally and geographically belongs to a town or district nearer to such source'. This advice appears to have had some impact, the 1878 Act authorising Manchester's Thirlmere scheme representing a step towards a less unfair method of development. When small undertakings, *en route*, had no other sources of supply, it enabled them to take water from the aqueduct. The provision was repeated in later legislation, specifically in the Acts applying to Liverpool, Birmingham and Birkenhead, and was a first step towards the principle of bulk supply agreement and co-operation among water authorities (Smith 1972: 129–30). In other respects the Manchester–Thirlmere project was less progressive. Like Birmingham's bid to secure control over catchment areas in central Wales in the 1890s, it stemmed from a powerful borough's attempt to pre-empt others from acquiring control over gathering-grounds, despite the fact – in Birmingham's case at least – that the capacity of the scheme was well in excess of likely needs for many decades (Sheail 1986b: 48–9).

Regional co-operation among suppliers was rare. Because two Tyneside water companies missed the opportunity to amalgamate in the late nineteenth century, regionalisation was not achieved for another seventy years (Rennison 1979: 304). The scale, as well as the challenges, of the scheme designed to develop the Derbyshire Derwent were, however, impressive. The Derwent Valley Water Board (DVWB) was instigated in 1899 to better supply Sheffield, Derby, Nottingham and parts of Derbyshire, following the amalgamation of separate Bills which had been promoted by the East Midlands cities. Tapping the resources of the upper Derwent, the scheme in due course did permit resource development and distribution to be planned more effectively and on a much larger scale than had previously been possible in this region (Lockyer 1957: 33–4).

The regional scale of the DVWB was quite exceptional. But the largest undertaking created before 1973 was the Metropolitan Water Board (MWB). After decades of inquiry and debate the Royal Commission on the Metropolis Water Supply finally recommended in 1899 that in the view of the magnitude of the requirements of London and the inadvisability of relying upon company supplies, a permanent board should be created so as to ensure that the capital should receive a pure supply and efficient distribution of water (*Return of water undertakings* 1914: ix). The MWB had 6.7 million customers in 1914. Its formation in 1902 involved the acquisition of the assets of eight private companies, the new board consisting of sixty representatives of local authorities and river conservancies (Dickinson 1954: 124).

The DVWB and the MWB were exceptionally large undertakings. Somewhat like the northern river committees they did not, however, set precedents. In fact, the next seventy years of industrial regrouping and restructuring never produced water enterprises which remotely approached their scale. In general, an atomised approach to source developments persisted well into the twentieth century, leading to the misallocation of supply and demand within catchments.

The emergence of special interests

Besides leading to regionally uncoordinated provision, the policy framework which evolved in the nineteenth century had other significant effects. The process of Parliamentary approval not only led to groups of water users becoming more aware of their shared interests; it also provided the opportunity to lobby actively for the protection of these interests.

An exceptional example were the owners of riparian rights, who were affected by the impounding of streams and the consequent disruption of channel flow. To compensate them for water undertakers acquiring the power to abstract water from the source, Parliament required guaranteed releases of water to be made from the impounded streams. Industrialists, mill-owners in particular, were a formidable interest and dominated discussions in the setting of compensation flows from nineteenth-century water-supply schemes (Smith 1972: 25–6; Gustard *et al.* 1987). Local authorities 'all over Lancashire and Yorkshire', it was claimed, conceded generous compensation arrangements to the mill-owners, so as to avoid prolonged proceedings before parliamentary inquiries. 'Of course a millowner would like to have the Atlantic at his disposal', complained one exasperated witness (BRL 1889a: 25; 1889c: 117). Until the 1890s the principle of intermittent releases, even zero flows over the weekend, was retained to coincide with the working hours of the mills. In certain extreme cases, the delivery to mill-owners of piped, filtered water was even required by compensation awards, the supply of such clean water to riverside factories thereby protecting them against pollution from other works located upstream (Bolton 1947: 22; BA 1854: 40; BA 1864: 8–14).

Following Thomas Hawksley's suggestion in 1868, Parliament adopted a rule of thumb that one-third of the total yield of an impounding scheme should be reserved when industry was present, and one-quarter otherwise (Sheail 1987: 6–7). In certain cases even more generous provision was made. Bolton Waterworks Company was required to build Belmont Reservoir, completed in 1826, exclusively for the use of mill-owners. After 1843, the amount delivered as compensation water to mill-owners was nearly double that supplied to Bolton itself [Bolton 1947]. Drought in 1851 made the delivery of compensation water to mill-owners very difficult for Bristol Waterworks Company, obliging the undertaker to make very costly financial compensation (BRO, 40619/A/2/b, 5 June 1852). When large reservoirs, impounding the Chew, were eventually completed, they were used exclusively for compensation supply, deliveries almost exceeding Bristol's total water consumption (Chattock 1926: 232). These were not unusual conditions: several of the reservoirs in the Longdendale system constructed by Manchester were also used solely for satisfying compensation requirements (Hassan and Wilson 1979). Overall, the mill-owners did very well out of the compensation arrangements awarded to them by Parliament. They had first claim upon the capacity of the new works, thereby obtaining a security of supply which they had probably never enjoyed before, and being largely protected against the unpredictable effects of drought. But these arrangements, in 'sacrificing the well-being of the river to one sectional interest', proved detrimental to the river systems, the flow in periods of dry weather, for example, being inadequate for effluent dilution (Smith 1972: 27). They also imparted a serious distortion to the way in which the yield of source developments was distributed. Compensation awards undoubtedly contributed to the scramble for sources noted above, and may have encouraged municipalities to overdevelop sources in this period.

A very different kind of anomaly related to the exploitation of underground supplies, which remained important in the South-East and the West Midlands. The combination of common law and practice led to a pattern of resource-use emerging, which created dissatisfaction among all interested parties. The law recognised no property in underground water, unless flowing in a known and definite channel. All landowners had unrestricted rights to abstract such water, or even to allow the resource to run to waste. According to a legal opinion, the position under English law was that: 'If a man digs a well in his own field and thereby drains his neighbour's, he may do so unless he does it maliciously' (*Joint Select Committee* 1910: 3).

Water-supply undertakers believed they were seriously disadvantaged by this situation. Three companies, for example, were statutorily required to supply water from the chalk area to some 900,000 consumers to the north of London. But, they complained, (*Report from Joint Committee on water resources and supplies* [*JCWR*] 1935–36: 93): 'we have absolutely no security of tenure so far as the water supplies in our wells is concerned. At any time industrialists may come and buy land … and take the water which Parliament has authorised us to take for the supply of public needs.' Collieries, breweries or railway companies could extract water from the subsoil, but faced no statutory restriction as to how they used it, thereby jeopardising undertakings' obligations to provide public supplies.

On the other hand, it was complaints from other proprietors and groups *against* those water undertakings which abstracted underground supplies, which caused the most dispute towards the end of the nineteenth century. The undertakers' extractions of underground water caused considerable concern to a variety of interests, including the local authorities in the areas where the resources were situated. In the Home Counties there was evidence of falling water tables, due to the increased extractions of the undertakers serving London. When proposals came before it, Parliament sought to protect all parties, providing for compensation or regulating the use of underground supplies. This process, however, invariably generated costly petitioning and litigation. To generalise the protection granted under recent private Acts, a private Bill, drafted on behalf of interests believing themselves to be injured by the undertakings' abstractions, was introduced in 1909 (Sheail 1982: 462).

The Joint Select Committee appointed to consider the Bill described it as a proposal designed to 'restrict the powers of authorised water undertakings' (1910: iv). Avowedly it was introduced to create conditions to ensure that the public would be protected when users' claims were in conflict. In detail, it was proposed that local authorities should have the right to supplies piped across their district by another undertaking. Another proposed clause placed the burden of proof, in cases of compensation claims, on undertakings having to demonstrate their *innocence*, rather than the landowners having to prove their loss. The proposed Bill caused consternation in the water-supply industry, which made numerous and detailed objections to it.

Broadly the Joint Select Committee agreed with the objections, acknowledging the Bill to be 'too inquisitorial and too inflexible' (1910: iv; 'Discussion', *TWE* 1910: 221), and in general subjected it to much criticism. The broader significance of the episode was that it led Parliament to begin to evaluate the legal framework governing water-resource development. Defects were recognised and the case for industrial reform was raised. The Committee recommended that a Central Authority to supervise resource allocation should be established, the country to be divided into watershed boards responsible to it. Nevertheless, essentially the Committee supported the *status quo*, especially the continued authorisation of source developments by Parliamentary local Acts. War broke out with no further action taken.

The episode had provided an occasion for the mobilisation of special interests and accelerated the emergence of the type of interest-group lobbying which would dominate events after 1918. The role of the Association of Water Engineers (formed in 1899) in orchestrating opposition to the Bill was apparent ('Discussion', *TWE* 1910: 221; 'Report of water areas', *TWE* 1910). The Association took the initiative in convening a conference of all parties hostile to the proposal, at which it was mandated to represent virtually all the water authorities and other interests sharing its concerns. The Joint Select Committee inquiry itself provided the Association with an opportunity for self-publicity and the presentation of its case. This was also true for the Association of Municipal Corporations, which was at this time the main conduit for the representation of the municipal water interest.

The waterworks which had been built up by the bigger local authorities by the early twentieth century had become large, highly successful enterprises. They frequently made a contribution to rate income, and their capitalizations, turnover and markets exceeded those of many of the country's leading companies. Municipal water supply had significant interconnections with other local author-ity responsibilities, including public health and the protection of property against fire. It is not surprising that the municipal water authorities developed a jealously protective attitude towards their enterprises and strove to maintain their autonomy. They demanded freedom from government supervision. The Municipal Corporations Association argued in relation to a proposed ministerial Order (quoted in Hassan 1995: 200): 'In order that the water authorities may discharge their responsibilities effectively, it is essential that they should have a free hand in the management of their undertakings ... and that they should not be interfered with by another body.' The municipal interest's claim to hegemony in the field of water management is reflected in the bitter emotions generated by the formation of the MWB. While it represented easily the biggest transfer of control from private to public enterprise in the industry's history, the municipal lobby's wrath was ignited because the London County Council was not to become the responsi-ble authority; this was to be a board representative of even wider (even if still pre-dominantly municipal) interests. An editorial comment in the *Municipal Journal* (12 December 1902: 1015) spluttered: 'The Bill [to establish the MWB] is not a "settlement" of the London water question: it is merely an attempt to degrade the County Council.'

By the early twentieth century a range of special interests had emerged with the fragmented, if rapid, growth of the industry. They displayed a myopic vision of the form which any future restructuring of the industry might take. Manufacturing industry, too, with its customary practice of using the water environment as a virtually costless resource for dumping its effluent, was develop-ing a narrow view of the form which a modernisation of water management should take, as the history of the attempts to strengthen pollution control illustrates. After a period of rapid, almost spontaneous change, growth began to decelerate from the early twentieth century, and industrial and political structures crystallised. A vested interest in the status quo was developing. Municipal enterprise, for example, did not wish to surrender its dominance in any future reorganisation of the industry. Such aspirations would complicate subsequent efforts to reform water management in England and Wales.

Environmental impacts and scientific insufficiency

Environmental impacts

A historical study of water obviously forms part of environmental history. This is partly because water is part of the natural environment. It is also because the way in which the water industry grew had significant environmental repercussions.

Elsewhere in the world clashes over water could assume a more overly political and violent form than in Britain. The marginalisation of certain groups by capitalist industrialisation could, on occasion, be symbolised by and associated with the endeavours of Big Capital to harness water resources for distant industry in ways detrimental to those living in the catchments. The damming of the Merrimack River by Boston capitalists to furnish energy for the New England cotton industry provoked violent protests in the twenty years after 1859 (Steinberg 1990). Outside Wales in the 1970s, while water was frequently enmeshed in local-political and public health controversies, it was rarely the subject of such polarised conflict in this country. Nevertheless, the economic and social impacts of the impounding of upland streams to meet the needs of distant urban markets were often considerable.

The acquisition of moorlands and the construction of reservoirs led to significant changes in land use. The fixed-supply, gravitation waterworks developed by energetic local authorities from the 1840s were often admired for their hydraulic innovation and scale. But they also involved, from a later perspective, the costly construction of long-distance mains and the 'sterilisation' of extensive gathering-grounds, including loss of access, reduction of amenity and the abandonment of many hill farms. Manchester ringed its Longdendale gathering-grounds with 'Trespassers Will Be Prosecuted' notices. The moors were patrolled by keepers, who effectively warded off intruders (Stephenson 1989). Birmingham secured Parliamentary authorisation for its River Elan scheme in Wales in 1892, and acquired extensive moorlands. By way of explanation, it was stated that the 45,562 acres supported only thirty-one sheep-farmers, 'who held their farms under strict regulations for preventing contamination of the streams and reservoirs' (Lees 1914: 501). Though the Acts of 1878 and 1892, authorising the Thirlmere and Elan schemes respectively, did make some provision for public access to gathering-grounds (Smith 1972: 129), this did not stop the municipal corporations from bringing about major changes in moorland management. In fact, it was the earlier experience of the original authorisation of the Rivington reservoirs, which provided only common-law protection to Liverpool against pollution of sources, which led the corporation to secure greater powers in 1871. These lessons were applied in the Vyrnwy scheme, where Liverpool purchased all the gathering-grounds (Liverpool 1903: 226–31). Such acquisitions did lead to land-use changes, afforestation in particular being adopted in pursuit of the local authorities' aim of minimising human or animal interference with the sources.

Corporations consistently refused fishing, for example, in their reservoirs. Afforestation was first introduced as a land-use policy at Oldham in 1885 (Hobbs 1950: 5; Hibbert 1948: 205). Liverpool's Vyrnwy project and Manchester's Thirlmere scheme displayed both aspects – extensive cultivation of out-of-character conifer plantations and restrictions upon sheep farming.

The dispute over Manchester's plans for Thirlmere anticipated later struggles over amenity. In the words of McFadzean (1987: 45–6), Manchester Corporation's policy here involved:

> the demolition of a number of farms and cottages ... the denial of access to any portion of the raised lake, and the prohibition of swimming, fishing and all other aquatic sports. The Committee ... was intent on establishing ... a forbidden country within the confines of the Cumbrian mountains where even the shepherds ... were to become employees of Manchester Corporation.

One of the most dramatic effects of the Thirlmere works was the doubling of the lake's acreage, an impact which had not occurred at earlier schemes by Glasgow and Whitehaven in taking water from Loch Katrine and Ennerdale. The publication of the Thirlmere proposals in 1878 generated a major dispute. The Select Committee investigating the petitions against the Bill, however, claimed that the appearance of the lake would be enhanced by the changes, and that the effect of the eight-foot difference between high- and low-water mark would be inconspicuous (Sheail 1986b: 52). Though defeated with the passing of the authorising Act of 1879, the Thirlmere Defence Association at least had registered notice that similar proposals in future could no longer be treated as purely a private matter between landowners and promoters (Kinnersley 1988: 65).

While the Thirlmere protests anticipated later environmental campaigns, they arose from a concern over landscape and habitats rather than a need to develop a sustainable approach to the exploitation of water resources. The way the water industry expanded in the nineteenth century did have seriously adverse consequences for the water environment. These effects became the focus for controversy and debate. Some of the disputes were ill-informed, and were often motivated by commercial or professional rivalries rather than environmental concerns. Among the factors, which contributed to the not always constructive debates surrounding these problems, was that the scientific understanding of the interrelationships between humanity and the natural environment was incompletely developed in the Victorian period.

Scientific insufficiency?

Science expanded enormously in the two centuries after 1700 and by the late Victorian period it enjoyed huge prestige (Russell 1983). Nevertheless the whole question of the contribution of science to industrial technology is problematic (Russell 1983: 98). Smith (1972: 10–20) has argued that the nineteenth century

witnessed a quickening of the development of many scientific disciplines relevant
to the aquatic sphere, including hydrology and meteorology. Yet, according to
Luckin (1986: 63) no science of the environment existed in this era, although
Newson (1992b) offers an alternative perspective. It is clear from recent studies
that the scientific analysis and conclusions utilised in a number of areas of water
resource management were based on very shaky foundations in this period.

Because the development of water policy occurred in a political 'context of
conflict' (Hamlin 1990: 8), science became very important to the lobbies. Hamlin
shows that science provided authority and legitimacy to proposals for the development of water supplies. Promoters of rival schemes hired experts to lend weight
and respectability to their projects. When the manipulation of science, itself
resting upon uncertain foundations, becomes an integral part of interest-group
politics, which exercised such a decisive influence upon water policy, it becomes
apparent that the calculation of the impact of science in the water services field
becomes complex indeed. The system of adversarial science was not always damaging. In the 1870s and 1880s Edward Frankland was an effective spokesperson for
those interests seeking to provide supplies, alternative to the questionable river
sources used by the London water companies: 'He was an effective witness, quick
witted, prestigious, in command of a wealth of facts', personifying activism and
authority (Hamlin 1990: 174). But it is clear that, in general, science was discredited by the cynical way it was used by the vested interests (Hamlin 1990:
212–13; 1982: 73). Nor was it only for proposals for London that eminent scientists could be recruited to support diametrically contradictory claims about, for
example, the quality of water supplies made available by rival schemes; this was
also common in the provinces (*Bolton Chronicle*, 2 February 1854).

Of the forces which influenced the water supply of mid-century London
Hamlin observes (1990: 101): 'A great deal more was at issue than the quality of the
water ... ; at stake were the values of the land from which the new supply would
come, the value of companies' shares, the careers of engineers who planned or built
new supplies.' Perhaps even more strikingly, along with Luckin, Hamlin has
demonstrated that the science employed in the water analysis and treatment field,
chemical analysis, was an 'empty orthodoxy' (Hamlin 1990: 205) which could not,
for example, distinguish foul from safe water.

Gradually, from the 1880s, the water question moved from the domain of
chemistry into that of biology. Until then chemical analysis continued to exercise
a significant influence upon the water industry. The methodology came under the
control of the London water companies, and a close, if openly criticised, relationship developed between them and scientific consultants (Luckin 1986: 52, 69).
Chemical analysis was indeed employed primarily to show that the sources used by
the companies were harmless, despite the fact that the river supply was indisput-
ably contaminated with sewage (Hamlin 1990: 89, 100). It is hard to avoid the
conclusion that professional rivalries and the sometimes cynical use of scientific

expertise by vested interests did not help expedite a resolution of the London water problem in this period.

The interplay between incompletely developed science and interest politics also had implications for river quality. Rivers became more polluted and fisheries disappeared partly because pollution controls were insufficiently tough. This, in turn, was partly due to the success of the manufacturing lobby in diluting the key reform of 1876. In accounting for 'a story mainly of failure, of a massive dose of science failing to provide the technical guidance needed to solve social problems of water supply, wastes disposal and rivers', Hamlin (1987: 547) does not support a theory of scientific insufficiency. Although acknowledging the existence of significant areas of scientific ignorance, his explanation favours two other themes. These are, first, 'the failure of political institutions' to solve the public health problem even where relevant scientific information was available, and, second, a lack of objectivity within the scientific community whose members were so bound up with adversarial conflicts and professional rivalries (Hamlin 1987: 548–53). His study of the development of fisheries policy led Macleod to a slightly different conclusion. Principles defined in the 1860s for the conservation of salmon fisheries required, in his view (1967: 149–50): 'more knowledge of natural history and fisheries technology than the Victorian scientific community possessed .... The endowment of environmental research implied a financial and constitutional commitment which the Victorian government was not prepared to accept.'

Hydrological and geological forces governing the behaviour of aquifers were also poorly understood. As in other areas, competing interests tried to gain access to, and utilise, the corpus of knowledge which did exist, by hiring 'experts' to speak on their behalf at inquiries. Significant abstractions from underground sources in the London basin since the 1770s had caused aquifers to dry out, so degrading their properties and allowing salt-water intrusion from the Thames (Addyman 1979: 245). By the late nineteenth century evidence of a fall in the water table in the South-East was emerging, leading to the drying-up of springs, water meadows and watercress beds. There were, however, disputes over the very facts of the matter. The Commission of the Metropolitan Water Supply in 1892–93 was sceptical about both the empirical evidence and the theoretical basis for arguing that pumping and increased abstractions could lead to a decline in water levels. It preferred a more reassuring theory, which implied that aquifers could resiliently tolerate heavy abstractions (Sheail 1982: 398). In fact, before long harder evidence of falling water tables made such a position untenable. In the meantime, however, the Commission's attitude had made more difficult the task of opposing abstraction schemes promoted by companies supplying London.

Conclusion

By 1914 the water industry had made impressive progress in expanding supplies, meeting growing demands and improving the quality of water provided to consumers. The relative neglect of the after-use side of water management, however, was associated with a hasty diffusion of water-carriage sewage disposal, without the effects of the increased effluent load upon river systems being fully taken into account. The unbalanced and atomistic growth of water services also reflected the vigorous free play of private interests over these years. Insights into the causes of these trends, and the emergence of a context of rivalry which became so typical of the water-policy field, can also be assisted by taking account of the natural characteristics of hydrological systems and the conflicting- and multiple-use nature of water. A situation was created, which was especially favourable to the presentation of special interests by powerful lobbies, whose claims were at times assisted by the uncertainties prevailing in the relevant scientific disciplines. However, the adoption of an approach to policy formation, in which the interest of private lobbies took precedence over public requirements was, given hydrological interdependencies, unsustainable in the long run.

3

The inter-war and post-war years: the paralysis of special interests

Water at the crossroads

In some senses, the water industry was at a crossroads in the early twentieth century. Decades of rapid growth were followed by a deceleration in the tempo of structural change and policy development. The regulatory framework had incorporated the seemingly sound principle that Parliament should scrutinise each project individually, with the terms of authorisation being informed by local circumstances. But this approach relied upon local initiatives to develop proposals and also provided the occasion for the mobilisation of special interests. Among the results were the development of a waterworks code with little uniformity of practice, and the provision of water services being singularly uncoordinated at the regional level.

For some time expert opinion had urged the adoption of a more coherent approach to water policy, for example through conferring on the government or a central authority more power to guide developments. That it was undesirable to meet urban water needs through long-distance gravitation projects was remarked upon by the Joint Committee on Water Resources (1934–35: 10), essentially reiterating a complaint which had been made as long ago as 1869 by the Royal Commission on Water Supply. Up to 1944, however, no effective moves were made to reform national water policy so as to modify the influence of sectional interests upon water resource development.

The need to modernise water management structures was widely acknowledged by the inter-war period. The issue began to assume a little more importance and was debated in Parliament. But on three occasions between 1914 and 1951 the 'tide of events' intervened to have the effect of aborting proposals which were under active consideration. Because it was under-prioritised, the process of reform was so long drawn out for events to repeatedly interrupt it (Hassan 1995: 195). This illustrates the difficulties of achieving change, when the strength of government commitment on the one hand was balanced against the influence of sundry interests anxious to modify or halt legislative proposals on the other.

Thus during the period under study, with the emergence of a lobbying system, in which groups were anxious to defend vested interests, with a government concerned with the need to consult all parties, and with a general disinclination to encroach on private property or other established rights, water reform proceeded at a snail's pace. Complete inaction there was not, however. Among measures of note were the Salmon Fisheries Act of 1923, which strengthened the powers of fishery boards, the Land Drainage Act of 1930, which established river-basin-based river conservancy (Catchment) Boards, and the Public Health (Drainage of Trade Premises) Act of 1937 (hereafter the Drainage of Trade Premises Act), which required local authority sewers to receive trade effluent. All of these measures, however, were circumscribed in various ways – the fishery boards could do nothing about fishless rivers, the Catchment Boards' duties were confined to land drainage matters, and the 1937 Act did not require traders to use sewers. The emergence of appropriately constituted bodies responsible for discharging specialist functions within river basins, and composed of a wider range of interests, did have significance for the subsequent development of water policy. For the time being, however, the framework governing water resource development inherited from the Victorian period remained largely intact.

To account for the failure of reform before the 1940s this chapter will look, first, into the interactions between supply and demand pressures, then examine the management of water quality and rivers, and finally consider the main influences upon water policy during the period.

Satisfying requirements: water demand and supply

Consumption trends and the pressure on supplies

By the early twentieth century the allocation of upland gathering-grounds was nearly complete. Yet, during the period under study, the water supply industry experienced little difficulty in meeting requirements. The principal reason for the lack of pressure upon the industry was that demand, as far as can be judged, grew at only a modest rate over the first forty years of the century relative to the preceding and succeeding periods. Estimates summarised in Table 3.1 suggest that demand for water grew at just over 1.5 per cent per annum over the first half of the twentieth century, a rate which had doubled by the 1960s.

The simple statistic, gallons consumed per head per day (ghd), although concealing a complexity of economic, social and cultural influences, does give a consistent measure of consumption at a moment in time. While noting the risks of making comparisons, especially across towns, estimates summarised in Tables 3.1–3.3, along with other evidence, confirm that a deceleration in the rate in the growth of water demand occurred in the inter-war years.

The reduction in the rate of growth of water consumption may have been partly due to industrial requirements growing less rapidly. Other factors, however, would have tended to increase water consumption. The belated transition to the

Table 3.1 *Rate of growth of public water supplies per head, 1900–71 (% annual compound rate of growth)*

1900–50	1.58
1950–61	2.70
1961–71	3.03

Source: WRB 1973: 29.

Table 3.2 *Water consumption in selected English cities, 1825–1978 (ghd)*

Newcastle	1851 11	1901 36	–	1951 40	1962 48	1978 62
Manchester	1841 12	1913 35	1938 41	–	1962 65	1974 84
Leeds	1851 8	1913 34	–	–	1962 44	–
London	1825 25	1913 34	1936 37	1952 49	1962 57	–
Birmingham	–	1913 27	1938 32	1948 47	1962 52	–
Liverpool	1846 8	1913 33	1938 37	1948 46	1962 53	–

Sources: Liverpool 1903; Parker 1913; Wegmann 1918; BWA 1950; Dickinson 1954; Twort 1963; Rennison 1979; Hassan 1985.

Table 3.3 *Annual rate of growth of water consumption in English cities, 1825–1978 (% p.a.)*

Newcastle	1851–1901	2.4	1901–51	0.2	1951–78	1.7
Manchester	1841–1914	1.5	1913–38	0.6	1938–74	2.0
Leeds	1851–1913	1.9	1913–62	1.0		
London	1825–1913	0.3	1913–36	0.3	1936–52	2.5
Birmingham	–		1913–38	0.7	1938–48	4.0
Liverpool	1846–1913	1.9	1913–38	0.4	1938–48	2.2

Sources: as for Table 3.2.

water-carriage system of waste removal in particular led to a large increase in water use. Sheffield, for example, was a town which had 68,000 houses and only 4,000 water-closets in 1887, but by 1947 had 161,000 houses and 171,000 water-closets. By the 1940s virtually all new houses were built with baths, sinks and water-closets installed (Hobbs 1950: 12).

Greater confidence in the purity of supplies, due to progress in water treatment techniques, also favoured increased domestic use of water. By the 1930s the principles of a four-stage treatment process, consisting of storage, rapid primary filtration, slow secondary filtration and chlorination, were widely understood by waterworks managers. Techniques of clarification and mechanical filtration became widespread and more sophisticated. Above all, from the 1920s the use of chemical reagents and the chlorination of supplies were developed extensively. After 1937 sterilisation of domestic supplies by chemical agents was adopted routinely by all major undertakers (Hobbs 1950: 14–16). The application of these techniques contributed to a 'very high standard of purity' being attained for London's water supplies, and the incidence of water-borne diseases falling to 'remarkably' low levels, only 195 cases of enteric fever being notified for the county of London by 1931 (Garner 1933: 683–4).

There were occasional water quality scares, notably those associated with typhoid epidemics in Epping in 1931 and Croydon in 1937; and serious gastroenteritis epidemics occurred in the leafy suburban retreats of Ewell, Sutton, Carshalton and Wallington in 1936, which were traced to a polluted well in Cheam ('The Epping epidemic', *WWE*, 20 July 1932: 340; *MYB*, 1939: li–liii; Jackson 1973: 123). These incidents, though isolated, led to efforts being made to correct perceived flaws in public health administration. In fact, the general safety of water delivered to the consumer had improved out of all recognition since the late nineteenth century. This was reflected in the drop of typhoid mortality from 160 per million living in 1896 to only ten per million in 1945 (Taylor 1946: 26–7).

Principally, the growth of domestic consumption was the result of a rise in the standard of living, as expressed in the increased installation and use of water fittings. The first few decades of the century saw the shared use of the communal tap by a number of households becoming a thing of the past. Working-class homes were being supplied with the novelty of abundant internal water supplies and even baths, as were middle-class homes, and by 1930, 'the bathing habit has become more general', affirmed Stilgoe (1930: 11). A further change was the introduction of increasingly sophisticated heating systems, evident in the typical private homes constructed by the speculative London builder of the inter-war period. After 1919, the vast majority of new London houses were fitted with a heated water system operated by a back boiler in the living-room fireplace, or a slow combustion stove or gas circulator in the kitchen. Heated towel-rails were found higher up the price range, while airing cupboards warmed by a hot-water tank were standard. Central heating, as such, was rare, being unavailable to the poor in America until after 1950 (Cowan 1983: 95), although a single radiator in the hall was not uncommon. As Jackson (1973: 144) said: 'Inside, the new houses reflected social change', the new fittings being partly a function of the increasingly servantless households.

These changes permitted increased water use and rising standards of personal hygiene and cleanliness. The introduction of automatic flush systems with large cisterns, and the increased laundering of clothes also led to higher water consumption in the 1930s and 1940s. Growing incomes by the late 1940s encouraged families to send washing to commercial laundries or even to acquire the new automatic washing-machines. To the extent the latter was replacing the former, increased water use occurred, as commercial laundering was more economical in water use than the home machine (PRO 1948b, 1949c).

Table 3.4   *Water consumption in Bradford, 1920–40*

	Houses with WCs (%)	Houses with baths (%)	Domestic consumption (ghd)
1920	43	29	25
1930	92	43	37
1940	95	56	42

Source: Hobbs 1950: 43.

The movement of the population into better-quality housing was a most significant factor in the growth of water consumption. The cost of water was not a constraint on use as it was generally an insignificant item in household budgets. In a representative semi-detached London home of 1935 the cost of annual water rates amounted only to £2.94, compared to £84.24 for mortgage payments, £16.50 for local rates and £12.50 for travelling to work (Jackson 1973: 199). The crucial factor was the demographic shift to better-class property with improved standard fittings, which led automatically to an increase in water use. The average consumption of a 'typical' London family in traditional accommodation was only 5.8 ghd in the inter-war years. On moving into corporation housing it increased immediately to 18–19 ghd, and rose over the following eighteen months to some 24 ghd (Hobbs 1950: 43). The consumption in better private property, well equipped with baths and water closets, might range from 23 to 53 ghd, as in South Staffordshire (PRO 1949b). The impact of improved access to water fittings is also reflected in figures on water consumption in Bradford summarised in Table 3.4.

Many of these changes in lifestyle, however, took place at the very end of the period and had more significance for the 1950s and 1960s. Contemporaries became aware of society's apparent new-found thirst for water and the pressure it was threatening to place on supplies in the post-war period. Increases in consumption were particularly noticed in 'water-loving London', where there was an increase in the number of 'bath-a-day addicts' who were using anything up to 90 ghd in comparison with typical pre-war consumption of 20–25 ghd. 'Fortunately' they were still a minority (Hall 1949). This was another example of London following American fashions, reflected in the 'best' new hotels of the 1930s being built with a bath in every bedroom ('Water supply', *WWE*, 1932: 344).

These, however, were new patterns, which barely touched much of the population. A surprisingly large percentage of houses possessed limited facilities, many with no more than a cold-water tap and water-closet. Despite a growth in consumption in Newcastle, for example, some sixty per cent of dwellings there were still without a bath (PRO 1949a,1949c). In 1946, throughout the MWB area and also in the larger provincial centres, forty-six per cent of domestic premises had only one tap and one water- closet (Hobbs 1950: 43). Despite the convenience of electricity, the dissemination of electric-powered domestic appliances was quite limited. Only from 1950 did reductions in price and marketing campaigns lead to a significant increase in the sale of washing-machines (Yarwood 1981: 151–2). Household penetration beyond one per cent of the market in England and Wales was achieved only in 1934 for clothes-washers and in 1957 for dishwashers (Bowden and Offer 1994: 729). In many rural areas in 1950 domestic consumption was under 20 ghd, and where standpipes were still relied upon it could be as low as 5 ghd. Overall, therefore, the increase in consumption was restrained.

Another favourable factor in the demand–supply equation was the tendency of Victorian developers to underestimate the capacity of schemes. Subsequently, minor engineering works to allow greater use of catchments, or the renegotiation of compensation awards, enabled waterworks' yields to be increased (Smith 1972: 130–1). For these reasons the pressures to modernise and expand water provision were not intense in the inter-war period. An analysis of requirements found a general sufficiency of supplies in Lancashire in 1935, for example, excess capacity being anticipated down to 1951 and a deficiency only being forecast by 1961 (PRO 1938). Sleeman (1953: 38) commented that, unlike electricity supply, the extent of the reorganisation carried out in the water and gas sectors in this period 'was very much less', because the needs were less pressing.

Drought and compensation supplies

This unexceptional situation was disturbed, nevertheless, in one or two respects. Low rainfall placed strain on the capacity of the water industry to meet demand over a succession of so-called drought years: 1887, 1911, 1921, 1933 and 1934. Drought did focus attention on deficiencies in the prevailing methods of allocating supplies. There was no general problem, with an estimated flow from surface and underground sources equivalent to fifteen times national requirements (Ministry of Health 1943–44: 26). For many undertakers the principal constraint was financial: they lacked the resources to carry out costly schemes, and were reluctant to embark on projects to meet occasional drought conditions. Some local authorities postponed schemes repeatedly through the 1920s. In 1921 the water shortage led to proposals being drawn up, only to be postponed in 1922, which 'set in wet' (Walters 1936: 211).

Ingenious, but highly inefficient, improvisations were often resorted to for overcoming shortages. In many cases water was pumped by inefficient machinery at heavy hire charges, or carried through improvised pipes underground. Polluted sources were frequently used in conjunction with temporary, expensively hired filtration plant (Walters 1936: 212).

Drought increased public interest in water supplies and stimulated debates about their organisation, the feasibility of a national water grid, and the need to co-ordinate, pool and centrally control resources (*Hansard*, 20 June 1934: para. 438). It focused attention upon compensation supplies, and the nineteenth-century practice of reserving from one- to two-thirds of a waterworks' yield for mill-owners. In 1923 the newly appointed Advisory Committee on Water (ACW) spoke of the need to 'abolish' such 'arbitrary' practices (PRO 1923). Although tempering its position subsequently, the Committee maintained that generous compensation awards led to a serious under-utilisation of resources and argued, in 1930, that the existing arrangements were wasteful, obsolescent and unfair. It proposed an alternative method of calculating awards, which would have effectively reduced compensation supplies by fifty per cent from the prevailing one-third of yield (Walters 1936: 203).

The issue was subsequently considered by the Joint Committee on Water Resources and Supplies (JCWR). This influential Parliamentary committee, however, was strongly disposed to maintain the status quo, and was against revising existing awards (*JCWR* 1935–36: xiv–xv). The Joint Committee appears to have been influenced by pressure from the Riparian Owners' Committee of the Federation of British Industry (FBI), which argued forcefully against the ACW's recommendations, maintaining that there was insufficient data to warrant their general application and arguing it had underestimated the importance of compensation water for industry (Sheail 1983: 388–9).

The government was indeed reluctant to act on a unilateral basis, but the drought conditions of the early 1930s did lead to some re-evaluation of the supply situation. The principal measure taken by the government to meet shortages was the Water Supplies (Exceptional Shortages Orders) Act of 1934. The Ministry of Health could make Orders under the Act to authorise local authorities to take steps to encourage economies in water consumption, or to modify restrictions on the taking of water. An Order, for example, was made which allowed the MWB to take more water from the Thames. The Act, significantly, also permitted the Minister to modify the release of compensation supplies. A number of voluntary arrangements were made, especially concerning compensation water, which led to some applications for Orders being dropped. In the event, no across-the-board reassessment of the proportion reserved for compensation supplies was undertaken. As in other spheres of water policy, only improvisation, rather than a full-scale review of the issue in question, was undertaken in this era.

Rural shortages

Drought did highlight the problems of rural supplies. Rural communities were often overlooked by source developments due to the relatively high cost of provision and their limited financial resources. In 1914 approximately sixty-two per cent of 12,869 rural parishes were without piped supplies (*Return of water undertakings* 1914: xxxvii). Formerly, the 'old-fashioned' system, by which each house or group of cottages provided its own source of water, usually in the form of a shallow well, had something to recommend it as a cheap and practical solution. However, it had disadvantages – the water was seldom pure, and it could not be raised sufficiently to allow a gravitational supply to sinks and baths (Veal 1950: 268). The lack of piped supplies also created difficulties for waste removal. A Women's Institute survey found that over half the houses in twenty-seven federation areas relied on earth, bucket or chemical closets. Many council houses built in Northamptonshire villages in the 1920s and 1930s were provided with only bucket sanitation. Even in 1945 many thousands living in rural areas had to carry water from standpipes over two hundred feet from cottages (*MYB 1945*: 296–7). Gradually the substandard levels of service delivered to the rural population came to be recognised as unacceptable.

Progress towards improving supplies was facilitated by the Local Government Act of 1926, which provided for cost-spreading among local authorities. Given the cost of laying mains to a handful of inhabitants in remoter districts, an ACW report to the Ministry of Health still suggested in 1929 that providing a piped supply to absolutely every village and hamlet in the country was impractical (Walters 1936: 209). The 1934 drought, however, emphasised the poor quality, unreliable nature and inadequacy of rural supplies. The Ministry of Health now adopted the view that everything should be done to complete the extension of piped water to sparsely populated areas. Consequently the government agreed to a £1 million grant to assist the development of rural supplies under the Water Act of 1934. This stimulated and encouraged county councils to promote further schemes to the value of £6 million, which represented the first systematic assault on the problem of rural water supply. By 1944 the proportion of the rural population without a piped supply had fallen to thirty per cent, or five per cent of the population of England and Wales (Ministry of Health 1943–44: 15). A further grant of £15 million was made available in 1945, as 'an essential part of the general reconstruction programme', to reduce the charges upon the rates from the building of new water and sewerage works (Ministry of Health 1943–44: 15).

Before 1945, therefore, those affected badly by drought restrictions and those living in rural districts were the groups most seriously disadvantaged by supply deficiencies. The government's response to these difficulties was a £1 million grant and legislation which allowed the Ministry of Health to make compulsory Orders; these, however, had an application of only six months.

Evidently the government did not regard the supply shortfalls as a serious problem. The experience of difficulties was transient, or felt by groups without political influence. By contrast, the government was receptive to arguments by well-organised parties, such as the FBI and Catchments Boards, against proposals to change compensation awards through ministerial action. A government spokesman in the debate on the drought recommended halving the amount of water used in baths as his contribution to ideas for countering the effect of shortages; the government placed faith in the consultative work of the weak regional committees as offering a future way out of the supply difficulties (*Hansard*, Shakespeare, 3 July 1934: para. 1812). Like the government, the JCWR (1935–36: ix–x), believed that the drought conditions of 1933 and 1934 were 'somewhat exaggerated in the minds of the public'. The committee feared that any alteration to existing procedures governing the allocation of water supplies might seriously affect property rights. Central authority was insufficiently bestirred by the shortage difficulties exposed in the 1930s to implement any changes to the prevailing system of distributing supplies, other than through temporary, *ad hoc* measures.

Industrial restructuring: policy aims and instruments

As already indicated, the inter-war water industry inherited a very fragmented structure. During this period there was a wide-ranging discussion of how industrial performance generally might be improved through restructuring and rationalisation (MacGregor *et al.* 1930; Lucas 1937; O'Brien 1937). A consensus developed that, for utilities, public regulation was desirable (Dimock 1933: 19–28). The Labour Party, in particular, envisaged that extending public ownership to such industries would contribute to its plans for promoting economic reconstruction, efficiency, investment, research and training and social justice. In the case of the water industry nationalisation was adopted as Labour Party policy in 1934. Labour, however, did not pursue this goal very resolutely, which forms part of a wider story of policy failure for this sector (Hassan 1995).

Nevertheless, that the water supply industry suffered structural weaknesses was widely admitted. Some engineers in the 1930s attempted to draw lessons from the electricity supply industry. Proposals were made for securing a more effective interregional exploitation and distribution of water supplies through the establishment of a national water grid. This was inspired by the successful rationalisation of electricity generation and supplies achieved by the Central Electricity Board set up in 1926. The proposal for a national water grid was made in 1933 and endorsed by the Institution of Mechanical Engineers. Professional opinion within the water industry, however, dismissed the idea. On hydrological, geographical and technical grounds attempts to draw parallels between electricity and water supplies were – to water engineers – a little absurd. For example, it was estimated that water mains performed an equivalent service to electricity mains at approximately thirty-six times the cost (*MYB 1935*: xxx). The economics of long-distance, interregional supply were not the same in the two sectors.

To encourage rationalisation, Parliament placed faith in the formation of *ad hoc* Joint Water Boards representing large areas, such as the South Potteries Water Board established in the 1920s. Their members were elected indirectly by constituent local authorities. By 1932 thirty-three had come into existence, rising to fifty-five by 1953. Among the largest of the new Joint Boards was the Durham County Water Board, which supplied over twenty local authorities. There were, however, a number of problems with the dependence on Joint Boards for achieving policy aims. Agreement was difficult to obtain among local authorities, and their creation was a slow and costly process involving statutory powers (Sleeman 1953: 55).

To promote regional co-operation and voluntary mergers among undertakers, the government also placed faith in regional advisory committees. They were advisory and data collection bodies and their compilation of information about local water resources and requirements would, it was hoped, encourage the adoption of a more regional perspective on water development. Despite government encouragement only four such committees had been created by 1929. In 1944 nine were operating, representing 354 undertakings and a population of sixteen million. The Regional Advisory Committees were singularly weak and ineffective bodies. The Minister of Health himself stressed that their only role was to advise the local authorities which set them up. In no way could a committee be 'a nucleus of a Joint Water Board of Joint Authority of any kind' (PRO 1925). The Yorkshire committee passed a resolution to the effect that their role was of no avail as they had no authority (*Hansard*, 19 February 1935: para. 79). It was eventually admitted in Parliament that they were weak bodies, which were 'made use of as the Minister ... desires' (*Hansard*, 3 May 1944: para. 1361). The Regional Committees, as a principal aid to the government's aspiration of promoting reorganisation in the water supply industry, had a limited impact.

That the atomistic structure of the water industry hindered the efficient provision of services was, however, recognised and, by the 1940s, strong arguments for reorganising the industry were being made within the Labour Party. It was envisaged that rationalisation would enable a better co-ordination and planning of water resource development and permit a wide variety of scale economies to be achieved – from improved standardisation in product quality, equipment and charges to more effective administration (*Hansard*, Mikardo, 30 June 1948: paras 1409–15; PRO 1948a). Both the Water Act of 1945 passed by the post-war, caretaker Churchill administration, however, and measures on water passed by the nationalising Labour government failed to address adequately the fundamental structural weaknesses of the water industry and did very little to accelerate the process of rationalisation.

Industrial organisation

The origins of the larger water undertakings like the MWB lay in the nineteenth century. By 1934 it distributed water to seven million consumers living in sixty-three local authorities. Manchester served one and a half million living throughout thirteen districts, Liverpool one million living in twelve districts and Birmingham one million in seven districts. Among the private companies, the South Staffordshire Water Company supplied one million living within thirty local authorities (*Joint Committee* 1934–35: 2). The DVWB had a complex pattern of distribution, part-supplying a number of authorities.

Turning from enterprise structures to source developments, the works promoted by the largest water authorities of the era, including Manchester and Liverpool, were conservative in conception, representing essentially a continuation of nineteenth-century practice. Their long-distance gravitation works exploited more intensively the resources of Cumbrian and Welsh catchments. But the tempo of development was slow. Although the Haweswater project received the Royal Assent in 1919, work on the first stage was delayed until 1929 and was not completed until 1955. Similarly, Liverpool's third Vyrnwy pipeline was also authorised in 1919, but the additional supply did not become available until 1938.

The inter-war years were not a time of great waterworks development. From the vantage-point of 1946, a President of the Institution of Water Engineers recognised the last quarter of the previous century as a period of relatively 'enormous' and 'prodigious' activity (Taylor 1946: 27). This was reflected in the fact that the second half of the nineteenth century witnessed about four times as many Acts of Parliament authorising waterworks undertakings as in the first fifty years of the twentieth century (Hobbs 1950: 19).

Among the reasons for the muted patterns of change in the period, with respect to both enterprise restructuring and source developments, were the following: the relatively depressed state of the economy which contributed to weaker demand pressures, especially from industry and trade (Hibbert 1948: 207; Manchester Corporation 1974: 10); inadequate policy instruments developed by government; financial constraints upon the construction of new works; and a parochial resistance to change.

The first two factors have already been discussed. A number of influences complicated the financing of large capital projects. The scope for self-finance was limited, partly because of the high level of fixed costs, with loan charges representing no less than fifty-one per cent of the entire expenditure of local authority waterworks spending between 1925/6 and 1934/5 (*Joint Committee* 1934–35: 7). The ability of the industry to attract resources for capital expenditure was also restricted. Statutory undertakings were limited as to what they could charge consumers for water under the terms of their authorisation, and also, in the case of private companies, as to what they could pay as dividends to shareholders. Statutorily required to extend mains to new housing developments, undertakings faced difficulties in raising capital for such projects which would provide reasonable returns for investors (Dixon 1920: 15). While the income-generating capacity of suppliers did not improve in the inter-war period, labour and material costs had increased substantially since before the First World War, allegedly having at least trebled over these years. After the post-war boom, costs may have declined somewhat, but even in the relatively depressed period of 1925–31 the cost of building trunk mains was almost exactly double what it had been from 1888 to 1903 (PRO 1933b).

Another factor undermining the finances of undertakers were inappropriate costing and charging methods. It was established practice for local government to subsidise unprofitable services, like sewerage, through the rate support grant. The device made no allowance for the renewal of ageing assets (Parker and Penning-Rowsell 1980: 30). The supply of water was regarded almost as a civic duty on the part of local government. Thus water, by most criteria, was one of the cheapest commodities available to the population, being collected, treated and distributed to consumers for only a few pence per ton or, in old money, from less than 2s per 1,000 gallons (Hall 1949). It was said to be well known that water was supplied to 'dwellings occupied by the poorer classes' at a loss, this being the case for seventy per cent of rated tenements in London, the loss being made up from income from the higher-rated properties and trade customers (Stilgoe 1930: 12).

Another reason for the experience of muted change in industrial structures in this period was resistance from the parochial-minded guardians of local auton- omy. Agreement on the formation of Joint Boards was difficult to achieve because the smaller local authorities feared absorption by the larger (Sleeman 1953: 255). Private companies in the South-East were especially reluctant to even co-operate with the MWB, fearing this would 'be a prelude to a tiger's meal'. Resistance to mergers generally was widespread (PRO 1934, 1944).

Concentration of ownership and output did increase between the wars. Larger enterprises became relatively more significant, and by 1944, of 1,196 undertakings, the largest 123 supplied seventy-five per cent of the population of England and Wales (Ministry of Health 1943–44: 4). But the process of change was slow. Table 3.5 outlines broad trends in ownership patterns in the water supply industry. Because of variations in data definitions, comparisons across time should be made with care. Nevertheless it is apparent that official attempts to promote rationalisation had a limited impact. While *concentration* of ownership did increase, the total number of undertakings apparently halving between 1914 and 1956, ownership still remained very dispersed indeed at the latter date. Regarding the *structure* of ownership, the period of great change was the later decades of the nineteenth century, when a rapid growth in the proportion of towns supplied municipally occurred. By contrast, between the 1900s and the 1970s the relative shares of public and private enterprise in the water supply industry remained fairly constant, with the tendency, if anything, for the proportion of supplies controlled by companies to rise above twenty per cent.

Financial constraints, relatively depressed economic conditions and parochi- alism all contributed to the slow pace of restructuring. The inefficiencies in the system of allocating water resources were widely recognised, but the policy tools developed to promote the much-discussed objective of rationalisation were weak. For such reasons pressure for change was limited and because most householders, despite some portents of future changes, continued to make do with basic facilities.

Water quality and river management

Waste management

Sidwick and Murray have stated (1976 IV: 404): 'Between the wars sewage treat- ment moved into the modern age, scientific thinking added technology to art and

Table 3.5   *Estimates of the number of undertakers in the water supply industry in England and Wales, 1904–70*[a]

	Local Authorities	Water Boards and Joint Committee	Water companies	Other	Total
1904	870	8	221	–	–
1914	786	34	200	1,139[b]	2,100
1934	790	48	173	c.1,000[b]	c.2,000
1944	–	–	–	–	1,196
1956	883	42	90	15	1,055
1970	64	101	33	–	198

Notes: [a] Survey numbers are not comparable as each estimate was carried out on a different basis.
[b] Includes very small private and/or non-statutory companies.
Source: Hassan 1995: 190.

habit, and most of the principles of modern sewage treatment were established.' The activated sludge process came to be regarded as the most progressive technique; the earliest experiments were carried out in Bolton in 1902, and by 1913 its effectiveness had been demonstrated at the Davyhulme works, Manchester. Engineers there sought to improve on the performance of the newly invented biological filter, on which an organic gel capable of purifying effluent could grow. The Davyhulme engineers showed that a flock built up from sewage solids could be used repeatedly and that the method promised major improvements in performance, cutting treatment time from days to hours. The importance of the process was also that it facilitated the development of schemes which drained entire catchments into one STW. The first full-scale plant was installed at Worcester in 1916. Following success there, the Activated Sludge Company sold the system in Denmark in 1923, India in 1924 and Canada in 1925 (Coleman 1994). Despite its evident superiority, its introduction was quite slow in Britain and, even in the 1930s, more traditional forms of biological filtration were more commonly employed (Sidwick and Murray 1976 IV: 404).

The disposal of residual sludge from STWs in an economical and acceptable manner was a major issue for scientists and engineers, and during the period attempts were made to perfect sludge digestion at the most modern works (Thompson 1935: 1249). There were a number of enthusiastic champions of sludge – sometimes described as 'inoffensive brown humus' – as a valuable, nitrogenous product which could be usefully employed as an agricultural fertiliser. New York and Milwaukee were able to find customers, and for some reason Kingston upon Thames found outlets on the Continent. In general, however, its commercial disposal remained problematic, and large centres like Manchester,

Glasgow and London preferred to pump sludge into specially designed barges for dumping at sea (Reynolds 1943).

Meanwhile, the goal of establishing sewage treatment on an efficient and rational basis throughout the country awaited not only the perfection of techniques, but also the reorganisation of sewage management and its integration into river-basin-based bodies exercising greater control over the water cycle. Nationally, this would not be realised for many decades.

Other factors which militated against the upgrading of sewage treatment facilities were severe restrictions on capital spending imposed by government during wartime, post-war and at times of economic crisis. Earlier gains were not always cumulative, and pre-1914 progress in river quality in south-east Lancashire was subsequently undermined. The LGB restricted loans and work on STWs fell into abeyance. Local authorities were indifferent to sewage in this unfavourable economic climate, and large authorities like Manchester set a bad example. Only from the late 1920s did Manchester begin to give a more positive lead and only from 1934, with the completion of a £1.5 million project at Davyhulme STW, incorporating a modern version of the activated sludge process, was there a significant improvement in effluent quality from Manchester (Richards 1982: 10.15). By the same year an important regional scheme for sewage disposal and treatment had been inaugurated, following the completion of the Coleshill works of the Birmingham, Tame and Lea Drainage Board, incorporating modern features and covering twenty-four square miles (Thompson 1935: 1249).

The rapid suburban development of housing estates and light industries in west London led to an increasing amount of land being covered in macadam, tiles and concrete. The changed volume, nature and behaviour of wastes and floodwater brought river management in the area to a critical state. Severe flooding occurred in 1927 and 1928, creating a serious public health risk. Sheail (1993d) has described the exceptional achievement of the West Middlesex Drainage Scheme, based on Mogden STW, as a comprehensive response to this 'unprecedented' suburban growth. Overcoming 'immense' political and technical difficulties, the scheme involved the integrated management of the output of several watersheds, in an area containing twenty-two sanitary authorities and twenty-eight STWs. Sewage treatment was established on a new basis, through taking the 'then courageous decision ... to rely solely on the activated sludge process' at a new site at Mogden (Sidwick and Murray 1976 IV: 407). Commissioned in 1935, despite having to receive a greater load than anticipated, Mogden consistently produced effluent of the highest quality over the first ten years of operation (Sheail 1993b: 152).

The achievements at Davyhulme, Coleshill and Mogden should not be denied. They were, unfortunately, untypical of the sewage treatment sector as a whole. It remained, more characteristically, disorganised and backward. The small scale of many district councils militated against the planning and realisation of appropriate drainage and sewerage works (LRO PWM/1, 1931–46). Many STWs in the 1930s were in a semi-derelict condition. Small towns in low-lying areas often resorted to running raw sewage into rivers (*Hansard*, 3 May 1944: para. 1388). Modern technology was alien to much British sewage treatment, which tended to rely on 'trial and error' (Sidwick and Murray 1976 IV: 609). There was a resistance to implement technical improvements, unless 'entirely new works' or 'extensive reconstruction' were required, and most works in use were old and ill-suited to mechanisation (Garner 1933: 700–3). Lack of co-ordination between sanitary and other authorities, and the occasional asymmetry in the expansion of waste management and water supply services, which had been a feature of developments in the nineteenth century, were among the causes of the outbreak of epidemics from water-borne diseases, such as the Epping typhoid epidemic of 1931.

By the end of the period the scientific and engineering impediments to effective sewage treatment had been largely overcome (Elsdon 1941: 479). The obstacles inherent in existing arrangements, which provided scope for 'local rivalry and misunderstanding', and the advantages of the regional management of sewerage, were widely recognised. The potential economies from integrated management by river boards, as on the German model, were well known. The major obstacle, and the expression of the sector's backwardness, *was* organisational fragmentation. In 1944 some 1,600 separate authorities had responsibility for sewage treatment, acting independently of one another, and often operating several STWs along the same stretch of river. Attempts to devise an ambitious regional solution to the growing sewerage problems of the expanding districts of south Manchester and north Chester foundered on the intricate technical and political difficulties of co-ordinating the interested parties; there continued to be 100 authorities within fifteen miles of Manchester city centre, sometimes with STWs facing one another across the river that marked local authorities' boundaries. More successful were attempts to co-ordinate drainage and pollution control in Hertfordshire, to the north of London. But even here, where local politicians 'always found a certain amount of decentralisation is more suited to the workings of local government', the scheme eventually approved in 1937 was on a smaller scale than would have been technically desirable (Sheail 1993c: 444).

Sewage treatment was a rather neglected sector over the first half of the twentieth century. Financial constraints were the other great impediment, Garner (1933: 698) admitting that sewerage had been 'one of the municipal services on which local authorities were least anxious to incur expenditure and in which they took the least interest without some measure of compulsion'. Investment was somewhat depressed, collapsing during the war decades of the 1910s and 1940s, and only rising sharply from the 1950s (NWC 1982: 13). Sheail (1993c) has demonstrated that in districts where urban growth outstripped the capacity of the sanitary infrastructure the 'most severely', as in parts of the Home Counties and the North-West, local government responded by proposing pioneering regional-management solutions based on watersheds. However, even in these exceptional instances, the stumbling-block of local autonomy often thwarted their full realisation. While Britain had developed a reputation as a technical leader in the development of STWs and sewerage, actual performance lagged, in particular because of the survival of inappropriate, local-authority-based jurisdictions. Central and local government alike was, as yet, opposed to the imposition of standard prescriptions, which may have provided for the establishment of specialised sewerage boards (Sheail 1993c: 445–6). While there was no actual widespread physical collapse of underground assets in the inter-war period (this happened later), that sewage treatment was a Cinderella sector within a Cinderella industry is hardly in question. 'There is no doubt that for many years', it was admitted in Parliament, 'the sewage business has been the cesspool of local government. The heavy cost alone has kept us from dealing with it' (*Hansard*, 3 May 1944: para. 1388). The dilapidation of the mainly late nineteenth-century effluent disposal system gradually got worse. Ultimately the challenge of redressing this neglect presented Britain, according to Parker and Penning-Rowsell (1980: 104–5), with 'a major task, not just for the water planning system but for the country as a whole'.

River pollution and river management

River pollution

The results of this neglect was a deterioration in river pollution. Trends were not uniform. In some regions river quality did improve. Elsewhere it declined. On balance, however, the inter-war years were not positive ones for the condition of the country's inland waters.

The underlying causes included an unfavourable institutional framework and a shortage of resources which factors, in turn, reflected a general public indifference and sectional opposition to tougher environmental protection measures. The two world wars, their aftermaths and the economic depression of the early 1930s were years when sewage treatment and river conservation received the lowest priority. Although the period also witnessed the increased use of water and new housing developments, which placed strain on utility infrastructures, these services were subject to restrictions on capital spending. Common and statutory law failed to protect rivers. Once their pollution over a number of years became established fact, common-law rights effectively fell into 'desuetude', and under their sporadic operation the interests of large industrial polluters tended to be privileged (PRO 1957b: 3–4). Fisheries Boards introduced in the 1920s and Catchment Boards in the 1930s embodied portents for the future. However, because their powers were circumscribed they did not appear to signify important progress beyond the river committees established in the nineteenth century. Radical change only came at the very end of the period. River Boards were created in 1948, covering the entire country and based on river basins. Under legislation of 1951 a system of discharge consents was introduced, with the River Boards replacing local authorities as the agencies responsible for administering pollution prevention law.

The main source of pressure for improved protection of rivers were fisheries and angling interests. By the 1910s the plight of rivers led to an outcry. This prompted the government to appoint a Standing Committee on Rivers Pollution (SCORP) in 1923, made up of fisheries' interests and representatives of the FBI. The government also allowed the passage of the Salmon and Freshwater Fisheries Act in that year. This measure consolidated nineteen earlier Fisheries Acts and empowered the Ministry of Agriculture and Fisheries (MAF) to define fisheries districts, which usually encompassed whole catchment areas, and to set up Fisheries Boards. By 1944 forty-eight boards had been established under this procedure. The Act gave the new Boards apparently wide pollution prevention powers; it provided protection for the insect life and spawning beds, which supported fisheries; and it established a more expeditious procedure for prosecuting polluters. Yet the Act's impact was circumscribed: the Boards suffered financial difficulties; the latter found it difficult to persuade courts that pollution injured fisheries; and the Act was inoperable for already fishless rivers (Parker and Penning-Rowsell 1980: 117; Turing 1952: 76).

Nevertheless fisheries' interests had succeeded in publicising the problem of river pollution. In response the government established a Water Pollution Research Laboratory (WPRL) within the Department of Scientific and Industrial Research (DSIR), and appointed an Advisory Committee on River Pollution. The WPRL, established in 1926, strove to collect information on the causes of river pollution, although its impact upon policy was limited. Before the Second World War its research focused upon two lines of inquiry: the treatment of milk effluent and the contamination of water by lead (*MYB 1941*: 391).

The Joint Advisory Committee, appointed in November 1927, made a greater immediate impact. A consistent theme through its three reports of 1928, 1930 and 1931 was the need for stronger, better-resourced pollution control bodies based on catchments. It also pressed the case for legislation to require local authorities to receive trade effluent. It had long been recognised that a major obstacle to improved river quality was the difficulties for manufacturers and traders in getting their effluent accepted into municipal sewers and STWs. Sustained pressure from interested parties, particularly fisheries, led eventually to legislation. Meanwhile the Public Health Act of 1936 affirmed, for the first time, the statutory duty of local authorities in England and Wales to undertake sewage disposal and treatment, and to carry on sewerage 'without creating a nuisance', that is, without discharging seriously polluted effluent.

The Drainage of Trade Premises Act of 1937 represented an important step forward in curtailing the industrial pollution of the water environment. Under the Act, any occupier of trade premises was entitled to turn wastes into local authority sewers with local authority consent; if the local authority did not consent, the industrial discharges would still have to be received as long as they complied with by-laws established for that purpose. The resulting system was, arguably, both inflexible and complex. Perhaps on account of this, local authorities and industry were encouraged to work out the practical application of the new situation through consultation and negotiation. According to Turing (1952: 17), very few local authorities actually put the requisite by-laws into place, and the parties involved gradually resolved the various problems associated with the municipal treatment of trade effluent in a non-confrontational manner. The 1937 measure, nevertheless, was not a complete solution to this issue. For example, local authorities for their part still could not require trade effluent to be received into municipal sewers and waste-treatment facilities.

River management

Pollution prevention was only one aspect of river management and, as already indicated, a variety of river bodies had come into existence by the early twentieth century. With the exception of the two London-based conservancies, none, however, performed more than a minority of relevant river management tasks and, moreover, there was a lack of uniformity in the duties which were statutorily conferred upon these bodies.

Even in the limited field of land drainage a highly diverse situation had evolved. The Royal Commission on Land Drainage spoke (1927: 15) of 'a confused tangle of Authorities, established by piecemeal legislation over 500 years', which exercised a variety of powers and functions. It also found that much agricultural land was waterlogged and that about one-third of the country was under the jurisdiction of no drainage authority whatsoever.

The recommendations of the 1927 Royal Commission echoed the conclusions of many earlier inquiries in advocating the integration of river management functions in unitary boards. The Land Drainage Act of 1930 was passed following the publication of these recommendations. It consolidated and amended drainage law and reorganised its administration. Catchment areas were to be specified and placed under the jurisdiction of Catchment Boards, each responsible for a major river basin or group of basins. In addition, in lowland areas smaller drainage districts, under the jurisdiction of Drainage Boards, were specified.

The Act provided for some progress in river management. But it is hard to interpret the resulting fifty-three Catchment Areas and 377 Drainage Boards as a radical improvement. Integrated management was not achieved. While land drainage and flood prevention responsibilities were defined under the Act, powers to control river pollution or influence source developments were not allocated to the new boards. It was a matter of grave concern and disappointment to the lobbies representing fisheries and fishmongers that the government decided to exclude pollution prevention from the new boards' responsibilities (WRO, RB 1930: 2–11). At the most basic level, this omission would undermine the drainage authorities' task of maintaining channels. The instances where a more comprehensive approach to flood and pollution control within watersheds was achieved in this period was, as with the West Middlesex drainage scheme, as a result of regional initiative and the employment of the administrative device of the local Bill (Sheail 1993c).

Recognising existing defects, the Joint Advisory Committee on River Pollution urged, in its 1937 report, that the multiplicity of bodies concerned with river pollution should be reduced and that source-to-mouth river authorities, in which land drainage and pollution prevention responsibilities would be central-ised, should be created. These proposals came close to realisation with the Rivers Board Act of 1948, which led to the Catchment Boards giving way to thirty-two River Boards.

The 1948 measure was a major reform. Within entire catchments, the new River Boards were to exercise the powers previously allocated to the Catchment Boards, the Fisheries Boards and the pollution prevention responsibilities hitherto carried out by the County Councils. An unprecedented integration of functions was achieved, although the Act fell well short of achieving comprehensive river management. The River Boards still exercised no control over source develop-ments or abstractions. Moreover, for pollution prevention, the tortuous procedure which included the need to apply to the Minister for permission to prosecute polluters, and the requirement to take into account economic impacts and the dis-chargers' use of 'practicable means', still remained in force.

Pollution control

The legislative and institutional framework permitted a variety of regional responses. In some cases river protection was pursued energetically and with some effect; elsewhere problems overwhelmed the responsible bodies and further deterioration occurred.

Despite the sluggishness of the inter-war economy, the cumulative conse-quences of industrialisation imposed greater strain on rivers. Industrial effluent, as opposed to municipal sewage, showed signs of becoming a relatively more impor-tant source of pollution, which was a serious trend, as river bacteria deals with factory wastes less effectively than with domestic effluent (Turing 1952: 40).

The measure of the deterioration of river quality in Lancashire, as well as a reflection of the intensity of river use, was that the industrial effluent discharged into streams like the Irwell was actually purer than the river it flowed into. It was this phenomenon which had discouraged magistrates from prosecuting manufacturers (BRL 1885a: 4; Biggs 1949: 24). Thus watercourses in industrial regions became very heavily overloaded, not only in terms of the abstractions for industrial and domestic supplies, but also for the task of purifying polluting emis-sions. Between 1912 and 1960 water use and effluent discharges in rivers in England and Wales increased by some 300 per cent (Lester, cited in Smith 1972: 180), thereby increasing the pollution threat due to the reduction of the amount of water available for dilution.

Among the endeavours to combat river pollution in the inter-war years there were some successes. Even in (northern) Lancashire, the readiness of the Rivers

Board to work in conjunction with the Fisheries Board brought dividends, reflected in a significant improvement in the stock of salmon in its rivers, calculated at only 551 in 1931, but climbing to 6,406 by 1943 (Turing 1952: 59).

The West Riding River Board emerged as possibly an outstanding model of a river-basin authority, its jurisdiction extending to 1,000 miles of river, in an area containing 166 local authorities, 400 STWs, and 2,000 premises discharging trade effluent. Pursuing its business energetically, it acted as an 'adviser and friend to manufacturers and authorities alike', checking pollution with a 'minimum of friction' (WRO, RB 1930: 4). It was responsible for over sixty per cent of all applications to the Minister of Health requesting permission to take legal action against polluters, which was granted in just under half of all such cases in the 1930s (Turing 1952: 82). But the more noticeable achievement of the Board was its ability to cajole and encourage traders and councils to co-operate for the improvement of local rivers, in particular through connecting trade premises with sewers. This led to a dramatic improvement in the quality of some local streams, and a considerable increase in the weight of the catch of migratory fish over the first three decades of the century was reported (WRO, RB reports: 1930–46). Recourse to legal proceedings became increasingly rare, in fact, between the 1900s and the 1930s. The Board was able to persuade traders of the reasonableness of the aims of 1937 Trade Effluent Act. Consequently, whereas in 1897 only 806 out of 2,103 trade premises discharged effluent into sewers, by the late 1930s the situation was exactly reversed (Sheail 1993b: 166).

But it has to be recalled that the achievements of the West Riding River Board have been described as unique in the annals of pollution history (Turing 1947: 27). It is too easy to discover less satisfactory evidence about river quality trends in the period. Despite the completion of the Mogden STW in 1935, for the Thames the first half of the twentieth century was a period of consistent deterioration as measured, for example, by dissolved oxygen levels (Wood 1982: 79–86). By the summer of 1947 conditions in the tidal Thames were the worst recorded (MHLG 1961: 9–10). When foreign ships moored in the river during the Festival of Britain they found it in a 'very poor' and polluted condition. The decline of the Tees was also a twentieth-century affair. Salmon catches of some 8,000 fish were made prior to the outbreak of the First World War, declining to only twenty-three in 1934 before disappearing altogether. The problem was the estuary, where ministerial officials were unable to persuade owners of coke ovens and other plants to purify their effluent before discharge (Turing 1952: 21). The Trent, one of the country's greatest rivers, became so polluted as to degenerate into a lifeless drain.

A government view (cited in Sheail 1993b: 167) of the Drainage of Trade Premises Act of 1937 was that it represented a 'great advance'. But the measure did not inaugurate sustained change. Until the 1960s there was little evidence that the country's rivers had recovered from the appallingly polluted condition into which many had fallen. Progress on improving rivers was so limited because, in the opinion of another official, other demands for public money had a higher claim. In the contemporary view: 'The country simply could not afford to clean its rivers properly' (cited in Sheail 1993b: 168).

A failure of public policy

The reform of water management

While hardly a major national issue, water management reform was under more or less continuous discussion during the inter-war years. At stake was the perceived need to, first, rationalise water provision; second, move towards an integrated management of the water cycle; and third, secure a more coherent development of water policy under the control of central, probably ministerial, authority.

For example, a Water Power Resources Committee convened after the war soon found that its brief needed to be extended to all aspects of water management. In its view, the 'allocation of water has become too serious a matter to be left solely to a succession of Parliamentary committees which are constituted from time to time to deal with a particular Bill and have no continuity of existence' (Board of Trade 1920: 5). Among other things, it recommended the establishment of a Water Commission to exercise general control over water allocation, responsible to the Ministry of Health.

The post-war climate, which had been conducive to reform, proved fleeting. The Ministry of Health had taken over responsibility for water matters from the LGB and it placed faith, for the development of water policies, in the work and advice delivered by the ACW and the regional advisory water committees which, as explained above, were not powerful aids for the realisation of policy objectives.

Drought in 1933 and 1934 helped to place water reform a little higher up the political agenda. Down to the outbreak of the Second World War the Ministry of Health did try to push the process of reform along. A White Paper set out proposals in 1934 for giving the Ministry powers to reorganise and restructure both water-supply enterprises and regional patterns of abstraction and distribution. The need to standardise and simplify the waterworks code was also officially acknowledged; it was felt that this should be done before the modernisation of the water supply industry itself was attempted. Hassan (1995) has outlined the painstaking parliamentary and other deliberations into these proposals, so deliberate and slow as to be inconclusive before the outbreak of hostilities in 1939 led to their being shelved.

Wartime discussions of industrial and social reconstruction in the future, however, encompassed the provision of water services. Their final outcome were the enactments of 1945 and 1948 which covered water supply and river management respectively. The 1945 Water Act and the 1948 Rivers Board Act closely followed the recommendations of the Central Advisory Committee on Water

(CACW), also known as the Milne Committee, after its chairman. The 1945 measure gave the Minister of Health the statutory duty of promoting water resource development, as well as the power, subject to parliamentary procedures, of creating Joint Boards, varying limits of supply and arranging for bulk distributions.

The significance of the 1945 legislation was that it gave the executive explicit responsibility, and some powers, to influence the development of the water supply industry. Yet, in many respects, it was a disappointing reform and made no progress at all, for example, in promoting integrated management. In this it followed the cautious advice of the Milne Committee that the new River Authorities, which were also being proposed, should be kept quite separate from the water supply undertakers. Consequently, as already noted, the 1948 measure established River Boards with no authority to control source developments.

The main test of the success of the 1945 Act, which charged the Minister of Health with the 'direction of a national policy relating to water', was, however, over the issue of restructuring. The overriding objective was to empower central government to accelerate the process of rationalisation in the water supply industry. This was the Act's main failure. It did not lead to significant restructuring. In 1944 there were 1,194 water supply undertakers in England and Wales and still 1,055 in 1956.

The reasons for this failure were that, despite the stated aims of the legislation, effective machinery was not given to the Minister of Health for discharging his duties regarding water. No powers, for example, were acquired to develop waterworks or storage reservoirs for conservation purposes. The Act did authorise the Minister of Health to form Joint Boards by compulsion. However, the stipulated process was lengthy and expensive and, if an objection was lodged, was equivalent to that of an opposed private Bill with all the expenses, consultation procedures, retaining of experts and witnesses, and the holding of Select Committees involved. As an official conceded: 'It is very doubtful whether more than a thousand undertakings can be reviewed on this basis' (PRO 1950a).

That a failure of public policy in relation to water occurred is argued because, despite the recommendations for a significant restructuring of water management which had been made repeatedly over many years, the measures passed in the 1940s had a limited impact. More than anything they reflected the ability of special interests to influence policy-making. After the reforms of the 1940s one still found: the continuance of common-law barriers to effective planning in the area of river management, water undertakers still being able to develop sources without reference to the new River Boards; sewage services remaining as fragmented as ever; and continued disorganisation of the water supply sector – for example in the Thames basin, despite the presence of the massive MWB, 177 local government bodies, sixty-five water supply undertakers and twenty-nine private companies shared responsibility for supplying water to the population. In fact, for another twenty years or more, the water industry remained beset by well-known structural deficiencies. Operators were too small and numerous from the point of view of technical efficiency, there were conflicts of interest over source developments between river and water supply authorities, and other obstacles which impeded the development of a regional approach to source development.

There is no suggestion that a crisis confronted the water industry during the first half of the twentieth century. No serious supply difficulties were experienced, and there was some improvement in the delivery of other water services. Some explanation for the weak dynamic behind the process of reform must, however, be made.

Local and central government clearly attached low importance to the water industry. This was reflected in the under-investment experienced throughout the period. As for legislative steps, the Labour government of 1945–51, for example, evidently was too preoccupied with other matters for it to wish to push through Parliament far-reaching measures providing for water reform.

Political indifference to water issues, however, was more a symptom than an underlying cause of environmental neglect. An explanation is favoured which explores interactions between the British approach to environmental reform and the economic characteristics of the water resource. The costs of a less than efficient delivery of water services tended to be borne by society as a whole. By contrast, well-organised interests in the water field frequently recognised a stake in the status quo, rather than vigorous restructuring or tough environmental protection measures. The part played by interest groups in the politics of water reform in this period requires, therefore, some attention.

Interest politics

Municipal water authorities

The local authorities had established an entrenched position in the water supply industry by the inter-war years. The historical roots of this situation have been referred to in Chapter 2. The municipal authorities were anxious to assert their autonomy and control in the water supply field, and they became a powerful lobby.

There are few cases of Parliament thwarting their plans for large-scale source developments. Sir A. M. Samuel acknowledged before the JCWR (1935–36: 41) that an impression had been created, 'that the claims of the water authorities are ... competitive with the claims of riparian owners, catchment boards, the Federation of British Industry'. And he affirmed that indeed, 'the claims and demands of the water authorities are absolutely paramount'. The municipal authorities, furthermore, insisted upon both their independence and their rights of consultation. A spokesperson for the Association of Municipal Corporations agreed in 1939 that 'a comprehensive scheme of water reform is desirable, if not overdue'; but the municipal lobby demanded, and was granted, close involvement in the process of preparing a revision to water legislation (*Joint Committee on Water Undertakings Bill* 1938–39: 41). Whitehall was anxious that reform proposals should not offend municipal prerogatives. Of plans to strengthen Regional Advisory Committees, a Ministry of Health official urged that they 'should not override the ancient and sovereign rights of the local authorities' (PRO 1943a). As noted above, a deficiency with water reform in the 1930s was the ignoring of much expert advice in denying Land Drainage Boards responsibility for pollution prevention. This caution can be attributed to an official unwillingness to proceed with any measure which did not have the full support of the Municipal Corporations Association, particularly where it might have the effect of relieving the local authorities of one of their traditional functions (WRO, RB 1930: 15–17).

As the reform of the water industry became imminent in the early 1940s the municipal corporations became fearful of a transfer of powers to central government, which they viewed 'with grave anxiety'. While broadly favourable to the 1944 White Paper, they had a number of concerns. The Municipal Corporations Association feared that members' representation on a new, statutory CACW would be 'most inadequate'. They advocated that legislation should be passed to facilitate the municipalisation of water companies still remaining in private hands. A key principle in the White Paper, namely the devolution of authority to local undertakings was, however, something they naturally supported (*MYB 1946*: 288).

It was crucially the Labour Party in government which was conscious of municipal susceptibilities. When the Cabinet got round to contemplating water nationalisation in the period 1948–1951, there was anxiety not to alienate the local authorities. Morrison stressed that it would be unwise to present the large local authorities 'with a scheme prepared in advance. We have to remember that large cities, for example, Manchester, Sheffield ... have become responsible for vast schemes and successful systems of supply' (PRO 1950b). He favoured 'socialisation under local ownership'. Officials recognised that any 'encroachment upon local government' would be 'much resented' (PRO 1951b).

There was a minimalist proposal, favoured by the Secretary of State for Scotland and some officials in the Ministry of Health, which simply involved the transfer of the remaining private water companies to the local authorities. The model preferred by Bevan consisted of the establishment of fifty to sixty Area Authorities. This would have led to the dissolution of existing municipal waterworks, yet much of local government's administrative and technical structures would have continued to operate as before, so the municipal element would have remained significant in such a nationalised water industry. Labour lost power before the reform was implemented. Nevertheless, Bevan's nationalisation model would have produced a much less radical reorganisation, preserving a more important local government role, than was achieved eventually by the reform of 1973. This reflects the considerable influence of the municipal lobby up to 1951.

Table 3.6 *Membership of the Association of Waterworks Engineers, 1896–1985*

1896	1925	1945	1960	1975	1985
142	443	874	1,950	3,808	5,870

Source: The Institution of Water Engineers and Scientists Handbook 1985–86

Professional associations

The municipal water authorities were a civic lobby. A distinct, if overlapping, area of concern was the professional interest of those whose work and careers were based in the water industry. Aside from the organisations representing local government were the professional associations formed on behalf of the private owners and directors, and the managers and engineers working in both sectors. They emerged in the late nineteenth and early twentieth centuries and came to exercise a significant influence upon government policy in the 1930s and 1940s.

The first and most professional of the three main bodies was the Association (later Institute) of Waterworks Engineers (AWE). Formed in 1896, its membership increased progressively, as can be seen from Table 3.6.

Most qualified waterworks engineers became members. The policy of the Association's Council was to admit only those with recognised and appropriate qualifications. By the late 1940s eighty-four per cent of the membership were also corporate members of the Institution of Civil Engineers. It had a research committee, which established ten research groups, working in close collaboration with the universities, as well as government and industry, on specific problems (Hobbs 1950: 866). The stress on formal academic qualifications as a prerequisite for a career in the sector, and the recognition by the civil and sanitary engineers of the relevance of theoretical training, contributed to the growing status and professionalisation of these groups (Taylor 1946: 23–4; Escritt and Rich 1949: ch. 1).

The British Waterworks Association (BWA) was more concerned with representing the interests of enterprises rather than the engineering profession. Established in 1912, by the mid-1930s 167 local authorities and seventy-six water companies in England and Wales were members. By the late 1940s it represented 570 water authorities in Britain, which supplied over forty million people. It claimed to be recognised, both officially as well as unofficially, 'as the representative organisation of the water authorities in the country' ('Water supply matters', *Municipal Journal* 1922: 493). The third professional group was the Water Companies Association, representing fifty-eight companies, which dealt with specific private-sector interests. These three organisations emerged as a lobby of significance. In the development of water policy it came to be heavily relied upon by the Ministry of Health for the provision of information and advice.

Immediately after the First World War, in the context of certain financial difficulties faced by the water undertakings and also the Water Power Resources Committee's proposals for industrial reorganisation, the President of AWE advocated the adoption of a co-ordinated approach 'with the British Waterworks Association and other kindred bodies for the purpose of enlightening Parliament and the public' on the water industry's position (Dixon 1920: 15). This initiative was seized upon by the BWA, and the two bodies collaborated closely together in presenting their point of view before the Committee and government. They also recognised the need for the creation of an extra-parliamentary body, representing water interests, to supply the government with information and advice. But they maintained: 'Such a body already exists in the British Waterworks Association acting jointly with its technical brother institution, the Institution of Waterworks Engineers.' They agreed to collaborate so as to 'bring their joint influence to bear on government' ('Memorandum', *WWE*, 20 July 1922: 244).

The newly established Ministry of Health accepted this self-interested advice when it agreed to the formation of ACW in 1922. It was made up of nominees from the three associations. It was a very small body, with only six members in 1929 and thirteen in 1935. It was replaced by the broader CACW in 1937. The Ministry of Health relied quite heavily upon both committees as sources of expert advice. The advisory committees liaised closely, if confidentially, with the professional associations in discussions over water reform, for example on proposals to modernise the waterworks code (PRO 1931). In such ways the professional lobby was able to exercise influence upon the development of policy and, ultimately, on the form which legislative reforms took. The emergence of these arrangements virtually formalised the presentation of special interests as an official component of the policy-making process.

The professional bodies adopted a conservative position towards water industry reform. A number of strong statements were made by the BWA and the AWE on the need for control of the national system of water resource allocation remaining vested, not in any government department, but in Parliament alone ('Water supply matters', *Municipal Journal* 1922: 493; 'Memorandum', *WWE*, 20 July 1922: 241). This stress on the sovereignty of Parliament was essentially a vote of confidence in the centrifugal approach to source development established in the nineteenth century. The commitment to the process of parliamentary scrutiny of each new scheme was reflected in advice given by the ACW to the Ministry of Health. Parliamentary authorisation, the Committee urged, was especially necessary for projects involving any 'prejudice to any private rights or vested interests' (PRO 1929a).

During the inter-war years, apart from the opinions and technical advice supplied by the ACW, the Ministry also occasionally liaised directly with other organisations, especially the BWA, in its formulation of proposals. It had direct communication with this body, for example, before releasing the White Paper of

1934. In the mid-1930s government made less use of the ACW, for the reasons noted below. The professional bodies, in the context of drought conditions and imminence of reform – even water nationalisation had been spoken of – became more anxious to influence events proactively. Steps were taken by the AWE to establish itself as *the* representative body of water engineers, members even being expected to resign membership of other organisations, in the view that this would increase the Association's influence. A number of initiatives were taken to mobilise interested parties and to exercise influence (Gourley 1935: 19–20). At a record attendance of a BWA conference in 1934, a motion in support of a pooling of water resources and the creation of a national water board was unanimously rejected ('Memorandum', *TWE* 1935: 11). The culmination of this phase of agitation was the Triple Conference of the three associations held in 1934 and 1935. This conference placed faith in the weak Regional Advisory Committee as a means of improving water resource allocation. It also agreed that: 'Water undertakers should remain autonomous .... Any outside interference with the local management of water undertakings would be disastrous' ('Report', *TWE* 1935: 4–5).

Between 1948 and 1951, when the Cabinet was considering the nationalisation of water, the Labour government tended to seek to accommodate more the municipal, rather than the professional, lobby. Time and again documents testify to the Cabinet's concern to take account of the municipal interest in its plans for water industry reform. Attlee was himself involved in these deliberations.

All three professional associations did have an opportunity to express their reactions to the Cabinet's proposal for large Area Boards. They opposed the plan, the three secretaries of the associations jointly signing a letter sent to the Ministry of Housing and Local Government, which reiterated the view that: 'They consider that the provision of water supplies should be in the hands of local authorities responsible under existing legislation for securing those supplies' (PRO 1951e). Far more disturbing to the professional lobby were signs, during discussions on water reorganisation, that it was losing its privileged lines of communication with government departments to the municipal interest. To its consternation, the BWA was not invited to a key meeting on this issue at which the local authorities and the municipal associations had been present (PRO 1951d). In fact it was less the prospect of reorganisation which affronted the BWA, as proposed departmental reforms in Whitehall which, it feared, would lead to the now traditional links between itself and a division within the Health Ministry being dissolved. The BWA feared that new arrangements would lead to the government's handling of water matters becoming 'merely an appendage of planning'. The BWA pleaded that this 'highly technical industry ... will continue to enjoy the advantages of a specialised and separate Department of the Ministry' (PRO 1951c).

So the BWA's worry was the possibility that the established relationship with the water industry's patron, the Ministry of Health, might wither. The significance of losing access to the ministerial ear would be considerable. In fact, the basis of

BWA's concerns was removed with the government's loss of office. Notwithstanding the BWA's momentary loss of influence just when the Labour government determined to make progress with water nationalisation in 1950–51, the impact of interest-group lobbying upon policy-making in this industry was clearly considerable. The co-ordination and purpose of the professional groups stands in contrast to the disorganised structure of the water industry. In so far as the limited aims of the professional lobby were conceded then the process of structural reform was slowed down.

The problem of policy co-ordination for a multiple-use resource

It will be noted that water's characteristic as a multiple-use resource was reflected in the range of interest groups active in this area. These elements served to complicate the process of water reform. Neither were the prospects for policy co-ordination assisted by the complex ways in which the responsibilities for water were assigned among government departments. No one department exercised overall control. Furthermore, the separate departments frankly viewed themselves as patrons of special interests (Sheail 1983: 391). The Minister of Health even argued in Parliament of the rights of the 'many sectional interests' to put their case and to be protected during the process of reform (*Hansard*, 3 May 1944: paras. 1388–42). This attitude had also been expressed by the JCWR (1935–36: xiii) in its statement that it was 'anxious that the rights of fisheries, mill and other riparian and land owners generally should be adequately protected'.

Both the wide range of water users' interests and also the at least partial perception of some government departments of themselves as protectors of these interests ensured that the development of environmental protection policies – to take one aspect of water reform – would be tortuous. The task of accommodating the variety of competitive interests was not made easier by a central tenet of the government's position, which was to take account of all interests in the policy-making process. On the problem of municipal reception of trade wastes Sheail (1993a) has shown, for example, how giving each interest – anglers, fishmongers, local government, separate factions within traders – its special say proved almost disastrous, leading to the failure of a private Bill, and the government having to put forward its own measure.

The difficulty of transcending divergent sectoral interests was increased by the manner in which responsibilities for water services were divided across a number of government departments. While the Ministry of Health had overall purview for water supply, the Board of Trade had some responsibilities for private companies; the Board had interests, too, in relation to canal navigation and water power, which it shared to some extent with the Ministry of Transport and the Central Electricity Generating Board; the province of the MAF was in the region of fisheries, land drainage and river conservancy; the Department of Scientific and Industrial Research (DSIR) had concerns with water pollution research, the geological survey and other special investigations; and finally, the Meteorological Office had obvious interests in water. Even within departments there could be conflicts. The MAF might discover that the interests of fisheries and other conservancy bodies were not identical; the Board of Trade might share with the Ministry of Health an interest in water reform so as to facilitate water-power schemes, although its client, manufacturing industry, had some interest in the status quo.

Sheail's examination of the Ministry of Health's proposals of 1934 demonstrates the conflicting positions within government (1983: 390–2). Heated and acrimonious discussions took place in Cabinet. There was opposition to the allegedly arbitrary nature of the powers being sought. To Sheail, the Minister of Health's position was fatally weakened by his failure to carry through the MAF and the President of Board of Trade with him. Both protested that the White Paper had been written entirely from the view of the water undertakers and was bound to excite violent criticism. Below ministerial level, bitter and sometimes petty grievances and rivalries existed between departments. Relationships became tetchy, for example, between the MAF and the Ministry of Health over proposals to reform land drainage. The MAF desired an extension to the powers of the Land Drainage Boards, but the water supply industry strongly opposed any moves by land drainage bodies to 'interfere with question affecting public water supplies' (PRO 1936). The perception by government departments that their role included the protection of client groups probably intensified the antagonistic features of interest politics in the water field.

As well as the various water supply interests, represented in their municipal and professional associations, many other water users were well organised to press their point of view. Among these was manufacturing industry. From a short-term perspective it appeared to have a strong interest in the survival of a number of practices governing water use which had been established in the nineteenth century. The attitude of some industrialists towards their perceived rights to exploit water resources was, according to Turing (1952: 49), expressed in a notice put up on a riverbank by a firm of calico printers. It stated that the firm retained and intended to use its right to pollute the river. In fact riparian proprietors did have the right to freely discharge effluent into streams, but only provided other owners' rights were not injured. Yet the calico printers' misconception about the nature of their rights was probably of less significance than their assumption regarding the freedom to pollute.

Commercial and manufacturing interests enjoyed other advantages from the unreformed water management system, in addition to the virtually uncontrolled discharge of effluent into rivers. As previously noted, manufacturers were big water consumers and, following the construction of waterworks, frequently obtained generous compensation supplies. The FBI and other industrial bodies argued the case strongly in defence of these established trade privileges. A plentiful supply of water to, for example, the paper-making industry, which needed 160 million gallons per working day, was seen as essential a 'public need' as supplies for sanitary purposes. The reaction of industry to the three reports of the ACW between 1922 and 1930 which advocated downward adjustments to compensation supplies was 'immense'. It led to protests to the Ministry of Health that industrial interests were entirely unrepresented, with consideration given solely to water undertakers and domestic supplies (*JCWR* 1935–36: 79–80).

The complexity of the issues involved in the modernisation of water institutions threatened to derail entirely the process of reform by the mid-1930s. The JCWR, after considering the Ministry of Health White Paper of 1934 and after holding a number of meetings, 'saw themselves becoming completely embogged in a mass of conflicting evidence, full of detail' (PRO 1943b). The conflicting nature of water users' interests may have led to the Joint Committee's problems. But it came to the conclusion – perhaps influenced by the proprietorial arguments of the holders of riparian rights like mill-owners – that the Minister of Health's proposals to acquire additional powers to control the development of water resources were excessive. It concluded that 'the rights of property owners [of underground and surface water] may be so seriously affected … that they are unable to recommend any procedure other than the continuance of that by private Bill' (*JCWR* 1935–36: x).

Another of the Joint Committee's conclusions was to favour the establishment of a Central Advisory Water Committee. This advice emerged naturally from the vexed and intricate nature of the politics and economics of water reform, which the Joint Committee encountered in its deliberations. Some water users became hostile to the ACW because of its recommendations and its unrepresentative nature, and government made less use of it for policy advice in the 1930s. Accordingly, the Minister of Health agreed to the appointment of the broader-based CACW, indicating, in his view, that it was, 'essential … that the views of all interests should be carefully considered before legislation was introduced' (PRO 1937). This non-statutory Committee, under the chair of Lord Milne, first met in 1937. For Smith (1972: 21), possibly overstating the case, this marked the beginning of a new phase in policy development. It was envisaged that it would act as an interdepartmental committee to advise on issues and legislative proposals relating to the development of water. Its constitution included two members each from the BWA and the Catchment Board Association, and one each from associations representing canal bodies, docks and harbour authorities, landowners, county councils, municipal corporations, urban district councils, rural district councils and the FBI, together with assessors from the main cognate departments (health, agriculture, trade, transport and the DSIR).

The Milne Committee exercised a crucial influence in the 1940s. While representing a much wider range of groups than its predecessor, the ACW, it still provided an important means for the promotion of the aims of the water supply interest, especially as far as structural reforms were concerned. The series of reports it produced informed Cabinet thinking. In considering post-war reconstruction the War Cabinet became convinced of the need for water reform, and proposals for a *National Water Policy* were published as a White Paper. Two of the three principles upon which the envisaged national policy would be based were to establish responsibilities for water supplies on democratic bodies, with government ministers at the centre, but with the local authorities at the 'circumference', and for all 'sectional interests' to have the right to be heard by government and Parliament.

When the White Paper was introduced to Parliament, there was derision in some quarters, with criticisms of the 'tame hand of the Milne Committee at work', 'a local, tin-pot, parish pump attitude', and of a 'hugger-mugger' of over a thousand undertakings being preserved (*Hansard*, 3 May 1944: paras. 1338–90). The water supply industry was, however, quite receptive to the proposal. After all, it had been extensively canvassed for its views. The Minister, Willink, referred to the need for the 'many sectional interests' among undertakers and users to put their case and be granted 'ample protection' (*Hansard*, 3 May 1944: para. 1342). While the Minister was not incapable of overriding all special pleading, in general great care was taken to note the concerns of vested interests. Consequently, the ensuing legislation in 1945 largely preserved existing structures. This was the dominant theme of the politics of water industry reform over the period under study: the determination of interested groups to press their claims vigorously and the readiness of government to accommodate the well-organised. It is not surprising that reform proceeded at a snail's pace in the first half of the twentieth century.

Environmentalism and the lobbying process

In view of the later importance of environmental pressure groups, it is of some interest to examine the inter-war agitation for cleaner rivers. As has been seen, some measures reflected the influence of this lobby, including the Salmon Fisheries Act, the Drainage of Trade Premises Act and the measures of 1948 and 1951, which provided for the creation of new River Boards. These partial reforms did at least provide the means to arrest the pollution of rivers. Given the government's anxiety not to infringe the rights of private property, questions arise as to the nature of this lobby and the reasons for even its limited success.

The preservationism and 'backward-looking environmentalism' of the pre-1940 years in the history of British nature conservation may be contrasted with the post-1960 phenomenon of popular and political environmentalism (Lowe 1983; Luckin 1990: 4–5). In terms of objectives and the 'mass' of interest, the single-issue campaign for less polluted fishing rivers in the first half of the century does not seem so very different from later crusades such as, for example, the headline-grabbing protests organised by Surfers Against Sewage. In terms of social relationships and ideology, however, there were differences. In the existence of a social control element, in particular, it is possible to distinguish between pre-war fisheries conservationism and modern activism, and to thereby obtain a better under-standing as to the former's modest success.

The free-rider and public goods problems associated with the provision of environmental services tend to make it difficult for environmental pressure groups to mobilise and to exercise political influence. The scale and specificity of interests represented by commercial and recreational fishers were, however, sufficient to override such disadvantages. The latter, in particular, grew significantly in number from the late nineteenth century, to the extent that Netbuoy (1968: 201) spoke of a 'democratisation of salmon and trout fishing'. By the 1860s some eighty anglers' clubs had been formed with a combined membership of not less than 50,000 (Bartrip 1985: 296). The anglers on their own did not amount to a particularly influential political force. They did, however, have powerful allies in riparian land-owners with their strong commercial interest in prosperous freshwater fisheries. In the late 1930s a thousand yards of the Lune could generate £30,000 annually from fishing rights.

As Sheail (1993a: 43) has explained, after the First World War there were a growing number of officials and politicians who were concerned about the contin-uing pollution of rivers. The Fisheries Minister, Lord Ancaster, stated that the government did not accept river pollution as an inevitable consequence of industri-alisation. Enthusiasm for tougher measures may have waned subsequently, but not before the Salmon Fisheries Act had been passed. Continued pressure from inter-ested parties led, moreover, to the appointment of SCORP and the passing of other pollution-prevention measures previously referred to.

The nature of the movement which sought action on the protection of inland waters, together with the reasons for their being listened to, to some extent, by government, can now be considered.

First, there was the combined political weight of the groups concerned. By the early 1920s there were at least 600,000 members of the Working Men's Anglers' Association (Sheail 1993a: 43). Angling associations were becoming more assertive in the inter-war period, more prepared, for example, to pursue legal action against sanitary authorities for adopting measures which obstructed the passage of fish (Turing 1952: 32). More to the point, angling interests, landowners and commer-cial fisheries – represented in the Salmon and Trout Association – together with the fishmongers and the National Association of Fisheries Boards, were coming together in the federal Central Council for Rivers Protection from 1927. This sug-gests the emergence of a coalition of forces which government could not ignore. By 1933 a wide range of bodies were calling on government to strengthen pollu-tion prevention law. Among them were the elusive 'Pure Rivers Society', the Oyster Merchants and Planters Society and the Fishmongers Company, as well as the National Association of Fisheries Boards (PRO 1933a).

Second, since the later nineteenth century shifts in attitudes towards the conservation of the natural heritage had been taking place. Environmentalism appeared to be broadening its base, although still influenced by the Victorian emphasis upon the protection of fauna. The conservation of habitats and landscapes themselves, however, emerged as popular themes in the inter-war period, especially among the urban population. These trends found expression in the national parks movement in the 1930s and the planning and national parks legislation passed in the 1940s (Luckin 1990: 95–114; Sheail 1981: 240–6). An interest in rivers and fisheries protection was in harmony with these concerns.

Third, there was a social control element to politicians' interest in the protection of rivers. Politicians from Left and Right might encourage measures to assist working-class angling for slightly different reasons. Leading Labour politicians like Arthur Greenwood and Ramsay Macdonald were sympathetic to environmental protection, and Alfred Short, Labour Member of Parliament for Sheffield, spoke of the polluted Don as 'flowing in agony, ashamed of itself'. He argued that the working-class quality of life was undermined by such an 'abuse and destruction of our rivers' (quoted by Sheail 1993b: 159). Clement Attlee was interested in water quality and access to the countryside. Other elements in the political establishment shared not dissimilar sentiments. Bartrip (1985: 296–9), in a nineteenth-century context, attributes parliamentary readiness to regulate river fishing to the distinction which was made between 'respectable' working-class anglers, who were worthy of encouragement, and netsmen, who were representative of the disreputable working class. A Whitehall official, Henry G. Maurice, stated in 1924 that river pollution had a demoralising effect upon the working class and might provoke discontent due to the threat to the healthy recreations of angling, boating and rowing (Sheail 1993a: 43). These were among the factors which led the MAF to actively promote pollution-prevention proposals in the inter-war period.

Fourth, as Sheail (1993a: 56) stated: 'The interest groups and professional bodies concerned with fisheries were among the first to enter into a dialogue with government, as attempts were made generally to recover the momentum of pre-war campaigns, whether by individual lobbying or by association.' The fact that the diverse groups with an interest in protecting fisheries became involved with the politics of lobbying is clearly crucial. The MAF, already with its strong landowning and agrarian links, was now actively being supported in its river-protection objectives by the Anglers' Association. The symbiotic relationship between patrons (the Ministry) and clients (riparian interests) emerged strongly in the inter-war period. It continued to develop in the post-war years to the extent that the landowners, farmers and river and drainage authorities were even said to have ultimately 'colonised' the MAF (Richardson *et al.* 1978).

In view of all these factors it is almost surprising that the rivers conservation movement achieved so little. This must be explained by reference to the several factors which have been identified in this study as detrimental to the prospects for effective environmental reform. They include: the less than complete scientific understanding of all the factors influencing river pollution and the health of fisheries; the presumption against environmental improvements which imposed unacceptable commercial costs; the strength of the manufacturing lobby and other interests opposed to tougher pollution controls; and the failure, until the end of the period, to make progress on establishing integrated water management based on catchments. The fisheries protection movement, even with significant landowning and Whitehall interests on its side, did represent a rather unwieldy coalition, and it was difficult for it to pursue its goals in a sustained manner. River pollution showed few signs of improving during this period and the movement still faced major struggles in subsequent decades.

4

A period of optimism, 1951–1973: the search for integrated management

Introduction

The 1950s and 1960s were in general a period of optimism and vision, of an unprecedented growth in the demand for water and, therefore, of an accelerated development of the nation's water resources. It was a period too, at least for some, of a growing faith in the efficacy of technology and planning. Its outlook was reflected in Twort's comment (1963: 9): 'We are in an era of giganticism, where nationwide economic survival depends on gigantic organisations for mass production. We no longer irrigate our own small-holdings and water our cattle from the village pump; we mass together for work, we mass-produce in mammoth factories … and, therefore, we must mass produce our water.'

As far as water was concerned, faith in the promise of large-scale engineering projects to facilitate the exploitation of Britain's natural resources encountered two difficulties in this period. Firstly, the incompletely modernised water industry lacked the institutional framework appropriate to the efficient conception and execution of large-scale, regional projects. Secondly, visionary plans to harness water resources through estuary barrages, interregional transfer schemes or a further building of reservoirs in upland valleys collided with the emergence of more acute environmental sensibilities. There was growing anxiety that such projects would cause unacceptable damage to natural ecologies.

Over the course of the period these two considerations were, to some extent, gradually incorporated into new thinking on water management. Notwithstanding some major exceptions there were signs of a search for 'softer', as opposed to 'hard' engineering solutions, although these terms were not, as yet, in common use. More emphasis was placed on river regulation, the conservation of groundwater deposits and, in particular, a greater protection and re-use of river water. All these strands could be encompassed in the concept of the integrated management of water, land and the environment in the context of catchments. The expert consensus was that through this approach the conflicting interests of water users could be reconciled.

However, in contrast to initial expectations, the reforms of 1945 and 1948 did not satisfactorily provide for the long-awaited modernisation of the industry. Restructuring proceeded painfully slowly. In the meantime Labour's electoral defeat in 1951 killed off their plans for the establishment of large, regional water boards as part of the proposed water nationalisation measure.

Nevertheless, between 1955 and 1973 more rapid and fundamental changes occurred in the water industry than during any comparable period in the industry's history – in the patterns of ownership and control, in the institutional framework and in the official analysis of the appropriate means and objectives of water policy. In the water supply sector a fairly significant regrouping of enterprises occurred. In 1963 a major step towards integrated river-basin management was taken with the creation of the River Authorities (RAs). Historically war has often been the great catalyst, accelerating the reform process and shifting perceptions of what can be achieved. For water this was less true, the traditional patterns of policy-making and bargaining among interests continuing to retard the dynamic of reform in the 1940s. While interest politics and the established systems of consultation did not disintegrate, a decade or so later barriers to reform proved less influential, for reasons to be explored in this chapter.

A significant factor was that by 1955 the Ministry of Housing and Local Government (MHLG) had become absolutely convinced of the need for modernisation, if necessary through coercion. This itself, however, can be linked to an aspect of the water industry's history during this period, which stands in strong contrast to the preceding half-century – namely that the economy, and with it the demand for water, was growing fairly rapidly. This imposed unaccustomed strains upon the physical and institutional structures of the water industry. It led directly to the reappointment of the CACW with a brief to investigate, and recommend responses to, the cause of the growing demand for water. Before long the CACW decided that it was necessary to interpret its remit more widely. This led it to make far-reaching recommendations for water reorganisation, realised in the Water Resources Act of 1963. Rapid demand growth, discussions about integrated water management, and moves towards more interventionist and planning-orientated approaches to economic management generally, all exercised important influences upon the development of water policy, with shifting nuances over time. By the late 1960s a supply-orientated, technocratic bias to water policy, exemplified in the outlook of the Water Resources Board (WRB) established under the Act of 1963, was rapidly giving way to a perception of quality, rather than quantity, as being the key water problem. This led to the truly revolutionary Water Act of 1973. This finally allocated responsibility for managing the entire water cycle, from conservation and water distribution, through to sewage treatment and pollution control, to new unitary bodies, the Regional Water Authorities (RWAs).

Needs and resources

The growth of water demand

In contrast to the relatively depressed inter-war years, the post-war era witnessed a much higher growth in the demand for water. Though springing from a variety of factors, the principal components of water demand remained relatively constant, trade and domestic consumption continuing to take public supplies furnished by the statutory water undertakings in a ratio of 1: 2.

It is not easy to find reliable and consistent estimates for the growth of industrial consumption. A CACW subcommittee estimated that industrial demand in selected districts had grown at 2.0 per cent per annum in the thirty years to 1955, and was likely to increase to 2.3 per cent per annum in the ten years to 1965 (PRO 1958). The forecast may have been an underestimate, as a source cited by Smith (1972: 139) indicated non-domestic water demand grew at 5.2 per cent per annum between 1955 and 1962. Certainly industrial demand was buoyant due to the relatively vigorous economic growth of the period.

In addition, there were specific factors influencing the nature of industrial water demand. The water undertakers were faced with large-scale, complex and growing industrial requirements in the post-war period. New plastics and chemical industries especially had grown up and needed millions of gallons of water daily for cooling and processing (MHLG *1957*: 46). Water had many characteristics of great value to the chemical industry due to its physical, chemical and electrical qualities. It was used for steam production, process purposes, cooling, domestic uses in laundries and canteens, fire-fighting and water-borne disposal of wastes (Cooper and Smith 1960: 1).

Traditionally, statutory water undertakings had not placed great emphasis upon meeting trade requirements, one result being that a uniform standard of potable water was supplied indifferently to all consumers (Smith 1972: 139). Consequently, many industrial enterprises found it cheaper and more convenient to develop their own sources of raw water. After 1945 some obligation was placed on the water supply industry to respond to industrial needs. Controls on new wells and boreholes were introduced. As a result, during its post-war expansion industry looked to public supplies for meeting some of its additional requirements. Providing potable water supplies for industrial use was wasteful and by 1958 some twenty undertakings were supplying untreated or partially treated water for industry. The increasing industrial use of water was an important factor in the promotion of many new water schemes. In 1955 the West Hampshire Water Company obtained authorisation for the supply of four million gallons of untreated water daily for the Esso Petroleum Company's refinery at Fawley (MHLG *1957*: 51–2), and a scheme yielding twenty-five million gpd for a new ICI plant at Avonmouth was approved in 1960 (Hodgson 1991: 24–30).

Within industrial consumption, the demand for cooling water represented easily the largest category of consumption. This water was recycled and did not constitute a serious abstraction load upon the system. In the 1960s the CEGB accounted for a large share of the seventy-five per cent of abstractions, authorised by the River Authorities under the 1963 Act, which went to industry (WRB *1966/67*: 5). At Imperial Chemical Industries (ICI) Billingham the total 'normal consumption' of water in 1960 was about 7 million gallons per day of town water (from the public supplies); about 3.5 million gallons daily of 'medium-quality water' was drawn from local streams and boreholes, but 230 million gallons of estuary water was used every day for cooling purposes where requirements were less stringent (Cooper and Smith 1960: 9).

In this period agriculture was a major factor in the growth of non-domestic water demand. Water was used increasingly, especially by horticulturists, for irrigation purposes. The scale of their abstractions threatened to adversely affect river flow (Twort 1963: 12), raising concerns which ultimately culminated in sweeping reforms. The government referred the problem to the CACW who, in a 1961 subcommittee report, argued that all abstractions of whatever nature should be placed under the control of the new RAs. The government concurred with this conclusion, which led to the passing of the Water Resources Act of 1963, which, in so far as it established the RAs which achieved a much greater degree of integration than before over large territories, foreshadowed the reform of 1973.

Turning to household consumption, the product's cheapness and the by now widespread confidence in the quality of tap water interacted with improved living standards to lead to increased water use. Outside Malvern, domestic consumption was unmetered, and fixing water charges upon the rateable value of properties encouraged heavy household use. Fluoridisation provoked controversy, but its introduction, for instance by Birmingham Corporation to 1.25 million people in 1964, reflected the continuing attention of authorities to drinking-water quality (MHLG *1965–66*: 24).

Studies show that the major determinants of residential usage in the period included living standards, household densities, types of dwelling, and household technology, such as access to washing-machines (CWPU 1975: 4). Slum clearance and the movement of the population to improved property, often with bathrooms installed, were important factors. While water use in back-to-backs, according to Bradford Corporation in 1957, was less than 8 ghd, for a modern terraced house it was some 13 ghd, while 17 ghd on average was consumed by the inhabitants of a new semi-detached house (Smith 1972: 138). The ease with which water could be heated in the home was a particularly important consideration. Hot-water systems constituted, in fact, a principal component of household demand, even approaching the water-closet's importance as the biggest individual item of domestic water consumption (CWPU 1975: 5). The uses to which water was put to within the home varied, with the accent increasingly upon personal hygiene and sanitation. An analysis of how consumers used water in the south-east of England identified eight main components, but cooking, dishwashing and laundry, let alone car-washing and garden use were, as yet, relatively unimportant in comparison with 'personal washing and bathing', water-closets and refuse disposal. These last two categories each took an estimated one-third of total domestic consumption (Smith 1972: 137, citing Sharp 1967).

The taking of piped supplies into rural areas both permitted and encouraged increased water use. The Rural Water Supplies and Sewage Act of 1944 provided for government assistance to the cost of schemes and led to substantially improved provision. Numerous old-fashioned sources of water could be abandoned following the construction of modern waterworks in many country districts. Whereas in 1945 some thirty per cent of the population living in rural areas in England and forty-two per cent in Wales were without piped supplies, by 1957 the proportions had fallen to ten and twenty-one per cent respectively. By 1970 only about three per cent of the rural population were still without piped supplies (MHLG *1957*: 53–4; *1969–70*: 72).

The combined effect of increased use of water in the home, factory and farm was that, apart from when piped supplies were first introduced in the middle decades of the nineteenth century, water consumption probably grew faster than it had ever done before. Nationally, water demand grew at about 2.5 per cent per annum in the 1950s and at 3 per cent in the 1960s (Table 3.1; DoE 1971: 29). All official forecasts, especially those of the WRB (1973: 61), expected these rates to continue so that in the North, for example, consumption would double between 1971 and the end of the century.

Given existing structures, the ability of the water supply industry to expand capacity and to develop schemes on the required scale was increasingly brought into question. A subcommittee was appointed by the reactivated CACW in 1955 to examine the implications of the growing demand for water. Its first report of 1958 did not betray concern, as yet, regarding the balance between supply and demand. This was, however, evident in the subcommittee's 1961 report, especially over the effect of agricultural use of surface water for irrigation, which was 'growing apace'. The *Final Report* of 1962 under Professor Proudman offered a more far-reaching analysis of the situation in the water industry and of the reforms needed to overcome, in its opinion, organisational defects.

In addition to the fear that agricultural abstractions might deplete the natural flow of many rivers, the precariousness of the situation in urban centres, especially in periods of shortage, as demonstrated in the drought of 1959, was beginning to animate many officials. It was believed in its aftermath that the schemes which had been proposed in MHLG Inspector surveys for south-east Lancashire and the West Riding of Yorkshire could 'well be too small', and that it would be necessary to press ahead with 'controversial' schemes to tap additional resources in the Lake District and Wales. A Cabinet Paper pointed out that by mid-October 1959 many large cities in the West Riding and Lancashire were 'within measurable distance of exhausting their supplies'. In places like Leeds and Stockport, resources were strained 'to the limits' (PRO 1959).

The critical, if unusual, situation of 1959 had encouraged officials and politicians to adopt a more strategic approach to the water industry's problems. The important reform of river management in 1963 soon followed. In the meantime, central government was even prepared to modify its traditionally parsimonious attitude to capital spending in the water and sewage sectors. Reversing its earlier intention to impose cutbacks, after the drought of 1959 it proposed to increase investment. A planned expenditure of £89.4 million on water and sewage for 1961/2 may be compared with spending of £55.8 million in 1958/9. The Chancellor of the Exchequer explained that the investment was for the purpose of augmenting inadequate supplies and to meet rapidly growing demand, principally from industry but also for domestic use (HM Government 1960: 23–4).

Water supply reorganisation

In principle, from 1945 the conduct of water policy was established upon a more secure footing than hitherto. The Act of that year laid down the Minister of Health's responsibility for developing a national policy, covering elements which ranged from the broadest aims for water conservation to a detailed remit to require undertakings to carry out specific works. The MHLG (*1957*) indicated that three principles set out in the 1944 White Paper guided its actions. These involved commitment to: (a) a sufficient degree of central control to prevent a haphazard and wasteful development of water resources; (b) responsibility for water administration lying equally between government at the centre and local undertakings at the 'circumference'; and (c) ample protection to be provided for all interests. These principles reflected the influence exercised by lobbies in the policy-making process. The contradictions involved in pursuing them were difficult to conceal.

On the first point, the MHLG found itself with inadequate powers to influence source developments, especially for surface water. This undermined its ability to realise the policy objectives set by the 1945 Act. In fact, it is probable that many elements within the cognate departments had come to the conclusion by the mid-1950s, if not earlier, that the 1945 Act suffered major defects in this respect (PRO 1954).

The second principle involved conceding influence and authority to statutory undertakings at the circumference. This collided with the aim of the regrouping policy, which was to secure the organisation of the water industry 'in units large enough to plan effectively for the future' (MHLG *1957*: 64). As a result restructuring initially made very little progress. Many of the 1,000 undertakings in England and Wales in 1956 were local authorities supplying a few hundred consumers. Concentration of ownership may have made more headway in the private sector, but control still remained very dispersed here, as the material covering eighty members of WCA summarised in Table 4.1 shows.

Table 4.1   *Analysis of members of the Water Companies Association, 1955*

Quantity of water supplied (million gpd)		No. of companies	% all member companies	% total supply of member companies
	<1	32	40	4.5
>1	<2	9	11	4.0
>2	<5	20	25	17.0
>5	<10	10	13	20.0
>10	<20	4	5	15.5
>20		5	6	39.0

Source: PRO 1955b.

In its discussion of the third principle – the commitment to give protection to all interests – the MHLG simply had to admit that its adoption had led to procedures for public inquiry and, in some cases, for special parliamentary investigation, being pursued when objections were raised over ministerial reorganisation plans. Moreover, the laborious procedures involved acted as a serious disincentive to seeking compulsory combination by Order under Section Nine of the Act (PRO 1953).

The 1945 Act disappointed in other respects. Practically no use whatsoever was made of the provision for the formation of statutory Joint Advisory Committees which, at the time of the Act, had been regarded as quite an important component of the modernisation policy. Another theme of the 1945 measure was the need to obtain more information about regional requirements and resources. As a result, throughout the country, water surveys were carried out by the MHLG's engineering inspectors, and their reports were sent to all interested parties. Some subsequent regrouping schemes were influenced by the inspectors' reports, such as that based on the new Chew valley reservoir serving both Bristol and Bath. The MHLG admitted, however, that the surveys were only a 'starting-point' for water reorganisation. A more dispassionate view recognised the 'elaborate series of regional surveys' as 'useful in their own way but containing no material not readily available' (PRO 1954).

The outcome was that the regrouping policy initially failed. A reappraisal took place between 1953 and 1955, after which Whitehall and leaders in the BWA launched, as Kinnersley (1988: 79) put it, 'a pragmatic campaign to achieve mergers substantially by agreement'. The new Conservative administration was coming to the following conclusions: that some of the smaller and less efficient water companies could not meet all the demands placed upon them; that the State possessed weak instruments to progress the reform of the water industry; and that voluntary regrouping had achieved very little, while the threat of nationalisation under a Labour government had not entirely disappeared (PRO HLG/127/102: *passim*). Following contacts between the water industry and the Ministry a significant change of approach was announced in 1956. In September a circular was issued to all undertakings, which emphasised the Minister's view that regrouping should proceed faster and more radically. All undertakings were asked to consider immediately the advantages of combining in the interests of efficiency.

The resultant merger movement did undoubtedly lead to dramatic changes in the structure of the water supply industry. The number of enterprises fell from over 1,000 in the mid-1950s to about 200 in 1970. In the urban areas of the North former municipal boroughs and urban district councils were largely absorbed by expanded County Borough areas of supply. Deficiencies in rural water provision and a more regional perspective to water resource development could be achieved by the growth of urban water undertakings into their 'hinterlands'. While the Newcastle and Gateshead Water Company still only supplied 153 square miles in 1945, after taking over the responsibilities of at least a dozen Northumbrian rural authorities, its area of supply by 1970 had increased to 1,854 square miles. Similarly, the district served by Bristol Water Company increased from 78 square miles in 1952 to 934 square miles in 1964. These two cases illustrate an interesting facet of the regrouping movement, which was the partial de-municipalisation it occasionally involved.

After 1955 the regrouping movement did have a significant impact. In 1956 almost half of the population of England and Wales was already served by the fifty-five largest undertakings, with the other half, however, supplied by almost a thousand (Smith 1972: 132). But by 1971, 198 undertakings served the entire country, and the six largest all supplied districts with populations in excess of one million (DoE 1971: 9).

Moreover, more order and control were being applied to the development of water resources through the development of the abstraction licence system. All abstractions from underground sources, including private industrial abstractions, were controlled through licensing powers conferred on the Minister by the Act of 1945. An argument for extending this procedure to rivers was made. With the establishment of River Boards in 1948 some control over new abstractions was secured. But in 1963 under the Water Resources Act, with only limited exceptions, all water abstractions from rivers, as well as from underground sources, had to be approved and licensed by the new River Authorities as from April 1965.

Returning to enterprise restructuring, the new element of a more coercive posture by government did strengthen its hand in promoting rationalisation. The main instrument for pursuing the policy was the Minister's power, provided for under the 1945 Act, to make Orders authorising undertakers to take water and carry out works. Authorisation of new waterworks by private legislation could, and still did, occur, but between 1945 and 1957, 246 ministerial Orders were made, against which only twenty-six local Acts were passed. This clearly represented a

Table 4.2 *Size distribution of water supply undertakings in terms of population served, 1971*

Population served	Local Boards	Joint Boards	Statutory companies	Total
< 50,000	26	6	2	34
50,000–100,000	9	21	3	33
100,000–250,000	12	49	15	76
250,000–1 million	14	24	11	49
> 1 million	3	1	2	6

Source: DoE 1971: 9.

significant change from the customary practice of leaving the development of resources and the authorisation of waterworks to local initiative and the private Bill.

Yet difficulties still remained to complicate the pursuit of a coherent national policy for water. There was still nothing to prevent individual enterprises from seeking authorisation of new projects through the traditional system of parliamentary private legislation. In fact, parliamentary approval was still required in cases involving adjustments to compensation awards and to contested proposals. Moreover, statutory undertakings still had complete control over existing source works and the possibility of conflict with river bodies was high. Among local authorities, joint boards and private companies, many small units, serving small populations, survived. As can be seen from Table 4.2, even after a decade and a half of regrouping about one-third of all undertakings served areas with populations under 100,000.

Few undertakings were large enough to conceive major regional, river regulation or conjunctive schemes, even in the unlikely event of their areas of jurisdiction being compatible with the boundaries of river catchments.

Notwithstanding these difficulties there is a tendency in the literature to judge the water industry's progress in this period favourably. It is certainly the case that these years did witness a decisive break with the past in a number of respects, especially the movement towards integrated river management and the squaring up, to some extent, to special interests. Such developments paved the way for even more fundamental changes in the near future. However, some reappraisal of the established view of this period in the water industry's history may be necessary.

Kinnersley (1988: 80) and Barty-King (1992: 158) describe the post-1955 regrouping movement as one characterised by pragmatism, flexibility and non-compulsion. Companies and local authorities are portrayed as content to see their identity disappear in Joint Boards. Barty-King stresses the importance of the Joint Board in facilitating restructuring, describing the co-ordination achieved under them as a first step 'in implementing a National Water Policy'. The British water industry, he says, 'was putting its house in order'.

This may be too generous an interpretation. A discussion of the nature and significance of the merger movement of the 1950s and 1960s can address several questions:

1   How far did regrouping of undertakings lead to an optimal restructuring of water supply provision?
2   What was the contribution of the Joint Board, the chief device to achieve reorganisation, in attaining these objectives?
3   How voluntary was the merger movement?
4   What was its long-term significance?

On the first point, some important regional projects were brought into existence in this period, such as the Great Ouse Water Authority. But they were not numerous. In general, the piecemeal nature of restructuring undermined the objective of basing water supply undertakings upon hydrologically sound principles.

On the second question, similarly the wielding together of a number of smaller undertakings in a Joint Board did not automatically lead to the realisation of significant cost gains or hydrological cohesion. Some of the new Boards were still such small organisations that their administrative and financial officers could only be employed on a part-time basis (DoE 1971: 11). Joint Boards did not necessarily enable flexible adjustments to supply being made in line with future shifts in demand, as each founding partner had its share of costs and supplies fixed at the outset and enshrined in the legislation establishing the Board. Subsequently the WRB (*1970/71*: 48) concluded that even a simple and static arrangement of the kind typical of most Boards was, in practice: 'an exercise of forbidding difficulty, involving protracted negotiation, complicated drafting, and all the expense and delay of private legislation. The procedure is quite inadequate for the kind of dynamic operational system which the regional approach requires.'

Thirdly, the pragmatic and voluntary character of the post-1955 regrouping movement was significantly qualified by an interventionist element. It is true that initially the Minister trod warily and was conscious of the likelihood of traditional, parochial resistance to rationalisation. An official concerned with promoting regrouping in south Lancashire observed (LRO, PHM/21: 9 May 1956): 'It is suggested that any move to ... regionalisation of water supplies might be strenuously opposed in some quarters if it were not made clear at the outset that regionalisation does not, in itself, necessarily mean the loss of identity of particular water undertakings in amalgamation with others.' This official reserve, however, was soon shaken off. In a number of statements in 1957, the Minister made it abundantly clear that the objective was to reorganise the water industry as rapidly as possible, hopefully through voluntary mergers, but by the application of compulsory powers if necessary (MHLG *1957*: 61).

Moreover, the Minister did indeed resort to coercion to achieve rationalisation, and many mergers were the result of an involuntary loss of identity. Following the resistance of the potential partners, a statutory Order was employed to achieve the compulsory amalgamation of five local authorities and two Joint Boards, thereby expanding the Cambridge Water Company's area of supply from 60 to 453 square miles (Barty-King 1992: 158). Likewise, following opposition by Essex County Council and in Parliament, several merger attempts in south Essex failed. This led the government to create the Essex Water Company by Order. By 1971 it supplied 1.3 million people, formerly served by six local authorities and two companies (Fabry 1991: 133).

Even where mergers were agreed to voluntarily, the potential threat of merger by coercion concentrated the minds of those who previously had so jealously defended enterprise autonomy. Water companies in the Durham area, for example, 'seized the opportunity' to regroup after the Minister's mid-1950s initiative, taking the view that voluntary agreement would secure better terms than compulsory measures (Fabry 1991: 129). At worst, if the water supply industry did not reorganise, an incoming Labour government might nationalise it. The BWA came round to supporting the post-1955 MHLG-led regrouping policy, because to resist it might lead to solutions being imposed very much less to their liking than an accelerated, if 'voluntary', merger process. The Association (PRO 1955b) recognised that unless: 'voluntary action is taken by such undertakings, the Minister will be compelled to exercise his compulsory powers and the result is likely to be the creation of regional boards or other large scale units under central control replacing the existing undertakings.'

Finally, the regrouping movement certainly did lead to a significant concentration of ownership. But largeness of undertaking did not, of itself, guarantee that the rational planning and development of river basins would thereby be achieved. The largest undertakings were faced with statutory responsibilities and still exercised financial power. Circumstances, therefore, tended to lead them to promote source-developments characterised by a disregard of regional needs (Mitchell 1971). In some senses the regrouping movement of the 1950s and 1960s was, historically, a dead-end. This may be an exaggerated overstatement, but certainly subsequent sweeping reforms of water management owed very little to the restructuring of water supply undertakings achieved before 1973. Meanwhile, a river-catchment-based reorganisation of water supply and sewage treatment was always going to be very difficult to achieve through a piecemeal restructuring of units defined essentially by local authority boundaries and jurisdictions.

Supply trends and reappraisals

Introduction

Rivers were subject to increasing pressures in this period. The discharge of effluent was, effectively, a major demand upon rivers. In addition, undertakings looked to them to provide additional supplies to fulfil their statutory requirements. Furthermore, because of large-scale abstractions, a high proportion of the summer flow of rivers like the Trent was composed of effluent discharges. Advances in water treatment made it practicable to abstract water nearer to the mouths of rivers. River authorities welcomed this as it led to rivers' natural flow being less disrupted. Nevertheless, undertakings still tended to prefer to take water from cleaner upper reaches whenever they could (MHLG *1957*: 51). But because of the pressures upon rivers, as well as the growth of opposition to dam building, it was becoming increasingly difficult to find suitable sites for reservoirs or groundwater pumps. Smith (1972: 140) has explained how, in the light of these constraints, the water industry undertook a reappraisal of how water resources should be used and existing works should be employed. Following on and adding to Smith's analysis, one may identify four major types of source utilisation to illustrate the nature of this reappraisal: more flexible use of existing sources, new river abstraction schemes, the promotion of river regulation projects and measures to enhance underground sources.

Source reappraisal

1] An example of more flexible use of an existing source were the steps taken by the Fylde Water Board (WB). Faced with an intense peaking of demand in the summer associated with the influx of tourists, the WB augmented its surface sources from boreholes in the Fylde sandstone during dry summer spells. In addition, it was able to call upon the Lake District aqueduct for bulk supplies, further diversifying its sources. Another example of flexible source use was the new Chew reservoir south of Bristol, to which Bath Corporation gained access through a co-operative scheme with three other undertakings, hence increasing Bath's water-storage capacity tenfold (MHLG *1957*: 51).

2] Smith also gives examples of new large-scale abstraction schemes requiring co-operative effort. For example, the Great Ouse Water Authority, created in 1961, constructed Grafham Water reservoir, into which water was pumped from the Great Ouse. The works came into operation in 1966 and the Authority provided bulk supplies to five undertakings in the East Midlands.

3] For Smith the most fruitful outcome of collective initiative was the increased emphasis upon river regulation. The inflexibility and high cost of direct-supply reservoirs, involving the 'total sterilisation of reservoired catchment', attracted adverse criticism in this period. The application of river regulation methods could produce many benefits. The natural opportunities for storage and distribution offered by the river itself are utilised, downstream abstraction means that the run-off from a much larger catchment is drawn upon, and a substantial increase in yield over a direct-supply system, based on identical reservoirs, can be achieved. A river's resources can be more purposefully utilised and managed – for flood control objectives; to maintain and regulate flows for fish runs, canals and recreational activities; to inhibit reverse saline flows in the lower reaches of rivers;

to maintain flows for the task of transporting water to consumers; and to mitigate the effects of channel scour and downstream erosion which can result from the build-up of reservoir sediment. There are a number of examples of some of these benefits being produced through the introduction of river regulation schemes, such as in the Hodder basin after 1933 and for the Tees from the 1960s (Smith 1972: 143–7; Petts and Lewin 1979).

A well-known example of river regulation is the Dee, where the approach was first applied in Britain. In fact the Dee has been managed, after a fashion, for hundreds of years; the Chester weir was built 700 years ago and Telford constructed a weir at Llyn Tegid in the 1800s to control releases into the Llangollen canal. The resources of the river were first utilised on a large scale through the construction of a direct supply reservoir by Birkenhead in the 1920s. Following the passing of the Dee and Clwyd Board Act in 1951, a consultative committee was formed and Llyn Tegid was employed as a flood-control reservoir. The scheme was subsequently modified, following further separate proposals being made to use the river basin's resources, especially Liverpool Corporation's plans in 1956 to build a large reservoir on the River Tryweryn. The modified scheme allowed Liverpool to make direct abstractions, led to improved flow and flood control, and enabled Tryweryn reservoir releases to be used for the generation of hydro-electric power. However, only after 1974, with the passing of the Dee and Clwyd River Authority Act, was the potential of river regulation and more flexible management fully realised (Smith 1972; Lambert 1988).

4] There was growing interest in the period in the conservation of underground water. Statutory undertakings considerably increased their use of underground sources, abstractions having risen by an estimated 125 per cent between 1914 and 1953, quite apart from large quantities used by industry (MHLG *1957*: 54). With no overall conservation policy, however, aquifers were degraded due to too rapid abstraction and the replacement of underground storage, not by rainfall, but by poorer quality river or sea-water. Aquifers were also damaged by the action of the 'drainage enthusiasts' who, by cleaning out ditches, dredging and canalising streams and rivers and removing growth from banks, accelerated the flow of water 'to a useless grave in the sea' (PRO 1949d).

Central authority had, however, now obtained the means to control the exploitation of underground water. According to the MHLG (*1957*: 54): 'The power to control the abstraction of underground water was perhaps the greatest innovation of the Water Act, 1945.' All new or increased abstractions were subject to ministerial control through licensing, and applied to designated areas, which included all the principal underground water-bearing regions. Henceforth the exploitation of aquifers in, for example, Nottinghamshire, East Anglia and the Thames basin was subject to orderly supervision.

The next stage was to consider means of restoring the depleted resource. The possibility of recharging aquifers had been discussed within the MHLG from

1949. By 1954 small aquifer recharge schemes were being proposed in several parts of the country and there was even one in operation, which employed effluent, treated to a very high standard, on the River Lee. The best prospects for large-scale recharge appeared to lie with replenishing the bunter sandstones of Nottinghamshire from the Trent. It was only by the 1970s, however, that such schemes were fully developed – Thames Water, for example, by then was recharging the chalk aquifer in the Lee valley on a large scale.

In the 1950s and 1960s, therefore, a reappraisal of water utilisation methods occurred and there was a greater readiness to endeavour to work with the natural characteristics of hydrological systems. However, prevailing institutional–industrial structures generally impeded their realisation. This was one reason why there remained a strong tendency for water authorities to continue to promote large-scale, direct supply waterworks, often traditional in conception, if not in scale.

Large-scale supply schemes

Many water authorities were concerned about the impending inadequacy of existing works and were anxious to respond to anticipated demand pressures arising from future economic and urban expansion. By 1954, for example, Liverpool Corporation felt that the search for new sources had to resume, given that demand was already being met by expedient overdrawing on existing sources (Mitchell 1971: 31). To justify its proposal to build a reservoir on the Tryweryn, Liverpool presented arguments to show that the city's economic regeneration might be jeopardised through inadequate water supplies.

Similarly, following severe drought in 1959 and growing demands for water, Manchester presented proposals to abstract water from Ullswater and to construct a reservoir in the nearby Bannisdale valley in 1961. Manchester's obligations as a water undertaker were considerable, with a responsibility to bulk supply fourteen other local authorities. A committee under Lord Jellicoe was appointed by the MHLG to investigate the options. The inquiry provided the occasion for the tabling of some exceptionally intrusive engineering proposals, such as a 'Grand Contour Canal' to take 100 million gpd of aquifer water from the upper Eden valley fifty miles south to Ribchester. While the committee agreed that many existing sources, such as Pennine catchments, were developed to the limits, it did not seriously entertain such outlandish projects. It concluded that abstractions from Windermere and the regulation of the Ribble could make significant contributions to satisfying long-term regional needs (MHLG 1963).

The immediate solution to Manchester's predicament was to allow the city to draw water from Ullswater, subject to sensitive controls. Liverpool and Manchester were criticised for developing projects, which were short-term in design and lacked a regional perspective, being the outcome and reflection of an inherited and anachronistic municipal perspective (Mitchell 1971: 59). Even if they dominated the regional supply picture because of bulk supply arrangements, the two authorities were driven to search for essentially expedient solutions to the problem of executing their statutory obligations in a period of rapidly growing demand.

A number of major new supply schemes were authorised or were under construction during the 1960s. As well as the works to draw water from Ullswater, they included the proposal to build a dam in upper Teesdale. Despite these new developments, the WRB, in particular, was much exercised by its projection of significantly expanding water demand over the rest of the century and the limited capacity of existing works. This was a time of grand design and high anxiety in the water planning world: in a series of reports the WRB warmed towards such proposals as the increased exploitation of Windermere, the building of a reservoir in Farndale in the North Yorkshire Moors, and the construction of barrages across Morecambe Bay and the Solway Firth. Other public authorities were swept up in the spirit of the times, with the Cumberland RA, Plymouth Corporation and the South West Devon WB being among those advocating the need for more dams and reservoirs within National Parks. On the WRB's recommendation, it was anticipated that 'only nine or ten substantial new surface storage schemes', including an estuary barrage, possibly on the Dee, would be required to meet the country's expanding requirements to the end of the century (MHLG *1969–70*: 69–70).

At this stage it was virtually taken for granted (Rydz 1974: 2) that new surface storage was urgently needed. The WRB's role in seeking a co-ordination of regional and interregional plans and the adoption of a long-term national strategy for water resource development was admired by many contemporaries. To be fair to the WRB, moreover, towards the end of its existence it became more than just an advocate of grand engineering solutions to perceived future shortfalls in supply; it aspired to a more flexible utilisation of resources within the overall framework of the water cycle; and it envisaged that new large storage facilities, such as the Kielder reservoir, would be employed so that river regulation and a more integrated approach to water management could be achieved.

Environmentalist opposition to water supply projects

The engineering bias and enthusiasm represented in much of the WRB's outlook, nevertheless, came into headlong collision with environmental concerns in this period. The opposition to new water supply projects evoked, to some extent, the preservationist impulse of seeking to defend habitats and the countryside. It also, however, displayed many features of post-1970 political environmentalism – in the mobilisation of mass interest, in the utilisation of scientific studies, and in the generally very politicised and public nature of the ensuing conflicts.

Public officials were becoming more aware of environmental sensitivities. As early as 1946 the CAWC (quoted in Twort 1963: 11) concluded that: 'Subject to reasonable safeguards we consider that gathering grounds should be so managed as to make the maximum contribution to the general welfare by providing facilities for healthy recreation and the production of food and timber.' In the past, the acquisition of catchment areas and minimising human activity were central planks of the water undertakings' efforts to protect water supplies. The issue was an important one during the Ullswater debate. In the 1940s and 1950s the attitude of water undertakings towards the principle of public access to gathering-grounds was still very hostile. The open-spaces movement had become well organised, however, and capably exposed the frailty of the position that ramblers represented a significant pollution risk (Stephenson 1989). The RAs had been enjoined under the Act of 1963 to promote the provision of recreational facilities, and they encouraged undertakings to open up their reservoirs to the public for these purposes; this policy was also supported by the BWA and MHLG (MHLG 1969–70: 71). Improving public access became an integral part of the authorities' responses when they came into conflict with groups angered by the environmental damage caused by reservoir building.

Throughout this period public bodies uttered statements which acknowledged that social, environmental and amenity impacts should be incorporated into assessments of new source developments, especially in areas of natural beauty. However, there was difficulty in reconciling this position with a determination to expand the capacity of the water supply industry. In the considered view of the WRB (1973: 1), for example, there would, in fact, not always be a practical alternative to development in the National Parks. Because they covered so much land, some ten per cent of the total, and comprised the rainiest parts of the country they could not, in its opinion, be regarded as 'sacrosanct from change'.

Some of the fiercest opposition to water supply projects had nationalist overtones, namely those to impound more valleys in Wales. Plaid Cmyru tried to stop the construction of the Clywedog dam in the 1960s by buying land and there were explosions at the dam site (Parker and Penning-Rowsell 1980: 69). With regard to the Trywern project, Liverpool conceded that there would be losses of amenity but that the poor-quality land and farming practices involved made these acceptable. Liverpool maintained that wider cultural and environmental costs were offset by the new reservoir's economic benefits and that the costs of the Tryweryn dam were the lowest among the available locations (Mitchell 1971: 46–7). Despite sabotage attempts and ferocious resistance the opposition was overruled and the scheme went ahead.

Highly sensitive issues of a different kind were involved at Cow Green in upper Teesdale, where the disruption of a unique upland ecosystem was threatened. The local WB was informed in 1964 that large extra volumes of water would be soon required by Teesside industries, especially ICI. In 1965 the Board deposited a Bill empowering them to construct a reservoir at Cow Green. 'The Bill was opposed by scientific interests and by amenity interests, and a national debate of perhaps unprecedented depth and passion was conducted in the press and before both Houses of Parliament', admitted the MHLG (1965–66: 84). Vital to the decision to overrule the opposition were the arguments, which persuaded the Minister and the WRB, concerning the vital economic need for additional water supplies and the lack of an alternative site. Public pressure, however, had significantly influenced the terms of approval. The Cow Green reservoir was part of a well-considered river-regulation scheme for the exploitation of the Tees and, as Mitchell (1971: 74) comments, accusations that it involved a haphazard approach to water management, as at Trywern, could not be invoked.

Perhaps more controversial were Manchester's attempts to increase its utilisation of Cumbrian water resources. Given parliamentary approval of schemes to build dams at Thirlmere in 1879 and Haweswater in 1919, the prospects for the agitation which sought to defend Ullswater did not seem especially auspicious. By 1960 Manchester concluded that the existing exploitation of Cumbrian resources was insufficient to meet the authority's long-term commitments. Manchester's plans to abstract water from Ullswater and to construct a reservoir in the nearby Bannisdale valley were contained in a Bill of 1961. This provoked enormous opposition from extensive and varied interests – from the Cumberland County Council to the Fell and Rock Climbing Club of the English Lake District. The scheme was scrutinised by the Jellicoe inquiry and in the House of Lords. The conclusion of the Jellicoe inquiry was that while Manchester had to act to respond to growing needs, in developing proposals it would have to take account of 'justifiable opposition' and all views expressed from the 'standpoint of amenity and planning' (MHLG 1963: 7). Although its first proposal was defeated, Manchester's need for water remained, and in 1964 a second attempt was made employing different strategy and tactics. A more controlled outcome was accepted by Manchester. This time, following a public inquiry in 1965, Manchester's plans to abstract water from Ullswater and Windermere were approved by the Minister. They were, however, subject to a series of modifications to preserve the unspoilt beauty of the surrounding countryside. For example, the duplicate aqueduct in Longsleddale which would have caused serious landscape damage was deleted, and stringent conditions on the appearance and landscape of the works were imposed. Manchester was also required to improve public access around Haweswater. There was no question of restricting access as the principal means of preserving water quality, as had been the case for Haweswater and Thirlmere, and separate treatment facilities had to be constructed (MHLG *1965–66*: 83; Porter 1978: 41–3).

Porter (1978: 39) stated that: 'The controversy which flared around the Ullswater proposal entirely changed the nature of surface water development in the Lake District.' More generally, that all large-scale proposals were likely to attract searching examination and that Parliament and the public felt that the National Parks required special consideration, were elements that the water industry professionals were obliged to incorporate into their thinking on water resource development. The WRB (*1966/67*: 2–3) strove to highlight the amenity benefits of schemes like Grafham Water. How far reassuring statements about a concern for nature conservation and the recreational value of reservoirs reflected a genuine sea-change in official attitudes, as opposed to skin-deep pragmatism, is problematic. On the one hand, the environmentalist opposition suffered many setbacks over the period and the WRB and other public authorities were still promoting major engineering schemes in the early 1970s. On the other hand, apart from the Kielder project, virtually none of those grandiose projects have subsequently been realised.

Environmentalist pressure certainly exercised a significant impact and even in cases of apparent defeat, its effect was tangible, as in the case of Cow Green reservoir, completed in the 1970s after huge opposition. The colony of Ice-Age flora may have suffered less seriously than was once anticipated (Rofe 1994: 120). If, however, the environmental damage proved less severe than worst fears, this must be attributed to the provisions included in the original authorisation, which ensured that local waterfalls were maintained and fish movements on the River Tees supported, as well as to redoubled efforts made subsequently to manage and conserve the area's valuable ecology.

Recognition of the great public interest in the environmental implications of water resource development, and of the need to improve policies regarding nature conservation and recreational use of the land and water owned by the water authorities, were among the factors which increased the need for an all-embracing reform of water management. With the passing of the Water Act of 1973, promotion of nature conservation and the amenity potential of waterworks were formally included among the aims of national water policy, and involvement in these fields became distinctive areas of RWA activity.

River management

River Boards and Authorities

River Boards

Kinnersley (1988: 71) has pointed out that the reform of water management in England and Wales in the recent past derived less from the attempts to reorganise water supply and more from the efforts to create integrated river authorities, and that this process can be traced back to the Fishery Boards established from 1923. It culminated in the creation of the RWAs in 1973.

The River Boards Act of 1948 led to the formation of thirty-two River Boards. Their boundaries were largely based on those of the preceding Catchment Boards. The River Boards acquired all the land drainage functions of Catchment Boards, the fishery protection duties of Fisheries Boards and also assumed responsibilities for pollution prevention.

Despite this, the River Boards represented a still far from ideal means of reconciling interests and ensuring the co-ordinated management of water resources within catchments. Above all, the public water supply still remained outside their jurisdiction and, 'water undertakings continued the largely independent appropriation of new sources' (Smith 1972: 31). Meanwhile, after 1955, CACW subcommittees were investigating water policy issues, especially with reference to the rising demand for water. What gave the process of inquiry greater urgency was the disruptive impact of drought in 1959 and flood in 1960. In a period of relatively rapid growth it was becoming clear that, notwithstanding the accelerated merger movement, the continuing *ad hoc*, localised approach to source development was inappropriate to contemporary conditions. The Proudman Committee of the CACW published its final report in 1962.

As it pointed out, the 1945 Water Act required the Minister to develop a national water policy, but there was only one provision which provided him with means to discharge this duty directly, namely Section Fourteen relating to powers to control the development of underground water resources. The thrust of the report was the need to create river authorities: 'comprehensive new authorities to manage the water resources of river basins as a whole and to be charged with the positive duty of water conservation'. Although the whole question of water-supply reorganisation was left unresolved, the Committee's constructive recommendations were largely accepted by the government and were embodied in the Water Resources Act of 1963.

The Water Act 1963 and the River Authorities

Under the Water Act of 1963 twenty-nine River Authorities were established. In addition, a national Water Resources Board was created with the task of collating the endeavours of the RAs and of preparing regional plans for different parts of the country and, ultimately, for producing a National Plan for water. This was published in 1973. The RAs inherited all the responsibilities of the River Boards – land drainage, pollution prevention, fisheries protection and some navigation duties. They were composed of the same range of interests as the River Boards, including those representing land drainage, fisheries, public water supply and manufacturing industry. But the RAs did not simply inherit the role of the River Boards. They were assigned enlarged, more specific and ambitious duties, especially for pollution control and resource planning.

The new authorities had wider responsibilities for managing rivers imposed upon them. The RAs were to use their enlarged information-gathering function to establish 'minimum acceptable flow' levels for rivers; this would inform planning on source developments and the setting of water-quality targets. In theory the RAs had the power to adjust works and to thereby control the amount of dilution water available for absorbing polluting discharges, though in practice this was not realised (Pitkethly 1990: 129).

The other potentially significant innovation under the 1963 Act was the provision made for water resource planning. It was hoped that the nation's use of water would be greatly improved through the introduction of the means to establish the nature of long-term demands, available resources and the claims of interests (WRB

1964/65: 10). The 1948 Act establishing the River Boards excluded water-supply responsibilities from their duties as it was believed this would create conflict with the rights of riparian owners. Under the 1963 measure, however, riparian rights to water resources were removed entirely in England and Wales. The abstraction and impounding of water was to be controlled through a system of licensing, and charges for all surface and underground water were introduced. It was envisaged that the RAs would act eventually as water wholesalers, identify and construct source works in their areas and sell bulk supplies as required to undertakings. In fact, as in the area of flow and dilution management, the RAs' interventions in the sphere of source developments were very limited.

Despite the failure to translate aspiration into achievement in these two potentially important areas, the 1963 measure as a whole is rightly viewed as significant. The RAs did represent a crucial move towards integrated river management. Barty-King (1992: 160) refers to the 'radical change' effected by the Act, making possible a co-ordinated management of water resources within river basins and on a regional basis for the first time. He approvingly quotes the President of the WCA's description of the Act as 'the most important piece of legislation affecting the water supply since the Water Act of 1945'. Also important was the introduction of the licensing system, described by Mitchell (1971: 22) as 'a radical change in philosophy by altering the status of traditional riparian rights'.

For Craine (1969: 42–3) the 1963 Act was a 'water management charter' which conferred upon the RAs not only all the responsibilities of the River Boards but also the 'initiative powers' of the MHLG for the conservation and proper use of water resources. The RAs had, therefore, been established with an apparently impressive range of powers – to collect data, conduct surveys, formulate proposals, establish minimum river flows, license all withdrawals, levy abstraction charges and construct, operate and co-ordinate reservoirs for water conservation purposes. The 1963 reform was significant, too, in reflecting the emerging international expert consensus on the need for institutional arrangements to reflect hydrological interdependencies. The progress made in this country towards integrated river management influenced reform elsewhere, notably France, where river-basin agencies were established in 1964 (Kneese and Bower 1968).

Of the reform of 1963, Barty-King (1992: 161) has spoken of 'the benefits which these changes brought to the statutory companies, hard pressed to find increased sources of supply to meet demand'. Reference was made in particular to the local RA's contribution to a resolution of Cambridge Water Company's difficulties in meeting a rapid increase in demand in the 1960s. Licences were granted to take water from sources, expert advice on a groundwater storage project was given and, following a pilot study, the RA prepared a scheme for drawing supplies from boreholes from the River Rhee.

No doubt the RAs were able to provide advisory and planning assistance to many undertakings. As will be seen below, however, relationships between the RAs and the water undertakings were often far from harmonious. The extent of the RAs' contribution to a solution to the country's water supply problems may be measured against the fact that they overviewed only one major inter-authority transfer project. This was the Ely Ouse–Essex scheme, which involved a vigorous and forward-looking water authority (Essex) that was anxious to overcome its water supply difficulties (WRB *1970/71*: 63; DoE 1971: 18).

The RAs ran into problems in the discharge of their remit to co-ordinate the use of resources. As Porter says, while under the 1963 Act these duties of the RAs were laid down, unlike the water undertakers they had no statutory obligation to find more water as such. The water undertakers did have this statutory obligation, but had no control over new sources. Frequently the water undertakers and the RAs were at odds when the former sought to acquire new sources and obtain a licence, while the latter might resist granting one because of conservation concerns. Porter (1978: 48) adds: 'While the water undertakers were at a disadvantage over new sources the River Authorities were at a disadvantage over existing works for direct supply .... In almost all cases the effect of the 1963 Act was to sanctify the undertakers' source patterns and patterns of supply.' This was hardly the intention of the 1963 reform.

With the benefit of hindsight it is clear that the powers of the RAs were quite circumscribed. Yet the 1963 measure looked forward to the 1973 Water Act. The national and regional bodies established by the 1963 measure represented new points of departure with respect to water planning (Mitchell 1971). The Regional Water Authorities (RWAs) followed the RAs and achieved the integration and authority which their predecessors lacked. The inability of the RAs to make significant progress in managing supplies and water quality within catchments was due to the continuing autonomy of the water supply and sewerage authorities. As long as these core activities remained under independent jurisdiction, the scope for conflict between the undertakers and the RAs in the interpretation of their respective responsibilities remained high, and integrated management would not be fully achieved.

The Water Resources Board

The WRB started its business in a temperate vein. As it launched itself into its tasks of preparing regional plans for the augmentation of resources and evaluating its forecast of a very large increment in water needs by the end of the century, an initially cautious mood was soon cast aside. The WRB recommended increasingly more ambitious supply projects so that an anticipated growth in demand could be met. Admittedly, the reports undertaken by the WRB were often commissioned by the government, to investigate, for example, the feasibility of barrage schemes. It was possibly outside its brief to question the assumptions underlying such investigations. By 1969/70 the WRB enthusiastically reported: 'We are fully engaged throughout England and Wales.' It outlined a significant number of large-scale regional studies which it had been involved in or was supporting (WRB

1969/70). By the following year it was giving more attention to interregional transfer schemes. The WRB also maintained that if its favoured strategy of meeting the North's future needs by a 'programme' of projects, including the Morecambe and Dee estuary barrages, was not adopted, an alternative programme based on 'seven major inland reservoirs' in northern uplands would have to be implemented (*1970/71*: 66).

Assessments of the WRB stress the occasionally considerable influence it was able to wield. It was, however, only an advisory body. It set up a national system for collecting water-resource data to better inform planning. It provided technical assistance to RAs in relation to hydrometric schemes and the investigation of underground strata. It carried out its own research activities and promoted and co-ordinated that undertaken by the RAs and other bodies. It did not, however, have any power to implement the conclusions of its reports. It could not construct or operate works itself, other than for research purposes. It could not require the RAs to co-operate.

Mitchell (1971: 24) noted, as a contemporary, that the WRB 'suffers from a bias towards engineering personnel, and the philosophy associated with such training'. Certainly it was preoccupied with the forecast doubling of water demand between 1970 and the end of the century. Regional plans were followed by a National Plan for the whole country. Kinnersley (1988: 90) called this plan 'not a future strategy but an engineering spree'. Porter (1978: 125) also criticised the WRB for its too narrow concern with source developments and bulk transfer. However, the case for undertaking a costly national strategic plan, such as was published in 1973, seemed strong at the time (DoE 1971: 47; Pitkethly 1990: 125).

Despite its narrow engineering bias, the WRB was not unaffected by the changing perception of the key water problem as being one of quality rather than quantity. It was thus drawn into considering issues like water quality, flood control, land drainage, fisheries and recreation which strictly lay outside its terms of reference (DoE 1971: 27). The WRB recognised the interdependency of the issues it was facing – the repeated recycling of river waters among successive users, the river's nature as a multi-functional resource, amenity issues and the interrelationships between functions such as water supply, pollution prevention and sewage treatment. This led the WRB to strongly advocate the case for a more fully integrated planning and development of the country's rivers (*1969/70*: 48–50).

There were problems, for example, in the sphere of effluent discharge and sewage treatment. RAs could withhold their consent for inadequate discharges, but their ability to enforce the maintenance of the right standards was limited, the only remedy being prosecution through vexatious proceedings. Also, sewage treatment being entirely a municipal responsibility, as long as it was financed through a charge on the rates rather than by a payment for a service, the interests of the river would inevitably be subordinated to those of local government. Further tensions arose between RAs and the statutory undertakings over the development of new sources of supply. The WRB catalogued the rich opportunities existing for administrative delay and paralysis in the prevailing abstraction licensing system, which put considerable strain on relationships between the water supply industry and the RAs. As the WRB (*1970/71*: 49) commented: 'Some river authorities have yet to win the full confidence of water undertakings dependent on them.'

In its very last reports the thematic diversity, almost contradictory nature, of its analysis of the water problem emerges strikingly (WRB 1973). On the one hand, the WRB still did not question the technique of extrapolating current trends to forecast a huge increase in water demand over the next generation, which underpinned its arguments over the need for, for example, an enlarging of the Haweswater dam and the building of two estuary barrages by the year 2000. On the other hand, the disadvantages of major, fixed-site schemes were recognised, river regulation and aquifer recharge projects were supported, and the need to develop a flexible approach to water resource planning was advocated.

River pollution

Introduction

By the beginning of the period the pollution of inland waters had become a dire problem. The filthy state of the rivers was partly the product of neglect over many decades in the past; but it was also the result of a continuation of neglect during the post-war years, in combination with the effects of new trends in water use.

Maintenance on sewage treatment virtually came to a standstill during the war years. Its end 'left a legacy of obsolete, worn out and necessarily inadequately maintained plant'. The impetus of prewar scientific research had been lost (Sidwick and Murray 1976 V: 515). Much plant was long overdue for replacement and a programme of investment was needed, if only because of the shortages of unsuitable labour, as well as the unpleasant nature of the labour-intensive methods of primary treatment at obsolescent plant, which produced objectionable detritus. The backlog of necessary maintenance or improvement work was ignored, however, and sewerage and sewage treatment were subject to severe restrictions on capital spending down to the mid-1950s. This forced the authorities to resort to many badly conceived improvisations: STWs were deliberately overloaded; storm overflows were operated to discharge crude sewage direct into rivers; and local authorities, in arrangement with River Boards, deliberately received substantially increased volumes of trade effluent into public sewers, although they did not have the capacity to deal with them (PRO 1957b: 8).

As intimated above, sewage management was complicated by economic and social progress, which led to the emergence of new waste-disposal problems. The improvement of water supplies in rural districts was a welcome development. Less so was the enormous expansion in the farm use of water when it led to the increased pollution of rural streams. New trends in domestic waste also bedevilled the task of sewage management. More disposable goods, including tissues, tampons and napkins, were being used and flushed into sewers, which had been designed to handle a load based on quite different standards of living (Jeger Report 1970: 3). After the war, also, synthetic detergents were introduced to the domestic market and their immediate popularity caused great difficulties. The accumulation of scum and foam presented unpleasant visual evidence of this new form of pollution. The situation improved with the marketing of 'soft' biodegradable detergents and the phasing-out of 'hard' detergents after 1964 (Sidwick and Murray 1976 V).

The pollution prevention system

The Royal Commission on Sewage Disposal set standards for effluent discharges in 1912. The parameters applied to the level of suspended solids in water and oxygen demand (BOD) and, because of the ratios attached to these two parameters, became known as the 30: 20 standard. They were widely accepted as reasonable targets for receiving waters, although many authorities set higher standards for slow-moving streams, in which oxygenation was less rapid, especially those used for public water supplies. In the 1960s, however, sixty per cent of the 5,000 STWs in England and Wales produced effluent which failed to meet the 30: 20 standard (Parker and Penning-Rowsell 1980: 118).

This poor performance may be partly accounted for by the intrinsic flaws in the pollution prevention system. Despite some modifications and improvements introduced in the inter-war period, the Rivers Pollution Act of 1876 remained the cornerstone of the system after the Second World War. Its principle of absolute prohibition of polluting discharges was fatally qualified, as has been noted, by clauses which protected polluters who used the 'best practicable means' of treatment or whose works were already in existence when the Act was passed.

These fundamental weaknesses were removed by post-war legislation. Under the Rivers (Prevention of Pollution) Act of 1951 each new discharge required the consent of the River Board, and individual consents defined qualitative and quantitative standards for the discharge. The Rivers (Pollution of Prevention) Act of 1961 extended the application of the 1951 Act to all discharges to inland waters, including those made before 1951. Meanwhile, the potential power to control new discharges to tidal water or estuaries (previously excluded by the legislation) through the application of ministerial Order was provided for by the Clean Rivers (Estuaries and Tidal Waters) Act of 1960, although a cumbersome procedure was involved and it was rarely used. The Water Resources Act of 1963 gave powers to prevent the pollution of underground waters from wells.

As mentioned above, the 1951 Act gave River Boards the power to specify effluent quality. In administering the Act the Board almost universally adopted the Royal Commission 30: 20 standard for STW effluent, 'so for the first time giving it general legal status' (Sidwick and Murray 1976 IV: 519). The RAs took over these responsibilities from the River Boards. Typically, most applications for consents were granted, subject to specific conditions. From 1963 it became illegal to discharge any sewage or trade effluent without appropriate RA consent. As Mitchell (1971: 20–1) says, the effect of post-war legislation was to provide the authorities with the power to manage pollution levels in rivers.

By the mid-1960s, therefore, the pollution prevention system had been comprehensively overhauled and discharges to all parts of the water environment were covered. Pollution was not eradicated, however, a major outstanding difficulty being that of enforcement. These problems were linked to the considerable expense of sufficiently improving STWs so that they could deal with mounting pollution loads now being imposed upon rivers. The major obstacle to pollution control in the past – the fact that the local authority enforcers were also major polluters – had been removed after 1948, with these duties being passed to River Boards and, later, RAs. There was, however, a legacy of municipal laxity in this field, which exercised an influence even after 1950. Nominees of local councils were included on River Boards to provide indirect, elected membership, and to reflect the financing role of local government. But as members of councils, which operated polluting STWs, they could press the Boards to turn a blind eye to breaches of consents by their own councils. Kinnersley provides an example of this tendency, which came to light when a RA determined to prosecute a polluting local authority. In the 1960s serious pollution occurred when Birmingham Corporation's Minworth sewage works suddenly discharged all its lagoons into the river and the Trent Authority moved to prosecute. As Kinnersley (1988: 78) observed: 'The city had four members on the Authority and they lobbied intensely against launching any prosecution in this case. In the event, the members from other downstream councils and other members of the Authority did not bow to this pressure, and the city was prosecuted, found guilty, fined and obliged to pay the costs of the court proceedings.'

It has also to be noted that invariably the penalties for breaking consent conditions, or otherwise being in breach of pollution prevention law, were derisory. For example, for 1965/6 only three sets of legal proceedings were taken by the Mersey and Weaver RA against polluters, including the Ford Motor Company for polluting a local brook near their Halewood factory, for which they were fined £25. By 1972/3 this RA prosecuted eight polluters, the fines in one case against a multiple 'offender' being quite severe. But for the rest, the financial penalty for breaking the country's pollution prevention code varied from £12 to £130, which hardly constituted a serious deterrent against malpractice in the future.

The most serious flaw in the consent discharge system, however, was that save for special purposes such as court proceedings, it was illegal for the authorities to publish compliance details, so that both good and bad performances were concealed from the public. Governments of both political parties retained this as a feature of the country's environmental protection system from 1951 to, effectively, 1985. A thin argument was used that it was necessary to preserve commercial confidentiality, but quite clearly it suited central government, unwilling to increase spending on STWs, local authorities with polluting STWs, and industry, failing to meet discharge consent standards (Kinnersley 1994: 44–5). The whole system operated under a cloud of secrecy. Pitkethly (1990: 129–31) cites the case of the Severn-Trent Water Authority which, on taking over from its predecessors in 1974, asked dischargers voluntarily to publish the current position on water quality in their area. Out of sixty-three agreeing to participate, only thirteen industrial premises were acknowledged to be complying with their consent conditions, a further eleven had not been given consent terms a dozen years after the relevant legislation, nineteen STWs were causing major problems – not one of which had ever been prosecuted – and forty companies would not allow effluent details to be disclosed.

The feeble pollution prevention system had its counterpart in public indifference towards infrastructural decay. The full extent of underground dereliction became brutally clear once the RWAs assumed their responsibilities after 1973 (see pp. 147–8).

Sewage treatment

By the time the Jeger Report (1970: 1) was published, it came to the conclusion that recent trends in the quality and quantity of sewage were threatening to destroy the natural assets of rivers and coastal waters. At this stage, about ninety-four per cent of the population of England and Wales were provided with main drainage, a higher proportion than anywhere else in the world. This was not as satisfactory as it appeared due to the problems caused by storm overflows, discussed below, and the outdated design and performance of many STWs.

By the 1940s the former dominance of land irrigation was finally giving way to more modern, scientific methods of sewage treatment. Primary treatment became increasingly mechanised, with the gradual displacement of unpleasant manual methods by mechanical screening and scraping. The development of secondary treatment in this period centred around two biological treatment techniques, biological filtration and activated sludge, which artificially intensified natural processes of purification. They were gradually refined through operational and technical improvements (Sidwick and Murray 1976 V). By 1970 the two processes each served a population of about twenty million. They both generated significant quantities of sludge, the disposal of which, therefore, remained a major problem for sanitary authorities. Although it continued, land disposal was more and more accepted as an unsatisfactory solution, and greater attention was given to refining digestion practices and de-watering equipment. Increasingly preferred, however, was tankering and disposal at sea.

Some attention was also given in this period to tertiary treatment, which involves an improvement of 30: 20 effluent to a standard of 10: 10 or even better. The problem of eutrophication became better understood, and changing expectations led to concern growing over the quality of rivers, used for domestic water supplies, but which were receiving steady discharges of nutrients from STWs.

However, the quality of the physical assets in the sewage treatment business did not keep pace with the improved understanding of the public health or environmental risks, such as the dangers arising from long-term ingestion of organic matter, associated with the new patterns of water use.

Pitkethly (1990: 131) states that in the 1960s and 1970s the system of granting consents to dischargers of effluent, for example from STWs, was not a major burden upon polluters. On the other hand, he discerns a permanent, if weak, pressure to produce improvements and indicates that a considerable amount of STW rebuilding was undertaken. RAs, certainly, pursued conscientiously their task of combating pollution. The Mersey and Weaver RA, for example, overviewed substantial repairs and reconstructions to STWs in its area and followed the policy of its predecessors, the Cheshire and Mersey River Boards, in encouraging the closure of smaller STWs, improving and concentrating treatment at larger works, and thereby enabling most trade effluent to be dealt with through the public sewers. Such improvements, however, should be kept in perspective. Just before the RA's responsibilities were assumed by the NWWA, the vast majority of the region's 179 STWs were still on sites which had been used for sewage treatment for over seventy years, and only three new significant works had been built on virgin sites (Mersey and Weaver RA, 1972/73).

In fact, Pitkethly's sanguine assessment of infrastructural improvement in the sewage treatment sector during the post-war period is not typical. Sewage treatment has been described as the most neglected of all parts of the water cycle before the 1973 reorganisation, and as a sector characterised by 'almost complete inertia' (Parker and Penning-Rowsell 1980: 121; Kinnersley 1994: 46). By the early 1970s the industry's underground assets were on the point of collapse, due to structural disorganisation and the failure to invest, these traits themselves being a reflection of public indifference and the low political priority attached to sewage.

Sewerage and sewage treatment were the water services probably least affected by attempts to modernise. They were solely a local government responsibility undertaken by some 1,400 authorities, including the Greater London Council serving a population of almost eight million, and the smallest sanitary authority with a population of 1,470 in 1970. In between were every sort of local council and some Joint Boards. The design of sewerage systems was constrained by the location of natural watersheds, which were usually unrelated to local council boundaries. Joint Sewerage Boards were formed in an attempt to overcome this problem. The largest, the Upper Tame Drainage Authority, managed the sewage for over two million people in the Birmingham area, but the smallest served less than 10,000. This solution, moreover, was resorted to infrequently. There were only twenty-four such Boards in 1971 and the majority had been created before 1914.

Compounding organisational fragmentation, sewerage and sewage treatment suffered from decades of under-investment. It is true that at 1970 prices expenditure on these activities climbed steadily from £14.6 million in 1948/49 to £112.8 million in 1968/69 (Smith 1972: 177). This increase, however, was from very low levels, investment having virtually ceased during the Second World War. Focusing on a regional experience, from 1875 to 1939 extension and maintenance of underground assets in the North-West took place in line with urban development. During the Second World War the ageing plant suffered from inadequate upkeep and repair. Although capital and equipment was relatively cheap, little renewal expenditure took place in the first post-war decade (Lloyd 1978: 7). Underground dereliction in the region subsequently manifested itself in various ways – frequent complaints of flooding by sewage in streets and houses; frequent sewer collapses, eventually reaching one major collapse per day; and a proliferation of storm overflows from the sewers into watercourses. A similar story was repeated elsewhere. Some 3,000 STWs, sixty per cent of the total, failed to meet basic standards (Jeger Report 1970: 9).

The government's role in this area should be noted. There was a clear contradiction between the government's aims, as expressed in the pollution prevention and other water legislation it passed in this period, and its public expenditure decisions. According to Gill (1953), the directives associated with the Rivers (Prevention of Pollution) Act of 1951 and the accompanying memorandum sent to River Boards were soon followed by a 'more influencing development, namely the need for economy'. Three MHLG circulars followed each other in quick succession in 1951 and 1952 which indicated that the resources available for new works would be very limited indeed. Broome (1971) observed that the efforts of the Mersey River Board, for example, were thwarted by the Ministry's delay of new sewerage schemes, unless there was an imminent danger to public health.

The organisational and financial defects bedevilling sewage treatment were investigated in the Jeger Report. It reiterated the by now familiar themes relating to the need to confer management of the entire water cycle upon integrated authorities based on river catchments, and the restrictive and inappropriate methods of financing local water services through the rate support grant. The report trusted that the forthcoming reorganisation of local government might produce a solution to these difficulties, although how this might deliver integrated river management was unclear.

Water quality trends and issues

Despite a general background of indifference, there was in certain official quarters a growing interest in the problem of water quality by the 1950s. This was undoubtedly due partly to reactions from specific sections of the public which, though uncoordinated and politically unsophisticated, expressed such strong feelings as to merit attention. Towards the end of this decade the MHLG was being inundated by complaints from groups positively enraged by the state of river and coastal waters. This growing dissatisfaction can be attributed to the increased recreational use of waters; the unpleasant visual and other evidence of pollution;

and growing awareness of a progressively deteriorating situation (PRO 1957b). Particularly vociferous were the angling associations. That representing Coventry and District, claiming 6,000 members, referred in a telegram sent to the Ministry to the 'vile and deplorable state' of rivers, 'this diabolical scourge' of pollution, which turned them into 'stinking sinks and cess pools', and demanded action, filthy rivers being a 'Sin against God in ruination of the lovely English countryside' (PRO 1957a). The Anglers' Cooperative Association spoke for 800 clubs, and by 1958, 850,000 anglers had fishing licences. Also beginning to provoke some intermittent public anger was the state of the beaches. There were fears that swimming in polluted sea-water might cause disease. The Coastal Anti-Pollution League was formed in 1957 by the parents of a child who had died of poliomyelitis after swimming off a polluted beach. Its establishment marked the start of a gradual increase in public interest in and awareness of the problem of coastal pollution.

By now it was beginning to be conceded by officials, at least privately, that a threshold of intolerability was being approached. An internal MHLG paper freely admitted past neglect and policy failures. The damaging effect of post-war spending restrictions upon infrastructural improvements was noted. It concluded (PRO 1957b: 11) that the 'serious pollution of the rivers may be likened to a cancerous growth which by the time it became evident could not be treated because of lack of resources and diversion of attention to other matters, and which has now become about as bad as it can be allowed to reach'.

While the subject requires further study, it appears reasonable to attribute the strengthening of the country's pollution prevention law, outlined in a previous section, at least partly to pressures exerted by an awakening public opinion. Official recognition of the need to act so as to improve water quality was demonstrated also by the steps taken to survey and classify British waters for the first time, on the basis of oxygen content, biological data and the presence of toxic substances. While it is possible to quibble about methodology and the comparability of the findings over time, nevertheless the figures duly adjusted do allow some assessment of water quality trends to be made. The first survey was carried out in 1958 and its results and those of later exercises are summarised in Table 5.8.

From the surveys Smith (1972: 177) concluded that a twenty-five per cent reduction in the length of rivers in the class four, 'grossly polluted category', occurred between 1958 and 1970. In general the improvement was made over short stretches of river, but noticeable gains were also achieved over longer lengths in East Anglia and in parts of the Severn basin. Parker and Penning-Rowsell (1980: 110–12) also referred to the 'continuing reduction in the amount of grossly polluted rivers'. They concluded that 'progress in river pollution control since the Second World War has been considerable'.

Trends varied greatly across the country. River bodies struggled to improve river quality and their endeavours had some impact. Even in one of the worst polluted areas, that for which the Mersey and Weaver RA had responsibility, there was some evidence of progress. Increased angling activity on certain stretches of water, an improvement in the quality of the Trent and Mersey Canal which allowed the establishment of a fishery below Middlewich, and record catches of fish taken from the Winsford Flashes were reported.

At first sight it may be difficult to square this evidence with that which has been cited concerning sewage treatment. In fact, writers caution against an over-enthusiastic interpretation of the survey results. Smith (1972: 177) noted that the 'overall situation' did not change greatly between 1958 and 1970, that slower improvement occurred in canals and tidal waters, and that many rivers in the industrial regions of the North and the West Midlands would remain 'highly polluted for some time to come'. Smith, furthermore, warned that the real extent of pollution was partly concealed by the method of compilation, since river length rather than volume of discharge was selected as the basic criterion. The long mileage of unpolluted headwaters was given as much weight as the more heavily polluted lower reaches, thus leading to an underestimation of the volume of pollution.

While the evidence on river quality suggested at worst a static situation and, possibly, a small net overall improvement in the post-war period up to 1970, contemporary assessment did not regard this as grounds for complacency. If anything, because of complex trends in the way rivers were being used, the need to improve, not simply maintain water quality, could legitimately be proposed as a prudent objective. Inland waters were under increased pressure from both recreational and urban supply purposes. As the WRB (*1973/74*: 49) stated: 'The problem of water quality and the disposal of water after use cannot be separated from the problem of providing clean water for abstraction.' To reiterate, rivers were also receiving a heavy pollution load. The effluent discharged from STWs into the River Lee, which incorporated significant quantities of treated industrial effluent, was equivalent to ninety per cent of its dry weather flow. But good treatment techniques meant that this river was a suitable source of drinking water for 600,000 people living in the north of London. In fact, two-thirds of London's water supply was drawn from the non-tidal Thames, which also received great volumes of municipal and trade sewage. 'This situation involves a high degree of reuse of water', it was stated (DoE 1971: 32) without exaggeration.

The contribution of industrial effluent to river pollution varied greatly across the country, and locally could be severe. One of the most heavy polluting loads received by the Irwell in Lancashire was from the Straw Pulp Manufacturing Co. of Radcliffe, the effluent of which was equivalent to the untreated sewage of a population of 250,000 (Mersey and Weaver *1965/66*: 28). The RAs pressed for pre-treatment at factories, in addition to the collective, municipal treatment of domestic and industrial waste, which was cost-effective and reduced the number of pollution points on rivers. In highly industrialised parts of the country more than half the discharges from STWs would have originated as trade effluent (Smith

1972: 173–6). The impact of agricultural pollution from the use of nitrogenous fertilisers, and thermal pollution caused by the release of cooling water from generating stations, were also explained by Smith.

To repeat, however, poor performance by municipal STWs was a principal cause of river pollution. According to Smith (1972: 178), river pollution could be attributed primarily to the overloading of the sewage system, 'which has not been expanded and modernised at a sufficient rate to keep pace with the increased consumption of water during recent decades'. Many older districts were still sewered on the combined system, where washings from roofs and paved areas ran to the drains, which were connected with foul domestic and trade sewage. During heavy rainfall, storm discharges, overflowing directly into natural watercourses, were characterised by high concentrations of 'particulates' and 'highly polluting slugs of solids materials' [sic], thereby causing serious pollution during storms (Jeger Report 1970; Ellis 1979). A major objective of the RAs was to encourage local authorities to adopt the separate system and to completely eliminate storm overflows. In the district for which the Mersey and Weaver RA was responsible, STW modernisation and other work were sufficiently advanced to permit some twenty sewage overflows to be abandoned by the early 1970s (Mersey and Weaver *1972/73*: 50).

Towards the end of the period under discussion official and semi-official assessments by, for example, the WRB, the CACW and the Jeger inquiry, placed particular emphasis upon the need to persist with efforts to curb river pollution. Summarising the findings of the last two sections, there is some evidence that – thanks to the endeavours of the river bodies and some modernisation of STWs – the problem of river pollution was being contained, with even some welcome instances of tangible improvement being achieved. Given contemporary pressures upon the water environment and the demands placed upon rivers, informed opinion still had reason to doubt, nevertheless, whether sufficient progress had been made in improving water quality.

Estuarine and coastal pollution

Unwillingness by the authorities since the industrial revolution to prioritise environmental protection in the aquatic sphere has been explained in this study by an analysis which stresses the multiple- and conflicting-use characteristics of water. The costs of any clean-up appeared enormous and the disadvantages of a tougher regime to economic interests, especially industry, seemed substantial. Consequently intervention, when it did occur, was often incomplete and reluctant in nature. The inconsistency between the evident aims of the reform of environmental legislation during the period under study and government spending plans has already been noted. More specifically, preferred waste-management policies were influenced by economism and a desire to push offending dirt away from sensitive areas like residential districts, rather than a wish to overcome the origin of the problem. Consequently, rather than its reduction at source, the spatial, and even the inter-generational displacement of pollution, emerges as a marked feature of environmental history. As Rose (1991) says, using the environment as a treatment works on the 'dilute and disperse' principle has been the salient feature of British environmental policy since the nineteenth century.

The unwillingness to commit significant financial resources to the conservation of rivers and coasts also often derived from a less than complete understanding of the nature and consequences of interactions between human activities and the natural world – for example, concerning the capacity of the coastal environment to dilute, or to absorb, retain and subsequently release, effluent which might contain toxic elements. At a time when Manchester's sludge ships were discharging small amounts of toxic substances, such as PCBs, phosphorus, mercury and lead into the Irish Sea, a DoE, Welsh Office (1973) study went out of its way to reassure readers that sludge dumped in coastal waters was rapidly dispersed, diluted and rendered harmless. Later scientific work enumerated the consequences of such waste-disposal practices in the very area in question – high loadings of toxic chemicals, the threatened extinction of marine mammals and the need to initiate an extremely costly, long-term rescue programme (Johnston *et al.* 1991).

To develop the argument further attention may now be directed at the English estuaries. These are a valuable resource – not only providing a channel of communication, vast quantities of cooling water and the means to disperse and dilute effluent, but also representing a significant natural and recreational amenity. They are the home of commercial fisheries and are internationally important nursery or over-wintering areas for numerous marine species. Too intensive use of the estuaries by industry may threaten their ability to perform these functions.

However, their exploitation as convenient dumping sites for industrial refuse virtually became government policy in the post-1945 period. This was reflected both by government favouring the development of industrial complexes at estuarial sites, as around Teesside, where ninety per cent of the pollution load received in the estuary came from industry, and also in the ways government sponsored and interpreted changes in pollution prevention law. Generalising, estuaries were largely exempt from the application of pollution prevention measures. Or, as the atomic scientist John Dunster commented in 1958, not the least attraction of coastal sites as a dumping ground in the post-war era was the 'lack of administrative controls' (quoted in Rose 1991: 10). Significantly, the displacement effects of this policy showed up in the official surveys of water quality. Smith (1972: 177) noted that the results of the surveys indicated that a slower improvement occurred in tidal waters between 1958 and 1970 than was registered overall, while Parker and Penning-Rowsell (1980: 112) commented of the survey findings that 'the state of our estuaries is cause of considerable concern ... Here pollution levels reflect a shift of effluent discharge from inland to tidal waters rather than a solution to the problem as a whole.'

Concern over the state of tidal waters was signified by the standing Royal

Table 4.3   *Industrial activity on British estuaries, 1950–70*

	1950	1970
Crude oil refining capacity in nine major estuaries ('000 tons)	9,500	109,000
Electrical generating capacity in estuarine and coastal sites (megawatts)	3,700	17,900
Steel production at British Steel Corporation (BSC) works discharging effluent into tidal waters ('000 tons)	5,064	10,722
Chemical industry fixed capital investment on eight estuaries (£m., 1970 values)	204	994

Source: RCEP 1972: 19–24.

Commission on Environmental Pollution (RCEP) devoting its third report, published in 1972, to an examination of the pollution of estuaries and coastal waters. The Commission remarked that, while the sea is a powerful scavenger, biologists, conscious of the degradation which had already affected inland seas like the Baltic and Mediterranean, were becoming apprehensive about its capacity to deal indefinitely with waste materials put into it. Gross pollution of estuaries, the Commission explained, does obvious harm to bird and sea mammals; the passage of migratory fish is prevented and commercial fisheries are destroyed. Pollution can cause the sea to look unpleasant and stink. More seriously, tides might not always immediately disperse wastes. Some potentially dangerous substances, such as mercury, could accumulate in bottoms or mud to lie inert, or eventually to be absorbed by living organisms.

The Commission, in fact, did not make any recommendations for sweeping legislative action or institutional reform. It did support the government's adoption of the PPP (polluter pays principle) and strongly recommended – well ahead of its time – the imposition of pollution charges; government supports such principles rhetorically but has proved singularly unwilling to put them into practice. The government obviously did not have access to the RCEP analysis until the end of the period under study. Its publication, however, did not trigger a significant policy change on coastal pollution.

From the late 1940s British industry, in its post-war expansion, became increasingly water-intensive, as has been seen. There was a significant movement of the large water-consuming industries to estuarine sites close to sources of cheap and abundant water, which is clearly reflected in the data summarised in Table 4.3.

To reiterate, this industrial relocation was encouraged by the government's environmental policies. The Minister could extend the application of the 1876 Rivers Pollution Act to tidal waters, if public health concerns were deemed to require it. Effectively, this almost excluded such extensions of the Act, only six tidal Orders being made under it before 1902. The limitation that the extension of the Act to tidal waters was contingent upon ministerial perception of a public health need was removed by the Rivers Pollution Act of 1951 which, *prima facie*, made it easier for pollution controls to be extended to coastal stretches. As an official at the MHLG put it, however, 'practical difficulties are not removed by a mere change of wording'. Furthermore (PRO 1951a), he emphasised to a Lancashire River Board representative: 'The Act specifically recognises the impossibility of looking at the elimination of pollution as anything save a long term problem, particularly in these times when industrial output is not lightly to be disturbed and until a portion of the National Investment Programme can be devoted to the reduction of pollution.' Application of Section Six of the 1951 Act might be conceivable the official went on, but 'if the extension of the Act to tidal waters was likely to involve industrialists or local authorities in substantial expenditure on treatment works the case for such an extension at the present time would have to be very strong indeed' (PRO 1951a).

Nevertheless, the River Boards were still actively exploring the possibility of extending their pollution prevention powers to tidal waters. The Wear and Tees Board discovered in 1951 that it lacked the legal powers to initiate, on its own, court proceedings against a chemical company polluting the Tees estuary; officials were anxious that the firm, which produced chromium compounds for the 'jet aircraft programme', would be forced out of business should such an action succeed (PRO 1951a, *passim*). Thus the River Boards had limited success up to 1955 and in only two cases did the Minister allow their jurisdiction to be extended to tidal waters – in both cases the channels involved being minor ones, behind tidal gates, almost indistinguishable from non-tidal streams. In that year, however, the Isle of Wight River Board applied for an ambitious extension of its responsibilities into open estuaries, which merged with coastal waters. The outcome would have important implications for the application of the 1951 Act. The departmental view was that while in theory its operation could be so extended, estuaries were receiving 'such immense quantities of sewage and trade wastes' that the costs to industry and local government would be 'crippling' and out of proportion to any benefits. Natural dilution in estuaries, it was believed, would make such an extension of River Board powers unwarranted and the application failed (PRO 1955a).

Thus arrangements for combating coastal pollution were both complex and ineffectual in this period. Under the Rivers Pollution Acts of 1951 and 1961 the Secretary of the Environment could make 'tidal waters orders', giving RAs control over new and existing discharges. However, pre-1960 discharges, which were 'substantially' a continuation of a previous discharge, were exempt from control. As a consequence, an acceptable annual increase in a discharge, continued over eight years, would result in a doubling of the volume of effluent being discharged (RCEP 1972: 11). Moreover, even for those qualifying as new discharges tidal orders could only be made on application by a RA, or other interested party, and after holding a public inquiry. Between 1960 and 1972 only fourteen such Orders were made and these did not include any for the major estuaries, except Milford Haven. The Royal Commission commented (RCEP 1972: 38): 'The less stringent control so far applied to tidal waters and estuaries has reflected the policy objective of progressively restoring and maintaining the wholesomeness of non-tidal rivers as a source of public water supply, while interfering to the minimum with the industrial development which has been attracted to the estuaries.' Thus most industrial discharges to estuaries, which had grown considerably since 1945, were outside regulatory control.

The prevailing government view was that the pollution of the great industrial estuaries was the inevitable outcome of economic development and, in any case, was a matter for local, not central, authorities to address. Responses to the problem were, indeed, local in nature, but they did involve co-ordinated action among a number of local authorities and other interests. Each estuary tended to have its own particular history of decline and renewal. There were some outstanding successes, above all for the Thames. The 'second restoration' of the river between 1950 and 1980 has been described by Wood (1982). It was the product of local initiatives, including the acquiring of special legislation in 1968 to strengthen the Port of London Authority's pollution control powers, although the river's improvement pre-dated this measure.

As the story of the Thames's recovery is relatively well known, it would be useful to make further observations about two estuaries, the experience of which illustrates themes which have been developed in this study – the Tyne and the Mersey.

The local authorities on the Tyne for long discharged raw sewage into the tidal waters of the river and its condition was the subject of representations from fishery and other interests over many years. The decline of the Tyne as a major salmon river has already been referred to. By the 1920s the visual evidence of the effects of effluent discharged from the numerous outfalls, including gases bubbling in the estuary from rotting wastes, prompted some concern but little action. Although the smell at some of the 180 major outfalls along the tidal stretch was so bad as to cause vomiting, medical opinion in the inter-war years did not believe that sewage treatment was necessary on health grounds (Tyneside 1974: 5–6). A committee appointed by the Special Areas Commission in 1935 came to a similar conclusion about the health implications of the river's pollution, ministerial intervention not, therefore, being warranted. Nevertheless, investigations now confirmed that the 'estuary had passed an unacceptable level of untreated sewage' (Tyneside 1974: 5–6). A 1936 report rather bizarrely suggested that 'though the sewage may increase in amount, the better type of house will result in a diluted effluent draining to the river'. Various collective sewage schemes were proposed during the 1930s, but as the Special Area Commission was not prepared to recommend a grant to assist them, and as the local authorities would not 'swallow' the scale of the expenditure involved – up to £2.5 million – they were stillborn (PRO 1955c).

In the context of post-war development plans it became necessary in 1949 to earmark land for the construction of STWs. Ten local authorities did agree to commission a feasibility study for a combined Tyneside sewage scheme, but nothing further was done until 1954, when the MHLG called two conferences to examine the problem. Insights into the rationale for municipal indifference towards the appalling deterioration of the local water environment were revealed in a council report. Essentially, compared to the improvement of other services, environmental protection was perceived as a postponable luxury (Newcastle upon Tyne 1958: 11):

> There is no doubt that with the general improvement in the standard of living, people
> are now becoming more sensitive to the condition of the river .... It is felt that the
> correct attitude ... is that the removal of sewage from the River Tyne is a problem
> which should be tackled, and that this should be done as soon as funds reasonably
> become available, in other words it is something of a luxury to be afforded when other
> necessary improvements in the standard of living of the people of Tyneside have
> been completed.

Nevertheless, the MHLG-sponsored conferences had prompted some response by the local authorities, who commissioned a further study of possible solutions to the sewage problem. The need for a co-ordinated plan for the renewal of the estuary was recognised. In 1958 proposals were made for a four- to five-mile sea outfall, no further discharge of untreated sewage beyond the capacity of existing sewers and the introduction of partial treatment along certain stretches of the estuary (Newcastle upon Tyne 1958: 12–17). Local authority representatives set up a working party to develop a joint strategy, and from this originated the Tyneside Sewerage Board which was set up in 1966.

With an appropriate administrative framework being put in place so slowly, the river's condition continued to deteriorate. The problem had, in fact, grown incrementally over the years not just because of increased discharges, but also because sludge solids, far from being scoured away by tidal action, were pushed back up the estuary by incoming tides to accumulate on the river bottoms (Tyneside 1974). By 1969 the condition of the estuary, by now receiving crude sewage from over a million people and large volumes of trade effluent, had become so bad that a public inquiry taking place in Newcastle's Moot Hall had to be adjourned because of the stench from the river, reminiscent of an incident during London's 'Great Stink' over a century earlier. There was, however, a promise of change. The sewage collection and disposal scheme now planned by the Tyneside Sewerage Board was the largest of its kind ever attempted in Britain. Interceptor sewers running parallel with each bank were constructed to divert most of the wastewater from the old outfalls to new major treatment works at Howdon and

Dunston. The Northumbrian Water Authority inherited the project in 1974, construction of which had begun the previous year. By 1983 more than half of the new treatment scheme was in service and the flow of raw sewage to the river had been reduced by sixty per cent. By 1990 twenty miles of the Tyne estuary and over eight miles of beaches had been cleaned up (Barty-King 1992). The improvement of the river was impressive. By 1988 the Tyne had once again become one of the country's top salmon rivers, with 1,500 salmon and around 1,000 sea trout being caught (though 120,000 salmon and 20,000 sea trout were caught in the estuary's coastal stretch in 1850). Formal completion of the sewage scheme took place in 1993.

The Mersey has long suffered from serious problems. The Mersey basin was one of the most intensively exploited catchments containing, perhaps, the most polluted inland waters in the country. These flowed into the estuary to join the raw sewage produced by a population which approached one million, together with industrial effluent from a wide range of chemical, petroleum and processing industries.

The seriousness of the estuary's pollution was recognised as long ago as 1899, when the Conservator of the Harbour Board, Admiral Sir George Ware stated: (cited in PRO 1927b):

> During the last fifty years the growth of Birkenhead and Liverpool has been great and the pouring of their crude sewage into this important estuary on the flood tide is certainly damaging for its conservancy interests .... Certainly the time will come when Liverpool and Birkenhead and the whole of these people who are contaminating the River will be obliged to do something for it and the question is whether a commencement cannot be made now.

This, however, would not occur for another eighty years. By 1922 not less than 400,000 tons were being discharged annually from the sewers. By this stage the Mersey Docks and Harbour Board had been demanding that sewage discharged into the estuary should receive some treatment, and at least that new discharges should be rendered free from solid matter. The enormous volume of effluent discharged into the river had adverse consequences for the state of the docks, affecting river and sea channels and altering river flows, causing silting, altering the nature of the mud in the estuary and obstructing dredging.

The City of Liverpool, however, opposed the Harbour Board's demands. It expressed a prevailing view that (PRO 1930): 'Apart from the statutory right of the Corporation to discharge sewage into the Mersey estuary, sewage disposal by dilution, especially as applied to tidal waters, is universally recognised as a right and proper method of sewage disposal.' By the early 1930s some thirty million gallons of sewage were daily discharged into the estuary. The extensive dredging required to preserve a navigable waterway prompted the Water Pollution Research Board to investigate the problem, but no change in practice was introduced. By the end of the decade a once flourishing fishing industry in the estuary had been destroyed.

Modern sediment core analysis enables the historic deposition of trace metals in the estuary to be analysed and a metallic emission record to be developed for as far back as 1860. A steep increase in the discharge of all six metals studied is shown from the third quarter of the nineteenth century, followed in most cases by emission reductions associated with industrial changes (NRA 1995: 23). Equally striking is the way this analysis underlines how estuary sediment can so effectively retain over extended period of time depositions of toxic metals, like arsenic, mercury and zinc. In the post-1945 period lack of authority by conservancy and river bodies to control discharges into tidal waters, and the complacency of the local authorities, ensured that the pollution of the Mersey estuary would not abate. It was still receiving massive amounts of contamination from grossly polluted feeder rivers and local sources. These conditions produced 'hydrogen sulphide in the upper estuary and nearer the sea ... lumps of crude sewage and balls of fat deposited on the foreshore' (Porter 1978: 120). After 1961 the Mersey and Weaver RA proved more effective in controlling new discharges and the very first signs of an arrestation in the decline of water quality were recorded. The immense scale of the problem was gradually recognised and the case for exceptional intervention was slowly being entertained.

In 1971, local authorities, industrialists and water interests set up a Steering Group on the Pollution of the Mersey Estuary to investigate and to make recommendations for the elimination of the more obvious manifestations of environmental pollution, namely odour nuisance and fouling of banks by crude sewage and industrial effluent. In 1974 consulting engineers recommended to this body the construction of interceptor sewers and STWs. In 1978 the cost of cleaning up the estuary was put at some £200 million, at a time when administrative and financial constraints restricted the North West Water Authority (NWWA)'s total expenditure on new capital projects to £7 million annually.

Eventually in 1984 the Mersey Basin Campaign was initiated with the aim of rescuing the entire catchment. As will be seen in the next chapter the government at last recognised the national importance and scale of this acute problem, resources were made available to assist the regeneration of the catchment area, and European Community (EC) funds were obtained. It was not until the 1990s, however, that the first significant signs of an improvement in the estuary were reported.

These two case-studies illustrate many of the themes which have been developed in this study – official reluctance to commit significant financial resources to environmental protection; the preference for waste-disposal methods which did not address or penalise pollution at source, but which had the effect of creating a spatial and generational displacement of the problem; and finally, when the negative externalities associated with previous policies proved unacceptable, the more determined putting in place of programmes to achieve environmental renewal.

These, however, because of almost a century of neglect, proved very expensive indeed.

The imperative of reform: the build-up to the 1973 Water Act

Originally it was anticipated that the 1963 Water Resources Act would achieve a relatively lasting settlement of the water question. It was never envisaged as a stopgap measure, certainly not one that would have a currency of only ten years. In 1966 the MHLG firmly dismissed ideas of a further integration of the bodies currently charged with water management responsibilities. The WRB (*1966/67*: 5), too, believed at this stage that no adjustment of functions between government, itself and the RAs was 'necessary or desirable'. Later (*1969/70*: 1–2), in response to MHLG requests to consider necessary modifications to the 1963 Act, the WRB admitted only to 'minor defects' in the measure, and sought amendments only of 'detail' to strengthen the RAs. Meanwhile a Royal Commission (the Redcliffe-Maud Commission) had been appointed in 1966 to review local government. This created an opportunity to reconsider whether it was desirable to maintain local authority provision of water services. However, the Commission had also formed the view by 1969 that water and sewage should be firmly retained within the sphere of local government (Richardson *et al.* 1978).

Very soon such gradualism would be swept aside and a much more radical reform of water management would be under active consideration. The driving force behind the change of outlook was the MHLG. It was searching for an administrative pattern to achieve a more effective reconciliation of interests, and had become convinced that the management of water services by 1,400 separate bodies was untenable. The view emerged that local government involvement in water institution should be replaced by new, all-purpose regional bodies, covering very large territories based on watershed boundaries.

A number of underlying factors, which have been noted above, account for the dramatic development of MHLG thinking. They include the rapid growth in water demand since 1945 which put considerable strain on existing structures; the growing dependence on relatively 'dirty' sources of lowland sources of water due to the full development of upland sites; and the evident incompleteness of the 1963 reform. Such factors contributed to the swift change in official attitudes, in particular the eclipsing of the WRB's technocratic stress on resource capacity by a growing concern about water quality.

Shifts in official policy were reflected in personnel changes in the MHLG, with the emergence of individuals with the ability to influence events. This has led some of the most authoritative accounts of the background to the 1973 Water Act to emphasise the impact of personalities (Jordan *et al.* 1977; Kinnersley 1988). Especially significant was the appointment of Jack Beddoe to the Head of the Water Division of the MHLG (later the Department of the Environment (DoE)) in 1969. He had become convinced that water re-use, quantity and quality were inextricably linked, and he became committed to the case for all-purpose authorities. The style of the individual and the vigour with which he pursued the policy led him to be particularly associated with the 1973 Act. Jordan *et al.* link these personnel changes with an 'organisational interpretation' of the 1973 reform. They describe the swift ascendancy of the 'management approach' in the MHLG, together with a belief in planning and efficiency, going so far as to claim (1977: 324–5) that 'the water industry would not have taken its new shape if the MHLG had not adopted "managerialism"'.

The reform of 1973 also, however, represented an attempt to resolve long-standing and widely recognised deficiencies in water management. Also, as is so often the case in the history of British administrative reform, the 1973 enactment was less of a discontinuity that it appeared to be at first sight.

The very processes established by the 1963 Water Act, themselves a response to the growth in water demand since 1945, contributed to the changing policy perceptions. The WRB and RAs, in pursuing their task of evaluating the supply situation, recognised the limits to which traditional solutions could meet growing requirements. The important Trent Model Research Programme demonstrated how functional co-ordination could permit the intensified use of water resources. Thus improved intelligence informed official judgements, including the perception that local government suffered a 'performance gap', was not competent to handle the water problem, and should be replaced by new all-purpose authorities.

Meanwhile the Redcliffe-Maud Commission published its report in 1969. The CACW, which had been in abeyance since 1963, was reconvened. It was asked to report on the existing system of water management, and as urgently as possible, given the possible need to co-ordinate any changes with local government reform.

By now the new thinking on water reform was fast becoming a consensus. In 1970 the WRB itself (*1970/71*: 47) emphasised that the principle of integrated, river-basin management was 'widely accepted all over the world'. It advocated reforms, which happened to be very close, in fact, to those achieved by the measure of 1973. Yet traditional influences continued to impose themselves upon the process of water reform, which had the effect of diluting the integration principle in the forthcoming enactment. The CACW, as before, reflected a myriad of separate water interests. Once reactivated it is noteworthy how horse-trading and departmental representation of client interests once again influenced the final outcome. As Jordan *et al.* indicate, the MHLG might aspire, heroically, to a more managerial system of water administration, but in reality it was soon forced to retreat to a more traditional style of policy-making.

Peter Walker's preference for a radical reform was balanced by a process of concession to the established lobbies. Rather than the creation of totally comprehensive regional authorities, assuming competencies throughout the field of water management, the final measure left private water companies largely untouched.

The municipal interest preserved an important place in the RWAs, retaining responsibility for sewerage as their agents and well represented on the new Authorities. The British Waterways Board retained responsibility for canals and river navigation. A particularly difficult area was land drainage. The MAF and the landowning lobby pressed very hard for farming interests to preserve their traditional influence in the field. Eventually the concession was secured whereby land drainage was to be placed in the hands of specially created regional and local land drainage committees, financed through the MAF. Kinnersley (1988: 100) interprets such concessions as only 'a limited qualification to the full integration of functions', while Richardson *et al.* (1978: 59) more dramatically speak of 'an almost unconditional surrender by the D.O.E.' It does seem that, with parliamentary time running out in 1973, without the concession the Bill would have been lost, a victim as often before of government having difficulty in finding time for water reform in its legislative plans. However, on this occasion the necessary political manoeuvres were undertaken and the Bill became law.

5

The Regional Water Authorities, 1973–89: the irresponsibility of government

The economic and institutional framework

The Water Act 1973

The Water Act of 1973 was the culmination of attempts to establish the integrated management of water resources in England and Wales. Responsibility for the entire water cycle was now allocated to ten RWAs, who took over the work previously carried out by 157 water undertakings, twenty-nine River Authorities and 1,393 Sanitary Authorities. Their jurisdiction was based not on arbitrary local authority boundaries, but on river catchments. Not only did the RWAs have the operational duties relating to water supply, river management, waste disposal and nature conservation and amenity conferred upon them. To achieve the perceived benefits of integrated management the RWAs were in addition to assume environmental protection duties.

The government set out a number of objectives for the reorganised water industry which reflected not only the broad remit conferred upon the RWAs, but also a recognition of the interrelatedness of water supply, sewage treatment, river quality and environmental protection issues. The first aim was to secure an ample supply of water to meet the population's needs. But this aim was linked to others that set out environmental improvement and other objectives for the industry (DoE, Welsh Office 1973: 8). These included:

1   providing adequate sewerage and sewage disposal facilities;
2   ensuring the maintenance of the contribution of land drainage to urban and agricultural areas;
3   achieving 'a massive clean-up of the country's rivers and estuaries by the early 1980s';
4   making 'the widest use of water space for other purposes including recreation and amenity';
5   protecting the interests of other water users, including fisheries and navigation.

A similar combination of supply, amenity and environmental aims informed

Table 5.1 *Public water supplied in England and Wales, 1961–94 (m. litres per day)*

1961	10,730	1973	14,840	1982/83	16,215
1962	11,030	1974	14,940	1983/84	16,453
1963	11,570	1975	15,140	1984/85	16,504
1964	11,810	1973/74	14,806	1985/86	16,576
1965	11,950	1974/75	14,904	1986/87	16,854
1966	12,280	1975/76	15,109	1987/88	17,879
1967	12,590	1976/77	14,417	1988/89	16,896
1968	13,000	1977/78	14,724	1989/90	17,273
1969	13,670	1978/79	15,343	1990/91	17,381
1970	14,050	1979/80	16,094	1991/92	17,209
1971	14,190	1980/81	15,876	1992/93	16,629
1972	14,440	1981/82	15,814	1993/94	16,559

Sources: CWPU 1978b: 2; WSA 1994: 2.

the ministerial guidance on planning priorities given to RWA chairmen in 1973. It was hoped that the long-awaited reconciliation of interests would be achieved through this sweeping reform.

Demand and supply trends

The economic background to the development of the water industry changed decisively in the 1970s. The UK Gross Domestic Product grew by some 3 per cent per annum between 1950 and 1973, while between 1973 and 1979 growth was only 1.3 per cent (Surrey 1982: 530). The changed economic environment rendered recent forecasts of water demand redundant. It also created new opportunities in that the expected supply pressures disappeared almost overnight. On the other hand, however, the effect of government's approach to economic difficulties was to starve the water industry of financial resources.

Although the expansion in water demand decelerated from the early 1970s, growth still did occur, if much more slowly and erratically, as reflected in the figures on public water supplies shown in Table 5.1. According to statistical analysis of data covering the years 1961 to 1974, the variables which appeared to have the most impact upon water consumption were changes in the number of private dwellings and industrial activity. Industrial recession would evidently have an important impact upon the level of water demand. In fact, the most vigorous component of demand during the 1970s was domestic consumption. The installation of washing-machines, showers and dishwashers contributed to increased water usage. Car-washing firms and swimming-pools also had growing requirements. However, among all these categories the biggest single user was the water-closet, consuming 650 million gpd out of a total supply of 3,300 million gpd in 1983

Table 5.2 *Effluent as a proportion of river flow, 1973 (%)*

River	Abstraction point	Average river flow	Dry river
Lee	New Gauge	16.5	81.4
Thames	Swinford	4.6	33.8
Thames	Surbiton	14.4	141.4

Source: RCEP 1992: 4

(Kirby 1984: 103). While in the past, domestic consumption typically accounted for some two-thirds of piped supplies, it was now clearly increasing its share of the total (NWC 1978: 5).

Effluent discharges were, effectively, another demand upon water resources. The natural capacity of the river, through the action of micro-organisms, sunlight and physical aeration, to purify polluting discharges, was a fundamentally important use of rivers. The heavier the pollutant load, the less the river could yield by way of abstractions. In some cases the double pressure upon rivers was particularly severe, especially in the London region where, on occasion, the effluent received exceeded the dry weather flow of the rivers themselves.

Although river pollution showed little signs of improving significantly, if at all, over this period as a whole there was, nevertheless, some evidence that pressure upon river systems from industrial effluent was diminishing. Part of the reason for the reduced pollution load placed upon STWs and rivers like the Calder in the Yorkshire region was the closure of textile plant (YWA *1980*: 14 and *1981*: 13). Industrial decline even led to trade demand contracting absolutely in some years, both private industrial abstractions from rivers and industrial demand for piped supplies showing signs of falling between the 1960s and 1980s (Lawson 1986; NWC 1978: 5). Demographic changes also contributed to water demand growing less vigorously than anticipated. By the late 1970s the population was growing at barely a quarter of the rate originally forecast (NWC *1976/77*: 16).

Due to such factors the balance between supply and demand swiftly altered in the 1970s. An almost linear growth of 2.5 per cent per annum in water consumption since the early 1960s was broken (CWPU 1975, 1978a, 1978b). Revised forecasts for water demand up to the end of the century were halved (NWC 1978: 5). The NWC (*1976/77*: 16) now believed that 'The lower demand means that much present service capacity will not be fully utilised for some considerable time.' The NWWA (*1978/79*: 13), also, on the basis of forecasts of future trends, envisaged a 'generally healthy situation ... with a surplus of available supplies over forecast demands into the future'.

Also contributing to what the NWC (*1977/78*: 19) described as a 'robust' supply/demand equation was the probability of resources being more effectively

Table 5.3   *Abstraction for public water supplies by source, 1980 (%)*

Region	Groundwater	Rivers and streams	Upland reservoirs
North-West	16	4	80
Northumbria	7	29	64
Severn-Trent	38	30	32
Yorkshire	25	23	52
Anglia	47	48	5
Thames	41	58	1
Southern	75	20	5
Wessex	56	10	34
South-West	13	33	56
Welsh	6	38	56
England and Wales	32	34	34

Source: NWC 1982: 6.

utilised following the creation of the RWAs (see pp. 133–6). Nor did work on water supply and treatment works suddenly cease. The RWAs developed major new programmes in these areas, about one-third of all their capital expenditure in the 1970s being devoted to water resource and supply schemes (see Table 5.4).

The completion of works in hand and the increasing use of groundwater resources contributed to an expansion in the water supply industry's capacity. In the aftermath of the handling of the drought of 1976, in the NWC's view (1978: 6), 'it would not appear to be economic sense to invest heavily for margins of security beyond those then demonstrated generally'. Moderate savings by consumers in cases of severe drought like that of 1976 seemed to constitute a reasonable basis for planning. The NWC (1978: 26) therefore concluded that there appeared 'to be only a very limited need for major new reservoir storage in the period up to the end of the century'. By 1986 it was optimistically claimed by Speight (1986: 195): 'The water industry, currently with no apparent need to construct major new water resources ... for the rest of the century may well be spared further public debate about general issues.'

Table 5.3 reveals that the utilisation of the three main sources of supply varied considerably across the country. Northern regions depended heavily upon impounded rivers and the south on underground sources. There was a trend, however, to depend increasingly upon river abstractions supported by storage reservoirs. In this way both reservoir yield and broader environmental values were enhanced. Such abstractions did, of course, usually involve an element of effluent re-use which, as indicated in the previous chapter, demanded the application of the most stringent standards of treatment to sewage and water supplies.

Some, however, were concerned as to whether the increased recycling of river water could be continued indefinitely to meet consumption requirements. On the one hand, sophisticated new methods of water treatment could, in theory, permit the production of pure water from any source, however poor (Gray 1994: 72). On the other hand, advances in analytical techniques in the 1970s and 1980s, the increased use of chemical compounds, and the increase in nitrate levels all drew attention to the potential public health risks inherent in the use of comparatively contaminated lowland sources. It was beginning to be realised that some micro-pollutants, even at extremely low concentrations, might be hazardous (NWC 1978, 1982). Before long the RCEP (1992: 4) favoured policies which promoted clean technologies at the place of work, rather than relying heavily on the water environment to purify pollution loads. Towards the end of this period, therefore, perceptions of how healthy the supply/balance was began to be modified. Reappraisal was also prompted by a succession of dry years and the re-emergence of supply difficulties. As will be seen in the next chapter the response was less to revert to traditional solutions, demanding costly new capital projects, and more to explore the potential of more subtle approaches to resource management.

The institutional framework

An institutional issue which was never adequately resolved during the period in question was the nature of the relationship between the regions and the centre. The solution favoured at the time of the Water Act of 1973 was to empower the regions so as to avoid excessive centralisation. A local perspective and a link with the municipal past were, moreover, preserved, in so far as local authority members initially were numerically dominant in the new RWAs. This concession met local government anxieties that their vital public health interests in the water field might be undermined by the reform. Responsibilities for the delivery of certain water services were also devolved away from RWA headquarters, as will be seen, in that land drainage, sewerage and even some water supply business were carried out through agency-type arrangements with pre-existing bodies.

Reformers had for long advocated the need for some co-ordination of source developments from the centre. The WRB had largely achieved this. The focus of much of its work – in advising how best to balance requirements and resources at a regional level – was after 1973 concentrated in the RWAs themselves. Succeeding the WRB, but not replacing it as it performed a different role to that body's planning-orientated functions, was the NWC. Consisting of the chairpersons of the RWAs and some government appointees, its general position was weak. As the NWC (*1974/75*: 29) stated: 'In practice the relationship between a constitutionally weak central body and constitutionally strong regional bodies must understandably be somewhat delicate.' Its prime statutory responsibility was to advise, liaise and to provide some form of informal co-ordination among the RWAs. The NWC was also given a number of functional duties, concerned with staff training and pensions, the water fittings scheme (to achieve a standardisation of parts), and the provision of machinery to negotiate terms and conditions of employment. But it had no planning responsibility, no executive powers and a small budget (Parker and Penning-Rowsell 1980: 41).

Porter (1978: 30), to closely paraphrase her argument, stated that the 1973 settlement led to a fragmentation of previous centrally-organised functions. National arrangements for data collection, research and planning were taken over by the DoE itself and a number of other bodies. Old unities achieved under the WRB were lost; no one national organisation stood above the others.

Before long a view emerged that decentralisation may have been taken too far. The large discrepancies in water charges across the country were cause for resentment. Disproportionately large increases were imposed upon rural areas, unable to take advantage of urban supply schemes. Anger over high charges was particularly strong in Wales, nationalism was waxing and a Labour government was dependent upon Nationalist support. Such factors led to the passing of the Water Charges Equalisation Act.

Debates over charge variations, regional supply imbalances and the anomalous position of the locally important private water companies encouraged the Labour government to seek to develop a more active water strategy. An independent National Water Authority was proposed to ensure that 'the combined operation of water authorities accord with national needs and objectives' (DoE, Welsh Office and MAF 1976: 4). In the late 1970s it was fashionable to argue that water research and planning activities needed a stronger national focus (NWC *1976/77*: 23; Porter 1978: 162).

In the event this was not the direction that water reform would take after the Thatcher government was returned to power in 1979. Nor did the politically expedient but in practical terms insignificant Water Equalisation Act survive for long (Prentice 1981: 293). Rather than developing the proposal for a national water body, the new Conservative government proceeded to abolish the NWC under the Water Act of 1983. It believed that most of its functions could be undertaken by the RWAs, who had considerably improved their planning expertise (DoE 1982a). The RWAs were also to become individually responsible for the training, pay and employment conditions of their employees. The NWC was replaced by the Water Authorities Association – purely a forum for discussing RWA matters of common concern.

From a later vantage, the late 1970s proposal for a national water authority looks anachronistically bureaucratic and not especially relevant to the key regulatory issues of environmental protection and the efficient delivery of water services. However, the abolition of the NWC hardly helped to further these goals either, and coincided with the onset of a period of drift in the conduct of national water policy. The government became preoccupied with the short-term aims of reducing costs and de-municipalising the RWAs. For some time it seemed as if all interest was lost in how the objectives set for the industry in 1973 should be achieved.

The work of the Regional Water Authorities

Management structures

The collapsing of almost 1,600 different water bodies into ten unitary authorities was, perhaps, the pivotal water reform of the twentieth century, facilitating the realisation of long-discussed objectives. The extent of the integration achieved in the first few years, however, can be exaggerated. Indeed, the degree to which the managements of 1,600 organisations, many of them very small, could be remade overnight into teams capable of assuming control over relatively vast, multifunctional enterprises was limited (Johnson 1986). The RWAs had to make the best use of the staff and structures they inherited. Reflecting the difficulties of adjustment the NWWA, for example, carried on business through no less than thirty-five units, before these were consolidated into eight operational divisions in January 1975 (NWWA *1975/76*: 2). Also, anomalies survived and much business continued to be carried on under devolved or agency-type arrangements. This can partly be attributed to the re-emergence of many of the traditional features of policy-making in the water industry during the preparation of the 1973 reform. Trade-offs between the sectional interests and government departments led to compromises. As a result, private water companies, regional land committees and local authorities remained, with active roles to play within the semi-nationalised industry.

Although the RWAs were able to gradually develop more effective divisional structures for the discharge of their responsibilities, the survival of bodies over which they exercised only general oversight created difficulties. Twenty-eight private water companies continued to provide twenty-two per cent of England's and Wales's water supplies to twenty-five per cent of the population. Ironically, their existence may have created fewer problems than other survivals from before 1973, although the DoE regarded the companies as anomalous and the Callaghan government proposed to abolish them. They levied charges on the same basis as the RWAs. Under agency arrangements, annual plans specified the companies' proposed works on supply and treatment works, which were submitted to the RWAs. In the view of Parker and Penning-Rowsell (1980: 36), the two parties appeared to operate 'well together'.

The second anomaly lay with land drainage. While the RWAs undertook supervisory and constructional tasks, executive and even financial responsibilities were devolved to regional land drainage committees. Membership of these committees was composed of nominees of county councils and the MAF. The finance of land drainage depended upon MAF grants. Although relationships between the various parties were cordial, Pitkethly (1990: 136–7) claims that these concessions to the landowning and farming lobbies led to cross-representation on committees, a failure to fully integrate the planning and co-ordination of land and water resources, and diminished operational effectiveness.

More obvious and practical difficulties arose from the third survival – that of a local government presence in sewerage (Parker and Derrick Sewell 1988: 33–6). Because of technical convenience and the significance to local government with regard to its public health and land planning functions, district councils were given the responsibility of carrying on the sewerage business as agencies for the RWAs, subject to the submission and approval of annual plans. Between 1974 and 1978 local authorities continued to collect sewerage charges and paid these over to the RWAs. Even after the introduction of direct billing (a uniform water and sewerage charge) local government continued to run sewerage services. Most coastal outfalls, certain trunk sewers and all STWs were the direct responsibility of the RWAs. But, in 1982, ninety-five per cent of all sewerage work was still handled by district councils under agency arrangements. Sewerage business constituted a large part of total RWA activity, accounting for twenty-three per cent of revenue expenditure in 1978. Over half of all capital spending by the RWAs was devoted to sewerage and sewage disposal between 1974 and 1981, including, admittedly, services managed directly by them (NWC 1982: 78).

Contracting out sewerage work to the district councils meant that the financial expenditure and technical management of a significant part of RWA business escaped their effective control. Professional and planning functions were duplicated. Such imperfections were inherent in the system, rather than the fault of the local authorities. But collaboration between the two bodies was less than perfect. The Monopolies and Mergers Commission had to emphasise that under the agency arrangements the RWAs did have the right to closely supervise the district councils and stipulate objectives defined by cost, technical and design parameters, and also to ensure that work was done cost-effectively – the implication being that this was not always achieved (NWWA *1982/83*: 6). The NWC (1978: 13) agreed that some local authorities did 'perform well', while 'some do not, usually more a reflection of their own limited resources than of their willingness to do what is needed'.

Naturally the RWAs strove to end agency agreements and gain control over the management of the water cycle in its entirety. The realisation that the RWAs did not have the right, even through private legislation, to abolish the arrangements for local authority sewerage agencies delayed the system's demise. Only after 1983 did the RWAs eventually obtain the right to terminate these arrangements and assume full control.

Integrated river management

It was anticipated that a number of benefits would flow from the creation of large-scale, regional organisations, for example that the RWAs would be able to attract scientific and managerial expertise more successfully. As Sidwick and Murray (1976 VI: 609) put it: 'Thus, instead of a widely scattered body of expertise usually with little power, authority or influence and with an image that failed to attract people of even average competence, there are now large, multi-disciplinary organ-isations offering status, scientific facilities and job-satisfaction.'

It was also anticipated that the introduction of integrated management would enable a more efficient use and co-ordination of water resources to be achieved. It had not been impossible in the past to conceive large-scale regional supply schemes. But with the new structures they did become much easier to develop and implement. More reliance could be placed upon the natural distribu-tion channels of river systems to redistribute resources, and greater flexibility could be achieved by converting direct supply reservoirs to river regulation schemes and by developing the conjunctive use of a number of water sources (Porter 1978: 34,48–9).

The reorganisation did enable these expectations to be realised. In the North-East, the Kielder reservoir, the largest man-made lake in Western Europe, was opened in 1982. It formed part of the first regional water grid in the UK and served to counteract the uneven distribution of supplies in that region. The poten-tial of the Tyne, Wear and Tees was enhanced, these rivers being linked to the reservoir by a network of cross-country pipes and pumping stations (Barty-King 1992: 224). Taking two years to fill after completion and with the capacity to satisfy the requirements of a population as great as that living in the south-east of England, the reservoir has been described as 'one of the most serious manifesta-tions of the incorrect forecasting of the late 1960s' (Gray 1994: 70). However, its strategic value might be better appreciated with the advent of more difficult supply conditions in the north of England.

The trend has certainly moved away from the development of vast fixed-site structures towards more complex and flexible solutions to meeting future needs. Replacing reliance upon long-distance aqueducts by downstream abstraction of river water enables the run-off from a much more extensive catchment to be tapped (Smith 1972: 143). Many schemes developed in the 1970s and 1980s illustrated the advantages from the application of a regional approach to water resource exploita-tion, including the Kielder project itself to some degree. For example, in the North-West, whereas all Thirlmere water had formerly been dispatched south by aqueduct, it was now possible to redirect some of the water, via the Derwent, to water-short districts of West Cumberland. The Lancashire conjunctive project drew on the resources of a wide area and provided the integration of groundwater, river and upland reservoirs in a sophisticated regional supply and distribution scheme. Regional solutions to water resource development were also applied in Yorkshire and East Anglia.

Some of these projects were envisaged before 1973. But it was only with the 1973 reorganisation together with, in the case of the Dee, the passing of the Dee and Clywd Rivers Authority Act, that earlier plans could be brought to fruition. For the Dee, the River Authority now possessed the powers to more flexibly employ impounding reservoirs for regulative and conjunctive uses. The scheme came to be regarded as an internationally important model. The harnessing of the resources of the Dee catchment for hydropower, fisheries, effluent dilution, abstractive and recreational purposes was accomplished much more effectively, and the impact of storm, drought and pollution incidents was accommodated or mitigated (Lambert 1988). It was not only in this river basin where the benefits of the application of integrated management were realised. The RWAs in general were in a much better position than any predecessors to conceive and use rivers as a multi-use resource, including the Tyne and the Thames, for example – to meet growing consumption demands through increased abstractions, to absorb a rising effluent load, and to satisfy amenity demands. More effective management of the hydrological cycle was complemented by other efficiency gains. The new framework enabled the RWAs to achieve economies of scale in water supply, sewage treatment, administration, research and training (Parker and Derrick Sewell 1988: 774). Even if local management continued to be employed, the collapsing of 1,400 separate sanitary authorities into ten RWAs enabled the management of sewerage services to be rationalised and its financial basis to be broadened (Kirby 1984: 27). In the Black Country the RWA's strategic sewage scheme enabled twelve out of fourteen old and overloaded STWs to be closed down (Barty-King 1992: 167–8). Lynk (1993: 99–106) confirms that the RWAs were better equipped to plan and control all uses of water within catchments, compared to the previous highly fragmented industry. His econometric study demonstrates that significant economies of scale and scope were achieved through the joint production of water supply, sewerage and environmental services.

The gains which arose from the RWAs' ability to manipulate the entire water cycle and to develop regional networks became evident during years of very low rainfall, which would normally have created great difficulties for suppliers and consumers. During the sixteen months to August 1976 England and Wales received its lowest rainfall for any comparable period since records began in 1727, and 1984 was almost as severe.

As these extreme conditions imposed themselves, the advantages of reorganisation became apparent. The regional unification of operational control within watersheds enabled local deficiencies to be met by supplies being switched from one locality to another, or by drawing upon strategic reserves. 'Reorganisation under the Water Act of 1973 was shown to provide the basis of organisation which can make a robust and resilient response to an unusual difficulty', concluded the NWC (*1976/77*: 11). Adequate supplies to most of the population had been maintained for long periods into the drought. Emergency powers, provided under the Drought Bill, were employed to only a limited degree in 1984. The NWWA (*1984/85*: 11) confidently reflected: 'The regional supply network allowed a high degree of flexibility in operation and enabled the most severely depleted sources to be adequately supported. Thus the region passed through the most severe drought on record with with only relatively minor inconvenience to the public.'

Such successes were a source of considerable gratification to the water industry and were the bedrock of the confident assessments of the robust supply/demand situation made about this time.

Notwithstanding the great changes it introduced, the 1973 reform did not deliver integrated management in its entirety. According to the analysis favoured by Newson (1992b: 385), 'land and water are a hydrological continuum and must be managed together'. However, apart from the very prescriptive municipal management of upland catchments arising from the Victorian scramble to control sources, the joint management of land and water has rarely been achieved in the UK. It was hoped that the reorganisation would enable the RWAs, for example, to open more reservoirs and gathering-grounds to recreational users. Movement towards this objective was less than was hoped, the prevalence of multiple ownership of much land and water in England and Wales proving a serious obstacle (Parker and Derrick Sewell 1988: 775–6).

Also, the principle of integrated management was undermined in so far as the RWAs could not exercise complete control over land drainage. The creation of separate regional drainage committees led to the division or duplication of responsibilities. The limitation on the RWAs' ability to encompass agricultural land-use in the execution of their duties leads Pitkethly (1990: 136–7) to observe that there was a failure to achieve a fully comprehensive approach to water management in this period. It was certainly the case that the integrated use of land and water under holistic management was not realised between 1973 and 1989, as landed and farming interests retained influence in the land drainage field.

Such complex, but practical, difficulties as the multiple ownership of land and water prompt the question of whether a complete reconciliation of all conflicts over resource-use can ever be entirely fulfilled – other than in a totalitarian world or, perhaps, in an ideal economist's one characterised by 'perfect' property rights. The complete elimination of tensions among water users, which integrated and holistic management might in theory produce, may in reality be extremely hard to obtain, such conflicts being inherent in the 'multiple-use nature of the water resource' (Tomkins and Wharton 1996). Some movement towards reducing and managing such conflicts might be made, gains in efficiency achieved and a greater security of supply obtained. All this the RWAs did secure impressively. The break with the past was decisive and significant progress towards establishing integrated management of the water cycle was made.

Sewage treatment

As noted previously, the municipal water industry tended to concentrate, historically, upon the development of supplies, rather than the improvement of sewerage services. Consequently, in 1973, the RWAs inherited a massive problem of underground dereliction, much of the sewer network pre-dating the First World War in origin and badly in need of renewal. There was even a serious want of basic

Table 5.4   *RWA expenditure by service, 1974–81*

Year	Water resources and water supply £m.	%	Sewerage and sewage disposal £m.	%	Land drainage £m.	%	Other £m.	%	Total £m.
1974/75	119	28	280	66	17	4	8	2	424
1975/76	164	31	310	61	27	5	11	3	512
1976/77	195	36	298	55	31	6	14	3	538
1977/78	192	37	261	51	41	8	20	4	514
1978/79	205	37	274	50	53	10	20	3	552
1979/80	213	36	298	49	73	12	21	3	605
1980/81	233	33	348	50	81	12	31	4	693

Source: NWC 1982: 78.

information regarding the exact size, age, diameter and condition of sewers and mains. Sewer recording was not a civic priority before 1973, and over seventy different record systems of varying quality were handed over to the Severn-Trent Water Authority alone (Styles and Robinson 1984: 3–4). Anglia Water Authority considered that they had adequate knowledge of only about eight per cent of the 22,000 km of sewers in their region (Kirby 1984: 105). Overall, only about thirty to forty per cent of all local authorities had reasonably satisfactory records of sewers and fifteen to thirty per cent of all public sewers had no records at all (NWC 1982: 35). Much of the early effort of the RWAs in relation to sewerage simply focused on the carrying-out of surveys to establish the extent of the problem. This was assisted by the development of closed-circuit television (CCTV), the only means of inspecting small sewers. In 1960 there were three or four CCTV contractors, rising to over fifty by 1984 (Styles and Robinson 1984: 4).

The RWAs were acutely conscious of the seriousness of their inherited sewerage problem and, within the financial resources at their disposal, addressed it energetically. In their first financial year of operation slightly over half of their total revenue was devoted to sewage collection and disposal and pollution prevention. Of the capital expenditure in 1973/4 nearly two-thirds went into these activities (NWC *1974/75*: 16–17.) Individual authorities, such as Severn-Trent, inaugurated large-scale survey and personnel training schemes in order to better equip themselves to undertake the necessary modernisations.

Table 5.4 indicates that sewerage and sewage disposal attracted the lion's share of capital expenditure in the 1970s. (The rising figures on land drainage capital expenditure in the 1970s, summarised in Table 5.4 ,were primarily due to increased investment on Thames tidal defences, which was largely financed through government grants.) The NWC was at pains to point out that by international standards the situation in England and Wales was good and claimed an improvement in reducing sewage pollution, outside some environmental 'black spots' (1978: 63). It

Table 5.5   *City of Manchester capital expenditure on sewerage, 1969–80*
(£m. at 1980 prices)

1969/70	1.34	1973/74	3.57	1977/78	0.21
1970/71	2.15	1974/75	2.26	1978/79	0.67
1971/72	1.47	1975/76	2.11	1979/80	1.97
1972/73	2.92	1976/77	1.32	1980/81[a]	2.16

Note: [a] Planned.
Source: Read 1979: n.p.

also pointed out that ninety-five per cent of households were connected to the public sewers in this country, compared to seventy-five per cent in the USA, eighty per cent in Western Germany and ninety-eight per cent in the Netherlands. Other comparative statistics suggested that the proportion of the pollution load of sewers provided with primary and secondary treatment was relatively high in Britain.

Yet despite good intentions and favourable international comparisons, it is doubtful whether the RWAs' endeavours in improving sewage treatment were adequate, both in relation to the basic requirements of maintenance and renewal, as well as with reference to the mounting demands being placed upon rivers to meet multiple needs. More probably the water industry struggled to keep abreast of the problem during the ten years following reorganisation. The figures in Table 5.4 not only show a declining share of resources allocated to sewage in this period, but also, after allowing for inflation, indicate that real spending on the sector was declining. In Manchester, for example, the dire extent of the sewer problem was finally recognised in the 1960s. Yet reorganisation appeared initially to have a very harmful impact upon a programme of sewerage renewal. For some years prior to 1974 the City of Manchester had been steadily increasing its expenditure on sewer improvements, but this was followed by an almost precipitous decline due to the limited resources available to the NWWA. Effectively, sewer renewal was given the lowest priority. The overall cost of renewal was greater than for the equivalent needs for highway replacement, yet expenditure on the former was only one-tenth of the latter in Manchester in 1979 (Read 1979).

The sheer scale of the problem threatened to overwhelm attempts to address it. In Yorkshire, where there were more sewer collapses than any other region, by 1985 the regional authority was spending some £100 million annually on capital programmes, including sewerage renewal. But due to large depreciation requirements this was said to be equivalent to a new net investment of only about £25 million (Jones 1985: 48), an expenditure unlikely to produce significant improvements.

From a very low ebb in the the early 1980s the situation slowly improved. The RWAs began to devote a greater share of capital spending on this sector again. Their annual reports catalogue a variety of new initiatives, in many of which the modernisation of STWs played a key role. By the mid-1980s the NWWA (*1984/85*: 13), for example, was able to document material progress in completing new sewers, renovating or abandoning old ones, and eliminating unsatisfactory storm overflows. Nationally, a sharp fall in the late 1980s in the proportion of STWs which were in breach of discharge consents possibly suggests improvement, although this may have been partly due to a relaxation of consent conditions.

It has to be said that sewage treatment was not a glorious area of RWA endeavour. External financial restraints were the principal factor choking off any chance of significant improvement. Faced with financial stringency, it is not surprising that the RWAs tended to favour, on occasion, economical methods of waste disposal, even if they were beginning to appear less appropriate in a more environmentally demanding world. The removal of the ever-growing volume of sewage sludge raised difficult environmental issues. Disposal to agricultural land was a traditional, relatively cheap and widely used solution, but was unsuitable when it originated from industrial areas due to chemicals in the sludge. Incineration was costly and could cause secondary air pollution. 'Carefully monitored' dumping at sea was frequently favoured, the NWC (1978: 11) claiming that studies of the Thames estuary and Liverpool Bay indicated that the impact upon marine ecology was not serious. By the late 1980s some nine million tonnes of sewage sludge, representing thirty per cent of total disposals, were dumped in the seas around Britain.

Yorkshire RWA originally recycled one-third of its sludge production to agricultural land, part of which was dried, processed and packed in plastic bags for sale as 'Yorkshire Bounty'; one-third was 'lagooned or dried and tipped'; and one-third 'was too contaminated for disposal by any of these methods and had to be incinerated or dumped at sea'. However, less reliance was being placed on the latter method and the proportion recycled to agricultural land was increased to about one-half by 1978 (YWA *1978*: 19).

Other regions, notably Thames and the North-West, were more heavily committed to dumping at sea. The development of Davyhulme, the most important STW in the North-West, was based on this approach. Facing difficulties in obtaining planning permission for incineration methods, the NWWA was reassured by feasibility studies that confirmed the economic viability of disposal at sea. It proceeded to invest in a 'regional sludge pipeline', replacing the use of barges on the Manchester Ship Canal, which would take the sludge from Davyhulme to a terminus at Liverpool, whence the cargo was taken by ship for disposal in the Irish Sea. The new pipeline was operational by 1987/8. The perseverance with this method was something of a wrong turn. European Community (EC) legislation would shortly ban the practice, requiring it to be phased out altogether by a decade after the completion of Lancashire's sludge pipeline; conversion to an alternative solution, at enormous cost to the industry, had to be made.

Environmental renewal in the North-West

In the 1970s further environmental deterioration and the physical collapse of its underground assets threatened the water industry. The problem was compounded by general public indifference. There was some awakening of interest in the North-West, with sewer collapses regularly underlining the extent of infrastructural decay. But at a seminar launching a campaign organised by NWWA in 1978 to raise awareness of dereliction, to which many MPs and Ministers were invited, a zero attendance from politicians was recorded.

This sub-section, by exploring events in the North-West, will seek to demonstrate that while financial pressures inhibited improvements, the RWAs were nevertheless extremely concerned about the massive environmental challenges which they had inherited. The NWWA became heavily involved in a number of ambitious programmes to reverse decline and bring about a renewal of the region's river systems.

A particularly serious problem of river pollution existed in the Greater Manchester area. In 1973 the NWWA acquired a higher proportion of classes three and four (poor and 'grossly polluted') rivers in the country, and most were concentrated in Greater Manchester. Against this background, the Greater Manchester Council and the ten district councils devised a regional programme to restore the area's major river valleys and establish a network of country parks. Agreement was reached on the River Valleys scheme in 1975, the NWWA becoming an active partner in a number of co-operative valley projects. Expenditure on river valleys and country parks in Greater Manchester increased from £59,000 in 1974/5 to over £1.3 million in 1981/2 (Maund 1982: 94). The transformation of the river valleys from their former derelict state into a more agreeable, greener condition where wildlife and recreational activities flourish is obvious to even the casual observer.

To some extent running parallel with the Greater Manchester valleys scheme, but on a considerably more ambitious scale, was the project which came to confront the issue of water quality throughout the Mersey river basin and estuary as a whole. The century-old causes of environmental decline throughout the catchment have been described on pp. 121–3. With the innovational assistance of helicopters, water quality and biological surveys were carried out in the mid- to late 1970s for the region's estuaries. Arising from such investigations and its analysis of the situation as regards inland waters, the Authority forecast an 'unacceptable deterioration' of forty-seven miles of rivers in the region between 1976 and 1980, and hardly less reassuring trends for other inland waters (NWWA *1976/77*: 39).

At this stage the NWWA adopted a 'Policy for river water quality', the long-term aim being essentially to protect and restore the region's rivers, and the short-term objective being, first, to prevent deterioration and second, as far as capital availability permitted, to improve the situation. These were limited objectives, aspiring to little more than a containing exercise at this stage.

A further series of initiatives, policy statements and consultative documents were launched between 1978 and 1984, which reflected the Authority's determination to safeguard the water environment in the North-West. The publication in 1978 of evidence relating to the physical dereliction of underground assets marked the beginning of a sustained attempt to redress neglect. In a seminar paper, the NWWA's chief executive, J. G. Lloyd (1978: 1) stressed that it was high time to settle a policy for replacing and maintaining underground installations, but that an 'essential first step must be a public airing of the whole affair'. For the next few years the Authority continued to refine its proposals, although the objectives specified and the financial resources earmarked for new programmes were, as yet, on a modest scale.

While epoch-making events are hardly the stuff of water-industry history, undoubtedly the arrival in Merseyside in 1981 of the charismatic Minister of the Environment, Michael Heseltine, was a significant moment. It offered the promise that the low importance attached to the region's environmental problems by the political establishment might be altered. Subsequently, in March 1983, Heseltine declared that the state of the Mersey was an 'affront to the standards a civilised society should demand of its citizens' (cited in NWWA *1982/83*: 14).

Meanwhile, a House of Lords Select Committee and a DoE consultative document acknowledged the need for capital investment to halt underground dereliction. The latter document, with a foreword written by Heseltine, pointed out that the Mersey was the most polluted estuary and river system in the UK, almost one-third of its river length being incapable of supporting life, and that it would probably take a generation to effect the necessary improvements (DoE 1982b). But the NWWA took considerable heart from what was, evidently, a shift in government attitude regarding the case for extra resources to be made available to assist environmental renewal in the North-West. Such an assessment had apparently been adopted by Heseltine, as part of his current interest and responsibility for reviving the economy and prospects of Merseyside. The new urgency was reflected in the ceilings for capital investment over a three-year period being increased considerably beyond the limits originally proposed (NWWA *1982/83*: 14–15).

The Mersey Basin Campaign was officially launched at a conference, convened by the Secretary of State for the Environment in March 1983, at which the DoE consultative document and detailed NWWA proposals were considered. In 1984 the Authority developed its key role in the campaign through applying for EC assistance in the funding of sewerage rehabilitation. It is noticeable that once the interest of the State in environmental degradation in the region had been registered, the figures produced by the NWWA to describe the expenditures required changed dramatically. A planned spending of £70 million over fifteen years for cleaning up the Mersey had been envisaged in 1980/1, but by 1983 and 1984 the NWWA put the long-term cost of regional renewal at between £3 billion and £3.7 billion (NWWA *1982/83*: 14; 1984: 6).

The campaign was supported by government and local authorities and other statutory bodies, with the RWA obviously a leading participant. It received a boost from the announcement of confirmation of government support by Patrick Jenkin in March 1984 and, particularly, from the news in 1985 that the application for EC funding had been successful, with the delivery of £67 million of assistance to cover the period, 1984 to 1987. The government further endorsed the campaign in 1986 at a second Mersey Conference.

As well as this programme, the NWWA involved itself with many other initiatives, which aimed to secure environmental improvement, promoting numerous volunteer and conservation projects, which assisted in the protection of wildlife, restoring sites, improving access to gathering-grounds and enhancing the amenity value of its property. From the early 1980s the Authority gave attention to achieving a workable balance between recreation and conservation. From the outset the basic imperative was to raise the quality of the effluent produced by its STWs. Even before the Mersey Basin Campaign could have had any effect, the NWWA was able to claim some progress over the first ten years of its existence, such as a reduction of nearly seventy-five per cent in the pollution load entering the estuary, and some quite marked figures on the return of wildlife to habitats. Significant improvement in water quality in the Mersey basin, however, had yet to be reported. From the mid-1980s projects were being commissioned whereby discharges of crude sewage from a number of towns were being progressively switched to STWs to afford at least primary treatment. For example, major new STWs were being built to serve a population of 500,000 in Liverpool, previously without such a facility (NWWA *1983/84*: 7–8). Such schemes took time to bear fruit. The condition of the Mersey estuary remained cause for grave concern for some while. In 1992 it was still referred to as one of the worst polluted estuaries in the country, with the campaign having, as yet, many years to run (RCEP 1992: 4). By the 1990s, nevertheless, reductions in the loads of organic pollution, heavy metals and dangerous substances entering the estuary were recorded. Evidence was also accumulating of a gradual return of estuarine and migratory fish (NRA 1995).

The under-performance of the RWAs?

Despite such endeavours, the performance of the RWAs in meeting the expectations of government and society came increasingly into question in the 1980s. Kinnersley observes (1994: 48) that in broad terms they 'turned out to be failing in what was clearly their key mission – the protection of both tap-water quality and river-water quality from increasing pollution by industry, agriculture and discharges from sewage works'. Although government had overarching responsibility for 'making' policy, the day-to-day task of managing the water environment was unquestionably the duty of the RWAs. Negative images about the RWAs were developing in the public mind, and government was able to pursue its privatisation proposal in the context of claims and assumptions about the under-performance of the industry.

The reorganised water industry, despite its worthy efforts in the field of environmental renewal and its success in realising some of the benefits of integrated management, was vulnerable to such criticisms. It under-performed in the sense of failing to convincingly achieve the objectives which had been adopted in 1973. A number of factors may have contributed to this failure, and to the perception that the RWAs were at fault. They include

1   the burden of their inheritance;
2   expectations and requirements rising more rapidly than the ability to fulfil them;
3   an inappropriate regulatory framework;
4   the harmful impact of the ownership and management structure established in 1974.

Firstly, the RWAs were certainly burdened with a legacy of neglect, and took over a dilapidated stock of physical assets. This was exacerbated by continuing financial restraints imposed by government from the mid-1970s, which made it difficult to fund improvements in water quality. The harmful impact of government interference, especially upon sewerage rehabilitation, was without doubt a principal cause of the industry's perceived failure to achieve environmental objectives. The burden of guilt, however, was to some extent shifted by some observers on to the RWAs (see Halsall 1989). The causes of this lie partly with factors examined in the following paragraphs.

Secondly, the 1970s and 1980s were an age of a more demanding consumerism. Consumer dissatisfaction with the RWAs derived from two separate influences: the rising cost of water services and growing environmental anxieties. British society, by the mid-twentieth century, had developed some confidence in the quality of drinking water. This was not entirely ill-founded, following a century of effort by the water industry in improving the supply and treatment of sources. It was widely assumed that water was a ubiquitous resource, for which users should be charged very low prices (Parker and Penning-Rowsell 1980: 68). This odd mixture of indifference and satisfaction with the quality of the product derived partly from the very low price charged for water services. The local authorities had generally delivered water supplies at a loss, making up the deficit from the general rate, while sewage disposal had been supported by the rate support grant. With reorganisation the government expected the RWAs to impose charges equivalent to the cost of supplying the service. Consumer angst intensified with the introduction of direct billing in the late 1970s. Public perceptions were that bills had been hiked up precipitously. The reasons for higher bills were that the full cost of water and sewerage services were being entered on a single bill, in a period of high inflation, and without the cushioning of the rate support grant. In 1980 charges were often increased by twenty per cent or more.

Consumer satisfaction with the RWAs was further undermined when, on top of having to pay higher bills, it gradually emerged that the good quality of potable supplies could not, after all, be taken for granted. Complacency about tap-water quality partly derived from the water industry's efforts in improving water treatment over the years. But it also stemmed from a less rational cause – namely the absence of the designation or enforcement of drinking-water standards. The consistent application of such standards would otherwise have exposed regional variations in water quality. From the 1970s World Health Organisation (WHO) standards were increasingly invoked, but the development which really began to expose deficiencies and undermine confidence was the advent of formal EC requirements. EC water directives laid down specific standards in relation to a wide range of parameters for drinking and other waters. Based on legislation agreed to in 1976, compliance with the drinking-water directives was supposed, originally, to be achieved within ten years. But when the target date, 17 July 1985, approached the British water industry was anything other than in a position to meet the specified standards. Studies, in fact, revealed that tap-water was failing to meet EC standards with respect to many of the parameters, including the presence of chemicals such as nitrates, which provoked considerable alarm (Lean and Pearce 1989).

The third factor contributing to the impression or reality of RWA under-performance was the impact of defective regulatory arrangements. According to Lynk (1993), poor attainment of environmental objectives was due to regulatory capture – a loosening of consent conditions due to the influence exercised by the RWAs. Regulatory failure there certainly was, but Lynk's analysis of causality may need a little modification. Although objectives were set by government for the RWAs in 1973, there was no provision made for measuring or monitoring how satisfactorily they were being met. Financial disciplines were introduced from the late 1970s and especially after 1983. It was claimed by government that financial targets and controls acted as a surrogate market, placing the nationalised industries under the kind of commercial pressures operating in the private sector (HM Treasury 1990: 5). As far as water was concerned, such claims cannot be taken seriously and the Tory government itself came to recognise them as poor substitutes for competitive disciplines – and therefore introduced privatisation proposals (HM Treasury 1990). In fact, while financial stringency certainly imposed strong downward pressures on costs in the RWAs and led to the elimination of certain types of gross inefficiency, the way targets were introduced in the water industry had perverse effects, as will be argued below; in conclusion, they can be dismissed as an inefficient and environmentally harmful way of promoting efficiency. Regarding 'regulatory capture', this is the wrong term to describe the RWAs' environmental protection functions which were conferred upon them by the 1973 Water Act. However, this did emerge as a misconceived solution which placed the RWAs in an untenable position. The clear responsibility for these failures lay less with the RWAs, and more with the

Table 5.6 *RWA environmental services: expenditure and income, 1984/5 (£,000)*

	Expenditure	Income	Support from the environmental services charge
Water quality regulation	17,328	115	17,213
Pollution alleviation	4,445	91	4,354
Recreation and amenity	6,961	2,630	4,331
Fisheries	8,296	4,290	4,006
Navigation	4,346	1,859	2,487
Total	41,376	8,985	32,391

Source: DoE, Welsh Office 1986: 2.15.

body which devised such mechanisms in the first place and which had ultimate authority for guiding water policy, and this was government.

Fourth, poor performance in the pursuit of environmental and other objectives may have been the product of the ownership structure prevailing in the water industry and, in particular, of the harmful effect of public ownership.

As has been seen, water management must not only deliver a wide range of services but also must attempt to reconcile the conflicting demands of different users. Arguably, a profit-seeking firm has less interest in efficiently delivering non-commercial environmental services than might be the case with a public enterprise, governed by more civic objectives. The DoE admitted that it would not be possible for most of the pollution-control and environmental functions to be undertaken on a profit-making basis by the water undertakings, once privatised (DoE, Welsh Office 1986: para. 2.14). The cost of supplying these services was reflected in the subsidies, with which the RWAs had to support their environmental services.

Note may also be made of the harmful effects of the under-regulation of private enterprise in the nineteenth century. These observations can be taken as a fairly conventional presentation of a case for public regulation, if not ownership, in a natural monopoly industry where there are significant externalities involved.

But the twentieth-century experience makes it more difficult to press this argument. In England and Wales the private water companies appear, if anything, to have increased their share of a growing national output, from possibly around twenty per cent in the 1900s to twenty-two per cent in the 1980s (Falkus 1977: 136; WSA 1992: 2,25). Given its resilient survival in the present century, the possibility emerges that the performance of the private sector had improved relative to the previous century and even in comparison, perhaps, with the semi-nationalised RWAs. An examination of the possible causes of such a shift may add further insights into causes of the apparent under-performance of the RWAs.

Empirical studies indicate that the form of ownership *per se* is not an important factor in determining how effectively services are supplied in utility industries. What does promote efficiency is the existence or threat of competition (Kay and Thompson 1986; Millward 1989). Competitive structures, which might foster lower costs and promote more effective asset management, are difficult to introduce in natural monopolies. Market failures under private ownership led these industries to be among the first to be brought under public ownership, and among the last to be privatised. Clearly, there is limited scope, in such cases, for the introduction of competition in the product market. There was, however, in the British private-sector water industry something akin to competition in the capital market. If a water company was not managing its assets effectively, there was a very real threat of elimination, either through bankruptcy, through take-over by a local authority, or incorporation into or merger with another water company or board. That the number of statutory water companies in existence fell from 221 in 1904 to twenty-eight in 1973 suggests that such disciplines were operating to some degree. The histories of private water companies provide some evidence that such forces did influence management, indicated by latter's attention to improving water quality, to maintaining services during droughts and to collaborating constructively with public health administration. It is of interest that the regrouping movement of the 1950s and 1960s provided the occasion for organisational and administrative improvements, and the acquisition of a significant number of waterworks hitherto under municipal management (Hodgson 1991).

Public-sector water undertakings, and especially the RWAs, were less subject to these influences. It is also unlikely that civic pride and the pursuit of the 'public good', as suggested in an older type of welfare economics, exercised public enterprise management in recent decades as strongly as was the case when municipalities were developing their towns' water supplies in the Victorian period. The property rights approach argues that firms with market power pursue objectives other than efficiency or profit-maximisation, and their managers, whether in public or private enterprises, seek to protect their salaries and are more concerned with the growth and survival of the organisation. With no competitive challenges, overstaffing typically ensues (Kay and Thompson 1986). This analysis does ring true for the RWAs to some extent. Political scientists have also drawn attention to the removal of water management from its democratic, municipal roots to the remote, 'regional states', which the RWAs embodied, with considerable managerial autonomy (Newson 1992a: 261).

It is difficult to carry out an analysis of the comparative efficiency of the RWAs and the private water companies due to data deficiencies and especially because the two groups furnished a different range of services. Lynk's study, nevertheless, does enable a snapshot comparison to be made of how close the RWAs and the water companies were operating to their cost frontiers immediately prior to privatisation. The extent to which a firm lies above its cost frontier can be regarded as a measure of inefficiency. Lynk (1993: 112) does make clear that the exercise does not permit a direct comparison of the efficiency levels in the two sectors to be made but it does, he maintains, 'provide information concerning the average levels of inefficiency prevailing within each sector prior to privatisation'. Lynk concludes: 'The average level of inefficiency within the privately owned water industry appears to have been substantially higher than that prevailing within the public sector in the period immediately prior to privatisation.'

Superficially these findings appear to conflict with the descriptive explanation of the apparent under-performance of the RWAs which is being suggested here. However, performance is being discussed in two different ways, in the case of Lynk's research it has to be said according to much more rigorous, technical criteria. Moreover his conclusions have to be placed in context: they apply to cost structures immediately prior to privatisation after a number of years of attrition imposed upon the RWAs, which had the effect of significantly reducing their labour forces and other operational expenditure, including those devoted to environmental protection. Prior to the purge, it has to be confessed that the RWAs did exhibit features of bureaucratic overload, including overstaffing and elaborate but undemocratic liaison and consultation procedures with water users' groups – characteristics neither likely to enhance performance nor their image with the public (Pitkethly 1990). Lynk's findings, therefore, tell us more about the impact of the intense cost-cutting campaigns imposed upon the RWAs in the 1980s and less about the long-term relative performance of public and private enterprise in the water industry.

This section has discussed factors which may have contributed to the unpopularity of the RWAs by the 1980s. It has also touched upon the obstacles they faced in improving water quality. The conclusions are less that anyone is to 'blame' for what happened in the water industry, but rather that the search for an appropriate market and regulatory structure for water management is a complex and difficult task, although some progress towards achieving solutions was made by the reforms of the 1970s.

Water quality and physical dereliction

The inheritance of the RWAs

In 1974 about 60,000 km of sewers out of a total network of 200,000 km, and 67,000 km of water mains originated from before the First World War. After decades of neglect the physical assets inherited by the RWAs had fallen into a sorry state. The carrying-out of the necessary renewals and repairs had been hampered by the dispersed nature of ownership and control which had formerly prevailed, especially characteristic of sewerage where fifty-eight separate authorities, for example, had been responsible for sixty-two STWs within Greater Manchester. But the poor state of the infrastructure was even more directly due to under-investment. Even in the 1970s, the annual expenditure on sewer replacement in England and Wales was only about one-half of the level estimated to be necessary simply to maintain the system (Parker and Penning-Rowsell 1980: 137). The situation varied considerably – in Severn-Trent only 2.1 per cent of the 34,000 km of sewers were deemed unsound, whereas in the North-West it was said, 'The majority of sewers so far inspected have had serious defects' (NWC 1982: 35).

Indeed the North-West illustrates general problems, but *in extremis*, and is emphasised in that context. The NWWA found itself with significantly less water treatment, less sewage treatment and more old mains and sewers than most other RWAs. One-sixth of Manchester's sewers were over 100 years old and often close to collapse. By 1868, 280 miles of its streets had been sewered, and about sixteen miles of small-sized sewers, without manholes, incapable, therefore, of being inspected before the advent of CCTV, had been built in the 1840s. There were even two to three miles in central Manchester which pre-dated 1830, uncharted and often discovered only by 'accident' (Read 1979). The NWWA, therefore, faced a huge problem of sewer dereliction, although the annual spending of £15 million in the late 1970s was thought to be only about one-sixth of the level required to clear the backlog of maintenance and replacement work. The NWWA reported (*1978/79*: 17): 'Sewer collapses and blockages continued throughout the year at a frequency of two collapses and forty blockages every day. Evidence of inherited underground dereliction in the North West is exemplified in the city centre of Manchester where in Spring 1978, eight major collapses and sewer repairs were causing serious traffic disruption.' The proliferation of storm overflows and the frequent flooding of streets and homes by sewage added to the mayhem.

Hitherto the public had been indifferent to out-of-sight dereliction, until inconvenienced by roads opening before them by sewer collapses. It was probably water-quality anxieties, however, rather than the resultant traffic difficulties, which would eventually politicise the issue and lead to a reassessment by the Authorities of the old adage that there were 'no votes in sewage'.

Legislative responses and system characteristics

Physical and financing problems, which have already been touched upon, limited the RWAs' ability to a manage an improvement in water quality. In addition, the position was complicated by legislative and system defects which will now be explored.

In 1974, the Control of Pollution Act (COPA), Part II, which applied to the water environment, passed into law. This measure superseded the Rivers Pollution Acts of 1951 and 1961. The granting of individual discharge consents remained the sole regulatory device. However, controls over discharges were now quite comprehensive and encompassed categories which had been previously exempt, including tidal waters and pre-1937 discharges. An important innovation was the introduction of a periodic review and alteration of consent conditions, which was designed to provide for a progressive improvement in effluent quality. Perhaps of greater potential significance, the previous regime of secrecy was removed. Whereas under earlier legislation it was forbidden to publish details of compliance with, or breaches of, discharge consents, now openness and publicity had been legislated for; these reforms were intended to create incentives to improve water quality (Kinnersley 1994: 8–9). Potentially, COPA, Part II was a major step forward in environmental legislation, providing the legislative means to effect a clean-up of the water environment. It has been described as one of the country's most important pieces of water-quality legislation (Parker and Penning-Rowsell 1980: 128). But its most striking feature was that under both Labour and Conservative governments its implementation, including provision for public registers, was delayed for over a decade; even when it was introduced, it was done so in a diluted form.

Initially (see Parker and Penning Rowsell 1980: 130) the view was taken that implementation was delayed because of recurring economic difficulties. Government and industry both claimed that the investment needed to make the STWs meet the standards required by consents could not be afforded. Secrecy over consent conditions was also advocated by industrial interests as being necessary to prevent sensitive commercial information being revealed to competitors. This was hardly a convincing argument for universal concealment. The reasons for the delay in implementing COPA Part II, for eleven years after Parliament had voted for it, for maintaining secrecy and for downgrading consent conditions are, however, open to another interpretation (RCEP 1992: 91; Kinnersley 1994: 9, 45). This would emphasise the use of the review of conditions in 1979/80 and 1983/4 to bring the consents into line with the historic performance of STWs. The object of the consequent relaxation of standards was to adapt the consent system, not to the quality requirements of the receiving waters, but to the performance of the RWAs.

During the period 1974–1985, moreover, widespread non-compliance was suspected. Incidents occasionally became public, for example as a result of court proceedings. Generally, though, the identity of polluters was kept secret. Non-implementation of the Act, therefore, particularly the delay in introducing openness and public registers, suited the under-performing water industry. But it suited the government, which blocked the extra infrastructural spending that might have led to improved STW performance, even more.

Another problem was the lack of a standardised approach to consent conditions. The tradition which evolved over many years was for the authorities to specify consent conditions which varied according to the circumstances of each case – the nature of the effluent, the diluting capacity and flow of the river, and the needs of other users. The 1912 30: 20 standard was frequently applied to discharge conditions but was also as frequently breached. WHO standards, based upon different criteria, were beginning to be used and during the 1980s the need for inland and other waters, particularly those intended for human consumption, to conform to EC environmental standards loomed as a forthcoming requirement.

For the time being, the quality of British waters frequently fell below WHO and EC standards.

The whole problem was exacerbated by a major flaw in the system. This was to confer upon the RWAs both operational and regulatory duties. While this combination of functions was introduced in 1973 in the belief that it would maximise the benefits created by integrated management, it was realised even at this stage that it might cause conflicts. To reduce them some safeguards were built into the settlement, notably RWA meetings being open to the public and open consent registers being provided for. The former innovation, however, was reversed after 1983, while the latter one was, as has been seen, buried for eleven years. The RWAs were aware of the difficulty of combining responsibility for implementing environmental law with the ownership of STWs. They sought to resolve this problem through an internal separation of roles with the creation of water quality advisory panels to oversee work in this area. The basic contradictions of the RWAs' position were not eradicated by this well-intentioned step. Meanwhile, the conceptual paradigm of integrated management still exercised considerable influence upon policy-making. As late as 1986 the DoE saw merit in the continued unification of functions. It proposed that after privatisation, the new water companies 'will continue to be the agencies responsible for protecting the water environment, as they must be if the benefits of integrated river basin management are preserved' (DoE, Welsh Office 1986: para. 3.1).

This outlook, however, was soon revised once work started on the development of an appropriate regulatory framework for privatisation. The conflicts of interest, which had beset the RWA, were well understood by Nicholas Ridley, the Minister in charge of the privatisation proposal. It was finally recognised that the combination of functions, which made the RWAs both poacher and gamekeeper, had not worked out well in practice. As owners of polluting STWs they were embarrassed to prosecute too energetically other enterprises which failed to fulfil consent conditions. COPA implementation delays had also encouraged the process of backsliding and half-hearted pursuit of environmental enforcement responsibilities. The NWWA, for example, initiated summons in barely one per cent of all cases where there had been 'pollution incidents' reported in the 1980s (NWWA 1981/82–1986/87). Even if all reported incidents did not justify summons, it is clear that the enforcement of environmental law by the RWAs lacked vigour. In 1978 the NWC commented that there was an understandable tendency for discharge consents to be set which were regarded as targets to be achieved over a period of years. COPA being non-operational, as yet, only RWAs could prosecute for failure to comply with discharge conditions, 'and they were expected to act reasonably by prosecuting only for flagrant and careless breaches of consent conditions' (NWC 1978, quoted in RCEP 1992: 91).

However, even if a sounder pollution control system had been devised, difficulties in achieving water quality improvements would have remained. STWs had to be physically capable of producing the desired effluent. The core weakness of the entire edifice for environmental protection in the aquatic sphere between 1973 and 1989 was the many outdated and overloaded STWs which remained in commission. A more rigorous enforcement policy itself would not have eradicated this flaw.

Water quality trends and problems

To reiterate, the present purpose is less to find fault with any agency, but rather to stress the difficulties which made water quality improvement hard to achieve. To inherited, historical causes of diffuse pollution were added complex, not fully understood causes of new types of pollution. That the country experienced far from uniform patterns of water quality trends in the 1970s and 1980s, including some important areas of improvement must, therefore, be stressed.

Such progress can be attributed to the endeavours of the RAs after 1963, as well as to the pursuit of integrated management and the launching of renewal programmes by the RWAs. Among localised successes was the Thames. There was no evidence of fish life in 1957 between Richmond and Gravesend, but the situation gradually changed, thanks to the introduction of a specific interventionist programme from 1963, so that by the early 1980s over eighty species, including one salmon, had been caught. Johnston et al. (1991: 56) refer to a 'spectacular improvement' in this river's biological quality between the 1960s and 1990. Another once badly polluted river which showed some improvement was the Trent. Between 1962–64 and 1978 the average concentration of ammonia fell from 3.5 parts per million at Trent Bridge, Nottingham to 0.9 ppm, and BOD loadings halved (Porter 1978: 125). A further improvement in the river's freshwater sections in the 1980s can be attributed to the upgrading of STWs as well as the removal of a substantial pollution load from the steel industry (NRA 1993: 43). The diversion of urban and industrial effluent to new STWs in the 1960s and 1970s led, eventually, to significant improvements in water quality for the tidal Avon, reflected in the increased number of estuarine and salmonoid fish in the 1980s (Gray 1986). The falling proportion of STWs in breach of consents in the late 1980s was possibly a source of comfort, although this still meant that in 1990, 333 STWs were failing what were, moreover, relaxed conditions (RCEP 1992: 92–3). As in the 1960s and 1970s, the middle reaches of rivers may have registering improvements, while downstream, tidal and some coastal waters remained seriously polluted.

Although the NWC tended to be quite upbeat in its evaluation of river quality trends, which it linked to the relatively high proportion of the population served by sewerage facilities, Kirby (1984: 108) found it difficult to discern a decisive improvement in river quality between 1975 and 1980. Like others, she was able to review the results of the river surveys, which have been carried out since 1958 and quinquennially since 1970. The system of classification changed in 1980 but after making adjustments some assessments of long-term trends can still be made.

Table 5.7 *Freshwater quality in England and Wales, 1958–90*

Class	1958 km.	%	1970 km.	%	1975 km.	%	1980 km.	%
Unpolluted	24,950	72	28,500	74	28,810	75	28,810	75
Doubtful	5,220	15	6,270	17	6,730	18	7,110	18
Poor	2,270	7	1,940	5	1,770	5	2,000	5
Grossly polluted	2,250	6	1,700	4	1,270	3	810	2
Total	34,690		38,400		38,590		38,740	

Class	1980 km.	%	1985 km.	%	1990 km.	%
Good 1A	13,830	34	13,470	33	12,408	29
Good 1B	14,220	35	13,990	34	14,536	34
Fair 2	8,670	21	9,730	24	10,750	25
Poor 3	3,260	8	3,560	9	4,022	9
Bad 4	640	2	650	2	662	2
X	–	–	–	–	39	–
Unclassified	–	–	–	–	17	–
Total	40,630		41,390		42,434	

Source: RCEP 1992: 6.

In 1991 the NRA published an eagerly awaited river quality survey covering the period from 1985 to 1990. There was some expectation that earlier signs of improvement would be maintained. However, the results disappointed. The RCEP commented that between 1958 and 1980 there had been a net improvement in national river quality, with the length of poorest quality rivers declining, and the length of the best increasing. The results for the 1980s, especially from 1985, were less reassuring. A net deterioration of 3.6 per cent occurred between 1985 and 1990. Notwithstanding some mitigating circumstances, the RCEP (1992: 6) concluded that there was cause for concern: 'Government policy in recent years has been to maintain or improve river quality and in particular to eliminate, over an undefined period, class 4 rivers and reduce steadily class 3. The results of the 1990 survey suggest that, modest though these policy aims have been, action to secure their achievement has so far been insufficient.'

In accounting for disappointing river quality trends over this period, on top of the previously discussed system flaws, the great complexity of an evolving problem must be borne in mind. As old problems were alleviated new threats to water quality arising from changes in industrial technology or agricultural practice emerged. New substances were synthesised and made their way into the water cycle. Concern over water quality was justified upon more than aesthetic grounds. The increased recycling of the water of rivers was the outcome of the contemporary tendency to increasingly exploit their multiple-use characteristics. It increased the threat of dangerous chemicals, even at very low concentrations, entering the system, with attendant public health risks (Kirby 1984: 116).

Complicating attempts to improve water quality are the historical, non-point nature of many sources of pollution. For instance, a serious source of pollution in Liverpool Bay are polychlorinated biphenyls (PCBs), which threaten the existence of marine life. Although in theory subject to the strictest controls, there are numerous local sources of PCBs, being the result of past permissive discharges and disposal practices. PCBs, mercury and other toxic substances have accumulated in coastal sediments and create major problems for pollution abatement (Johnston *et al.* 1991: 63). Not dissimilar problems are encountered in old industrial regions like the Black Country, where derelict and contaminated land is widespread. Although point sources of metal contamination in the Black Country have been tackled, seepage containing high concentrations of heavy metals continues, to flow into rivers from waste sites. The costly clean-up of derelict land is required of the UK to meet its international environmental obligations agreed to by treaty (RCEP 1992: 87).

Both old and new factors are at work in making agricultural pollution one of the most serious threats to water quality. The contamination of groundwater is caused by nitrate-based fertilisers and by pesticides, which leach into supplies. Pollution from agricultural sources caused a growing number of incidents in the 1980s. Many of these were traced to problems with silage, slurry or contaminated yard water. Fish farming also threatened serious effects on some of the cleanest rivers (Lawson 1986). The apparently worsening problem of nitrate pollution has been attributed to excessive spreading of manufactured fertiliser on farmland in the past, which can take forty years to percolate down into underground supplies (Brown *et al.* 1992). Concern is provoked because of the feared links between increased nitrate levels in water and the threat of methaemoglobinaemia in bottle-fed babies, and the possibility of carcinogenic links, although only 'about ten' cases of this disease had been reported in the UK between 1950 and 1978 (NWC 1978: 49; 1982: 15). Despite a long series of reports about gains in efficiency and the inception of pollution abatement projects, towards the late 1980s the NWWA had to acknowledge the existence of 'a net deterioration in classified length' of polluted rivers. This was attributable chiefly to the admittedly intractable problems of diffuse pollution from agricultural sources and industrial sites (*1986/87*: 21; *1987/88*: 19).

While much of the bad effluent received by rivers can be traced to inadequately treated municipal sewage, biodegradable domestic wastes do not pose the same problems as even trace quantities of chemical substances associated with industrial and agricultural processes. The question arises as to whether the discharge consent approach deals adequately with such pollution. One objection is that it quite openly and legally authorises pollution. For example, discharge consents permit a chemical firm to dispose of 600 tonnes annually of unspecified oxygen-depleting chemicals, 137 tonnes of ammonia and 45 tonnes of chlorinated solvent into a river (Cowe 1991).

Significant quantities of trace, but often persistent and toxic, industrial wastes enter the aquatic environment. Both the national consent approach, as well as EC water directives to some extent, are based upon the assumption that the natural ecosystem can assimilate certain loadings of harmful substances with, therefore, a limited financial impact upon industrial polluters (Johnston *et al.* 1991). This approach led to British estuaries being favoured as attractive industrial sites, due to their perceived powers to assimilate and dispose of industrial effluent. As a result they developed highly complex and varied pollution problems. Existing environmental policies seek to regulate chemical discharges on the basis of lists of prescribed substances – the EC black and grey lists, and the UK red list. These lists exclude many hundreds of sometimes dangerous substances which are daily discharged into estuarine waters. For Johnston *et al.* (1991: 68) the only way such problems can be tackled is through a zero-discharge policy, which requires clean technologies to be introduced at source. Also, only in this way, they argue, will the problem of the mere transfer of contamination from one medium to another be avoided.

However desirable the objectives, there are doubts as to whether a zero-discharge approach represents a politically practical policy. In any case some notable successes in reducing pollution can be claimed by exponents of EC/EU environmental policy. Specifically, the British chemical industry responded positively to the passing of directives in the mid-1970s which sought to reduce mercury emissions. Although the industry included powerful lobbyists like ICI, BASF, Bayer, Hoechst and BP, it appeared to accept the inevitability of having to comply with the legislation and invested heavily in on-site clean technologies and pollution abatement at source (Guruswamy *et al.* 1983). By the early 1990s, there were significant reductions in mercury emissions from British industry entering the water environment (Cowe 1991).

Both an absolute zero-discharge policy and the existing EU standards/consents system possess elements of a command-and-control approach. Current thinking tends to favour a genuine implementation of the PPP principle. An expansion of the market attributes of environmental policy, whereby polluters bear all the costs of their actions, including damage to third parties, would achieve this. It would not help the problem of much pollution which is historical in origin, and the actual effect of current British policy is to fund environmental improvement through the (water) consumer pays principle. There are certainly no inexpensive ways of tackling land-based sources of diffuse pollution, which has frequently been dispersed throughout the environment.

The impact and responsibility of government

The advent of a business culture and productivity gains

At the outset the government did not tell the RWAs how to run their businesses save in one respect. Their operations were to be self-financing. The aim was to end cross-subsidisation between divisions. The rate-support grant was withdrawn and the RWAs had to be self-sufficient.

Nevertheless, at first a civic rather than a commercial culture prevailed within the RWAs. Quite apart from the delivery of sewerage services through agency arrangements, the majority of RWA board members were local authority nominees. Although local authority members were encouraged to regard themselves as part of new corporate teams, rather than elected representatives, for the first eight to nine years of their existence the RWAs were run with a strong council ethos, eager to provide a reasonable service with, allegedly, little attention to cost (Jones 1985).

Between 1973 and 1989 the municipal tradition in the water industry was gradually eroded. This process started with the 1973 reorganisation and became definitive with the 1983 Water Act, which removed the requirement for local authority representatives to be nominated as RWA members, despite – not surprisingly – strong opposition from the still local-government-dominated RWAs (NWWA *1980/81*: 6). The government claimed it was dissatisfied with the contribution of local authority nominees, and there is evidence that the conduct of the RWAs in this phase of their history did suffer from bureaucratic overindulgence. Operating costs and staff levels increased, total employment in the ten RWAs as a whole growing from 58,385 in March 1975 to 63,664 in March 1979, despite the scope for rationalisation with the introduction of new regional structures (NWC *1974/75, 1978/79*). Johnson (1986: 4.2 2) claimed that the efficiency of the industry suffered in its early years. Pitkethly (1990: 139), generally very critical of the Tory government's water policies, spoke of the pre-1983 RWAs in uncomplimentary terms, of the 'smug self-satisfaction' of their administrative style.

The extent to which top-heavy administrative structures and overstaffing did characterise the RWA in the 1970s is revealed, at least to some degree, by the nature and scale of managerial reorganisations which followed. The 1983 Act enabled the government to reduce the size of RWA boards, which had memberships of up to eighty, to between nine and fifteen members. After 1983 the NWWA reduced the number of divisions, each with their own managers, financial and administrative support staff, from eight to three (NWWA *1982/83*: 6; *1983/84*: 8). Under the stimulus of the new performance indicators introduced by the government, there were significant reductions in numbers employed even before 1983. In the industry as a whole staff levels fell by some thirty per cent between 1979 and 1984.

According to Jones (1985: 9–10), the 1980s witnessed the eradication of procedural weaknesses and changes in management culture. Since the 1970s, this new government-appointed RWA chairman stated: 'the whole management style, at least in Yorkshire ... has become much more commercially orientated with a greater sharpness of the professional management cutting edge'. For Pitkethly (1990: 141), the changes promoted by the government forced the transition from a technocratic culture to one of business efficiency. A new 'breed' of water industry chairpersons were given the job of 'sorting out the industry'. After 1983 the pressure to reduce costs and improve efficiency intensified. In Yorkshire operating costs between 1983 and 1985 fell by about £2 million in real terms and 6,500 fewer people were employed. In the Northumbria Water Authority the numbers employed fell by over fifty per cent between 1979 and 1986 (Johnson 1986: 4.2 2). Business profitability improved considerably after 1983. Lynk's (1993) study indicates that significant productivity gains were made by the RWAs in the 1980s under the stimulus of operating targets imposed by government.

'Performance aims' were given to the RWAs throughout the 1980s. They were tough financial targets for operating costs. Generally these were achieved through labour and other savings. Most RWAs were able to report significant falls in their ratios in the 1980s. They claimed that economies were made without harming levels of service delivered to their customers.

Although businesses became 'leaner' and efficiency gains were secured alongside the associated revolution in management culture, it is evident that the agenda driving such changes was quite narrow. To Parker and Derrick Sewell (1988: 764) the government's objective was to transform the industry from a public service to a business organisation ripe for privatisation. The obsession with driving down costs and meeting performance targets, often based on quite simplistic criteria, ignored how the environmental and other long-term objectives set in 1973 could be achieved.

Financial cuts

The water industry bore the brunt of the government's macroeconomic priorities, in the shape of the severe cuts in spending and borrowing imposed upon it. From the outset the government wanted the industry to reduce borrowing and increase the proportion of capital expenditure financed out of current surpluses. Just before reorganisation the water industry had financed eighty per cent of its capital investment through borrowing and only twenty per cent from internal sources. Even in the late 1970s, the proportion of capital spending financed out of revenue was fairly low at thirty-three per cent (NWC 1978). This was a viable system, given guaranteed income and extended debt repayment arrangements. It was thrown into disarray, however, by the inflationary conditions of the 1970s which led to the renewal cost of loans far exceeding the value of the debt which had just matured (Kinnersley 1994: 7).

The scope for generating surpluses so as to reduce dependence on borrowing was limited, however, for a number of reasons. There was a high element of fixed costs in this very capital-intensive industry, due to the operation of STWs and treatment works, and high interest payments. At first, forty-five per cent of the current spending of the RWAs was attributable to finance charges (depreciation plus interest payments), twenty-five per cent to labour costs and thirty per cent to other operational expenses. By 1974/5 the burden of finance charges had grown to forty-eight per cent (NWC *1975/76*: 13). No less than seventy-six per cent of the NWWA sewerage budget, for example, was accounted for by loan charges (Parker and Penning-Rowsell 1980: 123).

In such circumstances it was difficult to finance investment other than by borrowing, despite the government's wish for it to fall. By statute the RWAs were restricted to two sources of external finance, long-term fixed-interest loans through the National Loan Fund (NLF), or in foreign currency from overseas sources. Foreign borrowing was attractive to the water industry, NLF loans being more expensive than the money which private firms could raise in the capital market, and left the RWAs, even after insurance costs, with a small interest advantage. But the government severely curtailed the opportunity to use foreign capital markets (NWC *1978/79*: 15).

Faced with such constraints, as the NWC and the RWAs were at pains to point out, the only way the industry could finance much needed expenditure was by increasing charges above the RPI. But there were certainly pressures not to do this because of inflation worries. Some RWA members were influenced by the tradition of providing vital services as cheaply as possible. In the late 1970s the Price Commission exercised an influence over the level of RWA charges, which reinforced inhibitions against increasing rates faster than costs (YWA *1980*: 47). RWA managers later became determined to override such restraints and, with the NWC, warned of the need for a substantial increase in charges, perhaps by as much as twenty per cent above the rate of inflation, to reflect true costs and to assist the financing of vital projects (Kirby 1984: 98).

Throughout almost the entire history of the RWAs, however, spending in the water industry was influenced above all by the exigencies of Britain's macro-economic predicament. In pursuit of national objectives, or more truthfully in response to economic crises, the Treasury exercised strict controls over public-sector borrowing and spending, including that of the water industry. The first oil shock was beginning to exercise its severe stagflationary impact upon the British economy (Maddison 1982) at the time that the 1973/4 reorganisation of the water industry was being carried through. The latter, after briefly experiencing its peak historic levels of capital expenditure, was subject to the imposition of stringent cuts in spending, in common with other public-sector industries. Tighter controls over public spending were once again applied following the Labour government's agreement with the IMF in 1976. In the aftermath of the second oil shock and with the new administration determined to pursue its medium-term financial strategy,

renewed efforts were made, in the early 1980s, to reduce the volume of public
spending and its share of national income. There was, however, little sign that
current public expenditure was falling; on the contrary an upward bias remained.
Consequently, to achieve its spending aims, the government took the politically
'soft' option of trimming capital expenditure.

Of all the public sectors, the water industry suffered most from the financial
cuts of the 1970s and 1980s, much more seriously than, for example, education, the
next worst case. Between 1955/6 and 1973/4 water service capital expenditure
tripled in real terms (NWC *1976/77*: 16). The industry would never recapture the
early 1970s level of spending before privatisation. In 1979 the new Thatcher
government instructed the industry to reduce its planned investment plans for the
following year by 11.2 per cent. The NWC (*1978/79*: 14) winced, stating that the
industry would co-operate: 'But the paring down process of the last five years does
mean that the current programmes are "lean" rather than "fat" and therefore cuts
will penetrate into the essential tissue of what is needed.' There was, however, to
be no respite, cuts continuing to be imposed for several years, and capital spending only began to recover as privatisation approached. By the early 1980s capital
investment in water and sewerage had fallen by from between a quarter to a half of
what it had been in real terms some ten years earlier, depending on choice of criteria and dates (Simon 1986: 3–5; Kirby 1984: 98). The water industry's share of
total fixed capital formation between 1964 and 1987 fell from an all-time high of
1.27 per cent in 1971 to an all-time low of 0.61 per cent in 1984, before struggling
back to 0.73 per cent by 1987 (CSO 1964–88).

The tools employed by government as instruments of financial control were
performance aims and external financing limits (EFLs). Both could have perverse
effects. Performance ratios were designed to encourage more efficient management
in a monopoly industry, and were first published under a Labour government for
1978/9. They placed limits on the operating costs of selected aspects of RWA business, expressed in spending per head of population equivalent. They did have negative effects. For example, it was claimed that they reduced managerial freedom to
control charge levels. More seriously, the ability to meet such targets could not
always be interpreted as the result of achieving higher levels of efficiency. Among
the reasons for low levels of sewage spending by the NWWA and, therefore, it
being able to record one of the lowest sewage performance ratios in the country,
was the practice of discharging untreated sewage from the entire Merseyside
conurbation into an already appallingly polluted estuary. As the NWWA (*1979/80*:
1) concluded, 'this performance ratio cannot be regarded with unqualified satisfaction'.

Cash limits on external borrowing were introduced in 1976 by the Labour
government. The imposition of EFLs could have the effect of cutting into the
whole revenue budget, as well as into the capital programme, thus powerfully con-
straining staffing levels. Like the performance aims, they might be presented as a

tool to promote efficiency, but both, above all, were used to curb public expenditure. Also the EFLs could have perverse effects. Their application diffused fatalism, rather than ingenuity, claimed a former manager: if the RWA had a bad year and the EFL remained unchanged investment would be reduced; if there was a good year charges might be reduced. 'Risks and rewards were not assumed by the business – they were either absorbed by the PSBR or they were passed onto the customer in price effect', stated Harper (1992: 105).

Undoubtedly there was some special pleading in earlier managerial comments on the impact of government policy. Considerable scope for improving efficiency did exist. As well as noting anomalies, subsequently the RWAs were not adverse to claiming credit when they did meet performance targets, and to link this with improved practice. But the government's preferred instruments were crude, if powerful, tools. Lynk (1993: 107) notes that the RWAs achieved technical advances and productivity gains. But this was clearly not due to new investment: 'Degradation of service and under-investment were, in part, the response to the operating cost reduction targets imposed upon the RWAs during this period.' It appears that the government's methods forced out some fairly inherent inefficiencies, but generated few concrete gains. The financial harness imposed upon the RWAs also led to deteriorating performance at smaller, now unstaffed, STWs (Kinnersley 1988: 117–20), a worsening in the fabric of the infrastructure, and a decline in water quality. 'There is little doubt that the Water Authorities are now more efficient than previously', observed Parker and Derrick Sewell (1988: 777), who, however, concluded that the methods of achieving this had 'dire' consequences for the renewal and replacement of assets.

The responsibility of government

No suggestion is being made that the RWAs were pusillanimous pawns, incapable of influencing the world they operated in. They were in part responsible for poor liaison with local planning authorities and the poor design of sewage treatment arrangements. STW mismanagement contributed to bad effluent being discharged and hence caused pollution.

Yet government departments even more self-evidently had overarching responsibility for water policy and for the creation of a framework which would assist the RWAs to achieve objectives which had been agreed in 1973. Under the 1973 Water Act the RWAs were required to publish an annual plan which would identify areas of corporate priority for the next five years. The ambition of these early years is reflected in the fact that initially the DoE asked the RWAs to extend the plans to cover their whole range of activities over a twenty-year period. But, argue Parker and Penning-Rowsell (1980: 34–5), this whole planning exercise turned out to be a sham, partly because of the excessive length of the planning period, but mainly because the imposition of financial cuts left the RWAs with insufficient time to accommodate to lower spending levels.

Thus the impact of the government's actions was not just to limit capital spending on necessary infrastructural projects. In addition, the arbitrariness of its interventions played havoc with the planning and implementation of programmes. Civil engineers continually pressed on government the need for the adoption of a long-term approach to the industry's infrastructural crisis. But their lobbying proved futile, an engineers' planning group complaining of the government failures to develop any 'overall policy for capital investment' and to put in place any 'machinery for monitoring the effectiveness of that investment' (Speight 1986: 195). Government interventions often turned the RWAs' short-term aims into long-term hopes. At the outset many Authorities attached the highest priority to upgrading river quality. But it was of little avail to devote a very large share of their capital budgets to sewerage and sewage treatment improvements when their overall size was subsequently drastically reduced. The YWA, for example, published river quality objectives that identified improvements it hoped to achieve within eight years. Capital expenditure cuts had the effect of postponing their expected realisation for a further ten years (YWA *1981*: 14).

With the government allowing its short-termism to dictate the water industry's financial structure, it was inevitably enticed into certain compromises. Spending controls halted the modernisation of STWs and reduced the number capable of producing acceptable effluent and meeting consent conditions. To accommodate this, the temptation to modify consents was not resisted. By 1977/8 the NWC, with no misgiving or opposition from the DoE, was stage-managing reviews and adjusting consents to reflect the poor quality of effluent being produced. A similar tactic was employed a decade later when the DoE encouraged the RWAs to apply for relaxed consent conditions, having the effect, in the run-up to privatisation, of obfuscating the extent to which STWs were being operated illegally (Kinnersley 1994: 150–1). The national failure to improve river quality in the 1980s was basically a reflection of official priorities. Barty-King (1992: 174) observed that it was difficult for politicians to admit that they had failed to maintain the 'great Victorian legacy', but investment in underground water pipes and sewers had always been less politically attractive than roads, houses, schools and hospitals. Kinnersley (1994) pursues a very even-handed approach in his treatment of these issues, but affirms that the progressiveness demonstrated by the RAs in the 1960s was subsequently smothered by the effects of Whitehall economic policies.

Claims were made that despite expenditure cutbacks, advances in 'corporate planning' and a 'reordering of priorities' enabled efficiency gains to be made without consumer service standards suffering (NWC 1982: 81; NEDO 1986: 7). Certainly, under the influence of new financial disciplines, productivity and profitability trends in the 1980s looked quite favourable. In the short run customer services may have been maintained. But in the long run what was being resorted to was a process of asset depletion, leading to a deterioration of the industry's

environmental and physical capital. In this period, the long overdue task of reversing these trends had once again been postponed. On this occasion, however, the
final reckoning would not be long delayed.

According to Pitkethly (1990: 119) the changes imposed by the Thatcher
governments of the 1980s led to the institutional structure of water management
in England and Wales being transformed from 'a model for reorganisation elsewhere to a model of how a hostile government can undermine concepts of holistic
management'. This strong conclusion may require some qualification. There are
now doubts as to whether maximalist versions of holistic water management are
politically and practically feasible (Winpenny 1994). As has been seen, the 1973
model of integrated water management was over-ambitious in the way operational
and regulatory duties were combined in the same bodies. The chief causes of the
comparative failure of the RWAs lay less with regulatory defects, which certainly
existed. The main problem was the damaging and arbitrary effects of the government's financial policies.

The enduring gains achieved by the 1973 reform should not be overlooked.
The introduction of source-to-mouth management of river systems by vast new
regional bodies was a sweeping innovation and in difficult circumstances the RWAs
accomplished much. After 1989 the financial and regulatory framework was transformed out of all recognition. Yet, significantly, the basic regional and organisational structures governing water supply and sewage provided for by the 1973
measure were retained largely intact.

6

Since 1989: the privatised water industry

The immediate prospects of the industry are complex and generate controversy but the objectives of this chapter are simple. They are, first, to provide a background to the decision to privatise the water industry in 1989, second, to discuss the changes created by the Act of that year and, third, to assess the impact of this latest reorganisation upon the water industry's ability to foster environmental improvement and satisfy consumers' needs. Attention will focus on the first five years of the privatised industry. It would be perilous to attempt to incorporate more recent events into a historical study of water. However, developments in 1995, such as the drought, have been so serious that they could not be entirely ignored and, therefore, some observations upon them have been included in a postscript.

The background to privatisation

The decision to privatise the water industry was largely a political one determined by the broad aims of the Thatcher administration. However, the form and the timing of the 1989 reform were also influenced by growing concerns about the deterioration of the natural environment during the 1980s and by national obligations to which the government had committed itself by agreeing to EC directives.

The politicisation of the environment

During the 1980s casual attitudes about tap-water quality and public confidence that the authorities, scientists and engineers would together guarantee high standards (Hamlin 1990: 1) became a thing of the past. Among the causes of this change was the advent of the more informed, questioning consumer. Apart from the impact of a number of scares like the case of aluminium poisoning following an accident at a treatment works near Camelford, Cornwall in 1988, more general worries about the environment created a background of unease over water quality. More specifically, agreement on the EC water directives exposed the extent to which British waters were failing to meet quality standards. This helped to increase worries about the potential health hazards associated with drinking and bathing

SINCE 1989   **163**

waters. A number of disquieting reports about drinking-water quality led the
public to turn increasingly to bottled water. By the early 1990s sales of bottled
water were growing rapidly, although by now tap-water was improving in quality.
(For detailed accounts of the disturbing potential health risks presented by contaminated water supplies, see Rose 1991; Maclean 1991.)

The origins of the greater concern about the environment, however, predate
these more specific consumer fears. Global resource shocks in the 1970s lifted the
environment on to the political agenda. During the 1980s the possibility that the
degradation of the environment might provoke serious climatic changes became
widely discussed. Evidence of the greater significance attached to environmental
problems was widespread and included the good showing of green parties at the
European parliamentary elections in 1989. It was also demonstrated in the huge
expansion in the membership of voluntary bodies with an environmental dimension. British membership of eight such organisations increased from half a million
in 1971 to 1.8 million in 1981 and almost four million in 1991. The impressive
growth of older conservation bodies like the RSPB (98,000 to 844,000 over the
twenty years) was more than matched by the dynamism of new groups like Friends
of the Earth, the British membership of which increased from 30,000 in 1981 to
372,000 in 1991 (Kinnersley 1994: 86).

Initially the politicisation of the environment did not appear to have a great
impact upon the conduct of public policy. Until the mid-1980s there appeared to
be an official tendency to underemphasise and misunderstand environmental
issues (see Rose 1991 for a full exposure of the 'great British pollution scandal').
For example, despite clear evidence that Scandinavian habitats were suffering
detrimental consequences from acid rain, there was official resistance to the idea
that a link might exist between transboundary emissions and environmental
degradation. It has even been claimed (Bidwell 1992: 18) that, 'Up until 1985 this
country had no real environment policy, where "environment policy" indicates a
clear strategy for clean-up and environmental protection.' For a whole variety of
reasons, however, as signified in the greening of Mrs Thatcher, towards the end of
the decade the political establishment began to attach far greater importance to
environmental problems. Environmental information was becoming more readily
available to the public, who became more aware and concerned about even quite
technical problems like sludge disposal (Kuchenrither and Gay 1994: 376). As
Barty-King commented (1992: 174), Victorian outfalls to the sea, for example,
which in their day were seen as an advance in public health and amenity, are now
no longer viewed as acceptable in a modern society. Reflecting such shifts in the
politics of the environment, since 1989 UK environmental policy has, in fact,
become much tougher. For example, the Water Industry Act of 1991 for the first
time made the supply of water which is unfit for human consumption, a criminal
offence (Gray 1994: 30). By contrast with the recent past, openness and implementation have become salient themes of UK environment policy.

European environmental legislation

Informed analysis concludes that EC/EU water legislation has exercised a beneficial impact upon the development of UK environmental policy (Howarth 1992: 120; Kinnersley 1994: 167). The history of the interactions between the British water industry, the water directives and government interpretations of the most expedient posture to adopt towards European environmental commitments is complex. Ideally it deserves more detailed discussion than can be afforded at this stage of this study. Comment will be limited to an observation of the manner in which the environmental directives reinforced the momentum behind the decision to privatise the water industry in England and Wales.

To simplify, there are broadly three types of water directives. First, legislation details quality objectives for specified categories of water, including bathing, drinking and shellfish waters and inland fisheries. Second, directives have been adopted with the aim of controlling the emission of dangerous substances into the aquatic environment. The intention is to eventually eliminate entirely the discharge of the most dangerous, 'black-list' substances, and to significantly reduce the discharge of grey-list substances. Third, there are directives which aim to protect the water environment against more generalised pollution risks. This includes the urban wastewater directive. Adopted in 1991, its effect will be to require the virtual phasing out of the widely practised discharge of raw sewage into the sea from anything other than very small coastal towns, and to end the dumping into the sea of sewage sludge produced by STWs.

The first water directives were adopted in the mid-1970s. Since then they have been progressively refined and added to. For a long time, by way of reception to this legislation, the tendency of the water industry and the Authorities in the UK was to underestimate and misunderstand the nature of the commitment which had been entered into when the British government agreed to the directives. For example, the NWC (1982: 9) claimed that: 'For inland waters ... so far as can be seen the effects will not be marked in this country which is well advanced in its general performance as far as water standards are concerned and has a stronger, more compact and flexible system of water administration than any other member of the Community.' A view also prevailed that somehow the directives would not fully apply in the UK. With respect to the bathing-water directive, the NWWA (1979/80: 80) genuinely did not believe that there would be any bathing beaches designated in their region which included, of course, the country's biggest coastal resorts. At the outset the British government did indeed designate only twenty-seven bathing beaches, excluding Blackpool and Brighton, in contrast to the 3,470 designated in France. This highlighted Britain's pragmatic approach to what was involved under EC environmental law.

The relaxed attitude towards the directives extended into the 1980s, the NWWA (1984/85: 15) claiming that most of the region's potable supplies easily complied with the minimum standards, and that, furthermore, 'on surface water abstractions, on discharges to groundwater, on bathing waters and on shellfish waters', the directives 'had little effect during the year'. But this confidence was followed a year later by the admission that nearly eighteen per cent of the Authority's drinking water sources did not comply with the necessary standards, especially in relation to concentrations of lead, aluminium and manganese.

Failure to take steps to apply the directives was by no means peculiar to Britain, and misconceptions about the obligations which they entailed derived from a number of factors. They included the unique nature of Britain's geography, the scope which existed for negotiating delays through derogation procedures, and the fact that it was left to each member state to decide on the details of how the directives should be implemented in practice. The result was that, as the dates for compliance approached, British waters often fell below the prescribed standards, especially for bathing and, above all, for drinking waters.

The effect of governments' misinterpretations of the nature of their EC environmental obligations was, perhaps, surprising. Coinciding with increased public concerns about the environment, it was actually to fuel fears over water quality. A 1980 agreement had specified rigorous standards for water intended for human consumption. Limits were set for forty-two parameters which, as well as prescribing limits for the penetration of chemical substances, laid down criteria for aesthetic quality, taste and colour. Little attention had been paid in the past to such standards for drinking water in the UK, but few practical steps were now taken to ensure compliance. Failure to reduce the level of nitrates and other pollutants in drinking water by 1985 under the terms of the 1980 agreement, the threat of EC court action against the British government, and the latter's attempt to get the deadline extended to 1995, all served to greatly publicise the whole question of water quality. All this was good copy for the press, and even in the more serious broadsheets reporting on such issues reached almost hysteria pitch – one report suggested that much of the population was threatened by poisoning from drinking tap water. Concerns over water quality throughout Europe were now expressed in many ways, such as a great increase in the number of complaints received by the European Commission over the application of the environmental directives, and the greater profile and militancy displayed by green activism on water issues.

Meanwhile the general problem throughout the Community of non-compliance led the European Commission to promote implementation as a central theme of the fourth Environmental Action Programme (1987–92). It became more prepared to instigate proceedings against member states; even if cases did not go all the way to the European Court of Justice, this could be fairly effective. The threat of proceedings, for example, led the UK government to designate an additional 362 bathing areas under the bathing-water directive, including thirty in the North-West. All these factors led to non-compliance with EC environmental law being recognised as a less viable option for the British and other governments by the late 1980s.

This realisation coincided with the emergence of more positive and proactive approaches to environmental protection at a time when the concept of sustainability was becoming increasingly influential. The green credentials of the UK government were underlined by its publication of its environmental strategy in *This Common Inheritance* in 1990. More concrete steps were also taken. To reinforce the dangerous substances water directives, the UK government adopted a 'red list' to supplement the grey and black lists. The government aimed to curtail the input of red-list substances into the North Sea by fifty per cent by 1995. This formed part of a wider agreement by countries bordering the North Sea to reduce marine pollution. The British government also decided to extend the target of fifty per cent pollution reductions by 1995 to all UK coastal waters.

The UK government would still experience difficulties over the environmental directives and, as it was again taken to court by the European Commission over non-compliance, an increasingly impatient attitude developed in the early 1990s. Some felt that the cost of implementing the directives was out of all proportion to the benefits. A view also emerged that there might, after all, be an alternative to compliance, namely renegotiation. These, however, are issues which do not bear on the impact of the directives upon water privatisation.

An important effect of the privatisation of the water industry was that, notwithstanding growing misgivings about the cost of implementing the water directives, the transfer of control out of public ownership did make it easier for the British government to accede to extensions to EU environmental law. The additional capital expenditure which this would involve would not have to be financed by the State. To the water industry's chagrin, for example, only one year after privatisation a fresh wave of initiatives on EU water legislation was announced by the Secretary of State for the Environment.

An example of the seeming paradox of the Conservative administration's disquiet about 'Brussels's interference' in national affairs, yet its agreement to tough new EU rules, was the urban wastewater directive. The UK water industry had been strongly opposed to this proposal. The problems which a ban on the dumping of sludge at sea would create for the UK arose from the fact that this country had made good progress in replacing the practice of discharging raw effluent into neighbouring water channels by preliminary sewage treatment. By 1992 the proportion of the British population served by sewerage networks was ninety-six per cent, compared to an EU average of sixty per cent. Consequently, however, a great deal of STW by-product, sludge, had to be disposed of. Despite these problems, partially shared by other member states, agreement on the urban wastewater directive was reached in 1991. Eventually it was agreed that implementation should be achieved by 1998. The cost of modernising disposal works to ensure compliance is enormous throughout the EU. Estimates of the required capital expenditure for the UK have varied from £5 billion to £14 billion.

To conclude this discussion on the impact of the water directives, it is necessary to return a few years to the time when the view prevailed that there were no practical long-term alternatives to compliance. One of the most important effects of this conclusion was a considerable increase in the attractiveness of water privat-isation to the Conservative government. This was an administration committed, above all, to driving down the scale of public ownership and expenditure. By the late 1980s it was realised that an investment programme approaching £24 billion would have to be undertaken to raise the quality of UK waters to required EU stan-dards, and the public also desired an improvement in the water environment. Demonstrably, much of the huge investment was to meet the backlog in infra-structure maintenance, rather than to fulfil new EU requirements (Maclean 1991: 5; Carney 1992: 7); but the directives imparted an imperative quality to the expen-diture, which was previously lacking. Soon estimates of the required investment increased to £30 billion. The government would not tolerate capital expenditures on this scale being financed through the public sector. Sir David Trippier, Minister in charge of the water industry after privatisation, agreed that such sums 'would never have been extracted out of the Treasury' (quoted in Barty-King 1992: 175). Or, as Kenneth Baker (1990) put it, 'No one would have expected as a nationalised industry the water authorities would ever have invested so much.' Privatisation provided a framework, acceptable to the government and the City, which allowed a massive increase in capital investment in the water industry to take place.

The decision to privatise

In April 1985 the DoE issued a discussion paper on water privatisation. It set out the general objectives of the government's privatisation programme. They dis-played parallels with the motives for privatisation as identified by Kay and Thompson (1986):

Objectives of the privatisation programme of the 1980s

Kay and Thompson (1986)	*Department of the Environment (1985)*
1. Improve economic performance;	1. Promote the competition and enterprise;
2. obtain revenue from the sale;	
3. discipline trade unions;	2. reduce the size of the public sector;
4. promote popular capitalism;	
5. resolve management problems between state and nationalised industries.	3. involve staff in companies;
	4. spread share ownership;
	5. free enterprise from state con-trols.

With respect to the specific advantages of water privatisation, the DoE was rather vague, other than referring to the 'many benefits' it would bring. In fact, most of the objectives of the Thatcher privatisation drive do not account for the 1989 water reform. The form it took was not the most effective way of promoting enterprise and competition; it did not raise revenue, the costs of the privatisation launch exceeding the proceeds accruing to government; the notion that it was especially designed to promote popular capitalism is discredited; and the labour relations dimension was unimportant. There were, however, two factors which strongly recommended water privatisation to the Conservative government. The fifth element noted above was certainly very important: privatisation would help to resolve the persistent problems of relating to finance and government–industry relationships. Secondly, and critically, towards the end of the twentieth century the urgent need to redress the consequences of generations of neglect and under-investment was finally recognised. The interacting influences of public concern and EU obligations drew the government to the solution of privatisation, as described above.

It was, however, initially the difficult state of RWA–government relationships which led the latter to consider going beyond the promotion of changes in management culture, which had hitherto informed its policy on the water industry. In the early 1980s the government and RWA leaders fell out over the price increases above the inflation rate which, the latter felt, were being forced through to bolster government revenue. The chairman of Thames Water charged the government of using the industry as a tax collector and it was he who proposed that the conflict over charges might be resolved by a change of ownership. This was the origin of the privatisation of water (Barty-King 1992: 173).

Once the decision had been made to transfer the responsibilities for providing water services to the private sector, the question arose as to what model of regulatory control and private ownership would be chosen for the industry. Millward (1989: 189) indicates that a number of motives influenced water privatisation and suggests that greater efficiency was a central concern. Yet his analysis and that of others shows that a mere change of ownership and the creation of uncontested regional monopolies, the solution adopted by the government, do little to promote cost-effectiveness and efficiency.

There are, of course, difficulties with introducing competition in a natural monopoly industry. Nevertheless, a number of options could be explored. While *regionalisation* confers market power upon privatised utilities, it is a method which provides comparative information about performance. This can help the regulator to control monopolistic practices. Regionalisation permits *yardstick competition* to be introduced. Under this arrangement the regulator fixes prices based on costs across the country as a whole, which provides an incentive to reduce costs below this level to achieve bigger profits. Furthermore, the threat of takeover is not removed – another incentive to manage assets efficiently.

The Conservative administration did indeed incorporate strong elements of regionalisation and yardstick, or at least comparative, competition into the 1989 water privatisation. There are, however, particular difficulties in applying comparative competition in the water industry, such as the different geographical and hydrological circumstances of each region and the varying condition of the inherited assets of each company (Wright 1992). It is also especially difficult to devise a plausible form of comparative competition in the provision of the waste disposal services executed by the companies, and to create such competition in the management of long-term assets (Kinnersley 1985: 5).

There was, however, a possible solution to these problems, namely *franchising*, which creates competition for, rather than in, the market. The right to supply water and sewerage services, generally on behalf of local or regional government, is auctioned and awarded to the most competitive bidder. Contracts tend to last from twelve to thirty years, and provide the means for regulating environmental standards and the quality of customer service. There are a number of potential difficulties with franchising, such as the transfer of assets at the end of the contract, and the choice of a length of contract which is long enough to provide reasonable security for the company but not so long as to encourage complacency. However, worldwide experience, particularly from France, indicates that flexible employment of franchising can reduce such difficulties to tolerable proportions and encourage the emergence of highly competitive, private-enterprise providers of utility services. Globally, it tends to be the preferred approach to water privatisation (Hassan *et al.* 1996).

In the UK it was decided to sell the RWAs to private investors almost intact as monopoly suppliers, with minimal enterprise or managerial reorganisation. The decision to opt for the asset-sale formula can be attributed to a number of factors. The viability of franchising was, perhaps, less evident in 1985 than it is today. The preference for a non-competitive market structure can be explained by the lack of time to develop an alternative, franchising mechanism, probable opposition from managers, and the reluctance of capital markets to accept profit-threatening competition, which might jeopardise the success of the flotation of the new companies' shares on the stock market. As early as 1985 Kinnersley detected franchising was not favoured officially. 'Possibly it is because it would give less scope for a successful flotation bringing in cash to the Treasury', he surmised (1985: 7). Franchising might also involve the survival of a public, even municipal, role in the water industry, which was, to reiterate, something a Conservative government had difficulty in countenancing.

Because the reform would create private monopolies with great market power, it was very important that the regulatory system should be devised with great care so as to, first, ensure that environmental protection responsibilities would be discharged effectively and that, second, the abuse of monopoly advantage should be prevented. At first it was assumed that the new companies would, as 'privatised authorities', retain the environmental functions of the RWAs. Managers felt it would be 'insulting' to strip the new bodies of their regulatory functions ('Regulatory aspects', *European Water and Sewage*, January 1987: 30). Also, to maintain integrated management, it was believed that the privatised companies should retain regulatory duties. The DoE (1986), furthermore, anticipated that external regulatory control would be 'simple, clearly justifiable, affordable'.

Kinnersley (1994) provides an informed account of the tortuous development of the privatisation proposal. In a generous critique of Nicholas Ridley's contribution to the process of reform, Kinnersley explains how and why a radical departure from the cosy solutions originally being entertained were insisted upon by the Secretary of the State for Environment; Ridley required that regulatory, environmental responsibilities should be conferred upon substantial new bodies in the public sector. It was inherently unsatisfactory to confer both regulatory and operational functions on the same body, as described in Chapter 5, and this was clearly understood by Ridley. The first set of proposals was withdrawn, to be replaced in July 1987 with a solution which was finally adopted: the RWAs were to be converted into water service companies (WSCs), providing water supply and wastewater treatment services, with other river-basin and regulatory duties, including environmental and consumer protection, conferred on new statutory bodies, the National Rivers Authority (NRA) and The Office of Water Services (Ofwat). There remained the question of the mechanism for Ofwat to employ so as to prevent the companies' abuse of monopoly power. The government opted for the price-capping formula, rather than the more traditional form of dividend limitation.

From the government's perspective the final form of the privatisation settlement was determined by powerful factors, which have been described above. But some constraints were self-imposed. From a neutral standpoint there was no particular necessity in having to reject franchising or deciding not to inject an element of comparative competition into a water industry still consisting primarily of RWAs. The determination that any large-scale investment should take place outside the public sector and that no vestige of municipalism should survive led, however, logically to the eventual solution. This involved the creation of powerful private monopolists and an elaborate regulatory system. Even if the form of the settlement was ideologically driven, it did display considerable ingenuity, and, especially in the environmental protection arrangements, contained elements that were a considerable improvement over past practice. It may be claimed that the current regulatory system is one of the toughest in the world. It was almost unavoidable, however, that the 1989 settlement, given its other features, including the creation of uncontested private monopolies, should incorporate the establishment of a tough regulatory regime. If the regulatory arrangements malfunction, the political, economic and environmental costs could be obvious and considerable. It is not surprising that the British privatisation model, incorporating complexity and risk, has few imitators.

Initially there was widespread opposition to the privatisation proposal, not just from the political opposition and the trade union and green movements. The Board of NWWA (*1984/85*) unanimously put forward a cogent argument for RWAs remaining in the public sector, on account of their unusual combination of natural monopoly, public health, regulatory and environmental protection characteristics. The NWWA doubted that 'enterprise' would be freed and competition encouraged by privatisation. While others remained sceptical to the last, decisively the industry's senior management was won round to private ownership. Kay and Thompson (1986) emphasise that a clear theme to emerge in the political history of privatisation was that by far the most effective and influential of the interest groups was the senior management of the industries in question.

Why were the industry's leading managers converted to privatisation, especially once it seemed a little less attractive after the separation of the regulatory role had been decided upon by 1987? The industry's official historian observed that privatisation always seemed more appealing to those in the industry, 'who knew what they were doing than to the industry's customers who had always pulled the chain and turned the tap without ever worrying where the water went or came from' (Barty-King 1992: 179). The prospect of being freed from irksome Treasury controls and the unpredictable effects of government interference was certainly attractive. But also appealing was that the government's solution would provide new managerial freedoms with little change in organisational structure or a move to a more competitive environment. Kinnersley (1985: 4) suggested that the main objective for changed ownership for the RWAs was an argument for the status quo.

A variety of RWA and industry spokespersons came round strongly in favour of privatisation in the course of the 1980s. Escape from the conflict of commercial and social objectives associated with the management of nationalised industries and advantages for consumers were among the envisaged benefits (Jones 1985; Bellak 1988; Brindley 1993). The chairman of one RWA believed customers would gain from tax changes and the conversion of debt to equity, which would enable the privatised companies to pay less on dividends than on debt interest (cited by Halsall 1989).

However, the industry's leaders may have had occasion to reflect upon events as the envisaged golden era approached. First, many observers were bemused by the purpose of a costly publicity campaign, commissioned by the RWAs, extolling the industry's high-tech achievements. Second, if the campaign's objective was to improve the image of the industry on the eve of privatisation, this was not helped by the effects of the severe drought of 1989. Following the public's experience of supply difficulties, the RWA chairpersons complained of 'an unprecedented campaign of vilification by opposition parties and environmental groups'; the RWAs were pilloried for ignoring warnings about water shortages and for over-concentrating on privatisation at the expense of the consumer (Renton 1989: 55). While there was a great deal of confused thinking in the criticism of the industry in the lead-up to privatisation, these events showed that the industry still had a major task on its hand in improving its public image.

The Water Act of 1989

The settlement of 1989

Among the main ingredients of the water reform of 1989 were the following:

1   There was a package of financial elements, discussed further below. The chief way that the modernisation of the industry would be financed was by allowing the WSCs to increase the prices of services supplied to the consumer above the rate of inflation, through the RPI+K formula. The K factor – how much companies could increase charges above the retail price index (RPI) – was to be controlled and monitored by Ofwat.

2   Efficiency was to be promoted. This was to be partly encouraged by the application of the pricing formula, which would encourage companies to improve performance, now that they would 'own' their profits. In addition, Ofwat was given specific duties in this field – it would promote efficiency through the application of a form of yardstick competition.

3   The industry's operational and regulatory activities were clearly separated. The RWAs' pollution control, resource conservation and river management duties were assigned to the NRA. Complementing the economic regulation executed by Ofwat and the environmental protection responsibilities of the NRA were the additional tasks performed by Her Majesty's Inspectorate of Pollution (HMIP) and the Drinking Water Inspectorate (DWI).

4   Virtually all other functions performed within the water industry, principally the delivery of water and wastewater services, were vested in the new WSCs formed out of the RWAs.

5   The statutory water supply-only companies (WOCs) were to be subject to the same regulatory supervision as the ten WSCs. The Act permitted them to convert to plcs if they wished.

To ensure the successful flotation of the new WSCs' shares on the stock market, it was necessary, particularly given the cost of improving water quality to EU standards, to add sweeteners to the 1989 settlement. The overall financial package included the following elements:

1   Under the RPI+K formula the water companies would be able to raise prices by an estimated average of 13.5 per cent over ten years.

2   The water industry's NLF debt of £5.2 billion was written off.

3   The industry was to receive a further cash injection, or 'green dowry', of £1.5 billion from the government.

4   Tax allowances of £7.7 billion were granted to the new companies.

5   A ten-year capital spending programme for each new company was outlined and approved by Ofwat.

Although an industry with limited potential for growth, guaranteed price increases above the rate of inflation ensured that resources required for its modernisation would be generated in the future. These conditions ensured that the share flotation in November 1989 was a success. In fact there was a massive oversubscription to the shares. Helm (1993) has likened the privatisation settlement to an 'investment contract' between the industry's management and shareholders on the one hand, and customers and society on the other. The £30 billion investment programme to be carried out by the year 2000 stood comparison with only a small handful of national projects, such as the Channel Tunnel.

Initially, this writer was impressed by the changes introduced by the 1989 reform. The means had been provided to finance a long overdue improvement in water quality. Potentially powerful new regulatory watchdogs had been created to encourage business efficiency, protect customers and promote environmental improvements.

The National Rivers Authority

The NRA was set up as an independent statutory body in September 1989 by the Water Act of that year. Its establishment was an innovatory moment in the history of water, breaking new ground particularly in relation to the industry's relationship with the State. It was easily the largest of the regulatory bodies with aquatic responsibilities, its staff of some 8,000 contrasting with Ofwat's 132 (WSA 1992). The NRA was assigned extensive and detailed duties with respect to river-basin management (including matters such as land drainage, flood defence and recreation), water conservation, pollution prevention and water quality. These responsibilities were allocated to a public-sector body, quite independent of the new WSCs. Yet the benefits of integrated management were essentially preserved under the new regime. The NRA was, in fact, largely formed from the parts of the RWAs which were concerned with river-basin functions. With specific powers to regulate river basins and license abstractions from any source, the regional divisions of the NRA evoke, but in a more muscular form, the RAs of the 1960s. Kinnersley (1994: 206) notes that as well as being an effective river-basin agency at a national level, the NRA devotes serious efforts to regional work and liaison with local interests.

While it engaged actively with its resource management and conservation duties, the NRA soon made the protection of the 'controlled waters' of rivers, lakes, reservoirs, aquifers and coastal waters to a distance of three miles, its first task. After decades of concealment and consent modification had brought it into disrepute, the NRA strove to raise the whole consent discharge system on to a level which would command respect (Kinnersley 1994: 206).

Water management has improved considerably since 1989, not only because of the creation of the NRA, but also because national policy aims with regard to water quality and the elimination of serious river pollution became much more precise and public than before. Under the Act the government was empowered, for the first time, to set statutory water-quality objectives (SWQOs) as a means of formalising the achievement of improvements. This measure, together with the

Water Act of 1991, enabled the Secretary of State for the Environment to prescribe a water classification scheme, which is based on the condition of the water, the uses to which it is put, BOD and other scientific criteria. These considerations, and also obligations under EU directives, are incorporated into the SWQOs. The NRA had a dual role in this process. First, it advised the Secretary of State and published SWQOs proposals, taking into account all the above considerations. Second, it was its duty to exercise its pollution prevention powers in order to secure the achievement of water-quality objectives which are set.

In addition, as noted above, the NRA had wide-ranging responsibilities to manage resources within catchments, and to ensure sources were adequate to the demands placed upon them. To fulfil such obligations the NRA took steps to replenish rivers suffering from reduced flows by pumping water from adjacent aquifers. Such measures, however, could threaten underground water levels and the existence of farm ponds. Flood prevention, the impounding of streams and authorising abstractions from rivers were, also, all potentially important aspects of the NRA's work, but equally all could negatively effect river quality and river levels. The NRA had, therefore, to carefully pursue a co-ordinated approach in its planning, regulatory and operational activities, to recognise the interactive nature of river systems and to balance the possible conflicts of interest among water users (Davies 1992; Pearce 1992; RCEP 1992: 161–2).

At the risk of simplifying, yet without wishing to labour the point, it could be said that the NRA's adoption of catchment management planning (CMP) illustrated and represented the agency's proactive approach to the resolution of a wide range of problems inherent in water management. For Gardiner and Cole (1992: 401): 'The fundamental aim of river catchment planning is to conserve, enhance, and, where appropriate, restore the total river environment through effective land and resource planning across the total catchment. As such, it can be regarded as the taproot of sustainable development.' CMP seeks to integrate policies in all aspects of river management within catchments, including the uses of surface and underground water and also other land uses. Through this approach the NRA endeavoured to address the timeless issue of the need to accommodate conflicting interests among water users. For example, the preparation and execution of the NRA's catchment plan for the River Lee in London involved numerous local agencies (Reid 1995). The integration of policies in all aspects of river management is also illustrated in the NRA–Thames region's much admired approach to the carrying out of its flood defence, land drainage and other environmental functions within the Thames basin (Newson 1992a: 273).

Some early critics of the NRA were sceptical as to whether the agency would operate effectively and independently of government. With the benefit of some years' experience one would not wish to argue with Haddon's view (1994: 11) of the NRA as 'arguably one of the most successful environmental agencies in Europe'. It was its autonomy, and particularly its active enforcement policy, which made the NRA so significant in the history of water. By July 1994 it had initiated 1,800 successful prosecutions against polluters. The complaints that the NRA pitched its quality requirements too high and overemphasised its environmental improvement role (Carney 1992) simply reflected the shock felt by some in the water industry at having to face an apparently all-powerful regulator pursuing a vigorous enforcement policy. Its active policy made an impact. Before 1989 industrialists considered it quite adequate to seek compliance with discharge consents ninety-five per cent of the time. Since the inception of the NRA, apparently, aims have been altered and industry realises it must endeavour to achieve no less than full compliance (Cowe 1991).

There were, nevertheless, some concerns, mainly over the future of the NRA and the policies associated with it. First, there has been lack of progress in implementing the PPP. The 1989 Water Act permitted the NRA to introduce charges for discharge consents, which it did after three years. These, however, do not impose costs upon dischargers which bear any resemblance to the external pollution costs which they caused; they merely cover the expense of administering the discharge consent system. The Tory government had a general presumption in favour of economic instruments. But until very recently it hardly promoted their implementation with any vigour. Official inertia, interdepartmental differences and resistance from business interests may account for this failure (Kinnersley 1994). Second, while the NRA actively advocates water demand management, progress by WSCs in introducing its most potent, market-based tool, domestic metering has been very slow. Finally, much of the positive impact of the NRA could be attributed to its autonomous status – in fact, to its imperviousness to 'capture' by politicians – and to the forthright, open policies championed by its chairman, Lord Crickhowell. As the separate identity and also, most probably, the leadership provided by Crickhowell, would not continue after the merger with the Environmental Protection Agency, there were fears that the work it had performed would not be so resolutely pursued in the future.

Ofwat

Ofwat was conceived as a substitute for competition and as a means of protecting consumers. Ofwat determines and monitors the pricing of services supplied to water consumers under the RPI+K formula. The intention was that the modernisation of the water industry should be financed internally and, therefore, Ofwat's job is to ensure that the companies carry out the appropriate capital expenditure and pricing decisions in line with their allotted K factors.

A major task of Ofwat is to promote efficiency and competition. Ofwat exercises leverage through the regulation of water charges; there is no control over profits as such. However as, in contrast to the situation before 1989, companies now 'own' their profits, and as in principle the K factor is set for long periods, there is an incentive to choose the most cost-effective way of carrying out new works. This is one reason why, despite the regulatory rigour, the 1989 settlement is so popular with the water industry – it now 'keeps' its efficiency gains.

That the companies own their profits does not of itself necessarily promote efficiency. Consequently Ofwat places store by yardstick competition. The application of yardstick competition is pursued through the preparation of comparative cost information in connection with the completion of asset management plans (AMPs). Established under the 1989 measure, these consist of capital expenditure plans drawn up by each company over a five- to ten-year period. The data they supply are utilised for the determination of individual companies' K factors, and provide information which helps Ofwat to determine how well companies are being managed.

There are a number of difficulties with the application of yardstick competition in the water industry previously alluded to, including asymmetry between companies regarding their local geography and the condition of inherited assets. Recognising such problems, Ofwat has investigated other ways of fulfilling its remit of promoting competition. During 1995 it explored the possibility of seeking legislation to force 'common carriage' arrangements upon companies, particularly for domestic customers. Under this companies would have to carry another undertaking's water, which household metering would help to make more technically feasible. The potential impact of competition was revealed in Croydon when it was discovered that due to the peculiarity of local circumstances the WSC could compete for customers normally served by the local statutory company. The possibility of competition led the latter to reduce their water bills by twenty per cent over a four-year period ('Croydon leads the way', *WB*, 23 June 1995: 5). Although the scope for introducing common carriage appears limited in the medium-term, the government now appears genuinely interested in promoting competition. In April 1996 it published consultation proposals, which were designed to encourage discussion on ways of introducing common carriage and other methods of increasing choice among users of both water and wastewater services.

Returning to the practical difficulties in applying yardstick competition, while the setting of long-term targets and K factors would be an appropriate way of promoting efficiency in the water industry where many projects are long-term in character (Brindley 1993), in fact between 1989 and 1994 revisions to Ks became virtually an annual exercise. As Helm and Rajah (1994: 74) observe, Ofwat's intervention in the pricing and investment decisions of the industry is provided for in the Interim Determination Mechanism, which allows for adjustments to be made to the K factor on account of external shocks. Having made exceptional profits due to an unexpected fall in construction costs, during 1992 Ofwat's intervention led the majority of the companies to 'voluntarily' agree to raise their prices by less than the levels permitted by the pricing formula. The mechanism also allows for prices to be raised to accommodate unexpected increases in costs arising, for example,

Table 6.1 *Water industry pricing limits for 1995/6 to 2004/5*
(% increases p.a.)

		Weighted average for		Average over ten years
	1995/96	1996/7–1999/00	2000/1–2004/5	
WSCs	1.5	1.5	0.6	1.0
WOCs	0.6	0.6	−1.3	−0.4
Industry	1.4	1.4	0.4	0.4

Source: WSA 1994: 33.

from new EU requirements. South West Water, undertaking major coastal improvement schemes in order to fulfil the bathing water directive, benefited from this concession. The uncertainty generated by regular renegotiations of Ks arguably evokes some of the less satisfactory aspects of the pre-1989 regime. Helm and Rajah (1994: 89–90) are sceptical whether this will diminish in the future, due to the characteristics of the system and the likelihood of frequent shocks in a real-world situation.

Over the first five years of privatisation the average K factor permitted companies to raise prices by an average of 4.5 per cent above the inflation rate. It enabled companies not only to make substantial profits but also to massively increase capital expenditure; a total investment of £15 billion was carried out between 1989 and 1994. The periodic review of the K factor was brought forward from 1999 to 1994. The companies' second development plans, AMP2s, were delivered to Ofwat during the spring of 1994 and were intended to provide information to assist in the determination of the second K factor. The outcome of the award is summarised in Table 6.1.

The second determination of K, which permits an average increase in water prices up to the end of the century of 1.5 per cent above the rate of inflation, received mixed reviews. It was met with some relief by the water industry. It had been anticipated that when Ofwat published its draft K factors, the figure would have been closer to zero than to two: this would have been a virtual price-cap, showing Ofwat resolute in its mission to protect consumers, as opposed to shareholders. Some consumer groups were also satisfied with the outcome. But some environmentalist response was little short of outraged, with the claim that consumers and the environment would continue to be 'ripped off to boost water company profits and shareholder dividends' (cited in Beavis 1994).

Analysis of the details of the Interim Review of 1994 suggests that a tougher regime was being imposed on the water industry although, admittedly, much less than this would have been very difficult to justify. The review provided for capital investment to continue at a high level of £14 billion over five years, and for companies to take on more debt but also to be more cost-effective. Ian Byatt, the Director-General of Ofwat, built into his calculations assumptions that companies would have to reduce the rate of return on investments and achieve efficiency improvements. There would be a deceleration in the growth of profits and share-holder pay-outs (Bannister 1994).

How effective has Ofwat been in pursuing its remit of promoting high levels of performance among WSCs and WOCs? While any judgements must be tentative when we are so close to such contentious events, some observations may be made. First, it has to be admitted that the Director-General of Ofwat faces an unenviable task. As Wright (1992: 79) notes, it is more difficult than for the other utility regulators: 'He is overseeing an industry with rising prices, significant investment requirements, little competition, and the right to seek cost pass through for certain expenditures.' This situation leaves Byatt with little room for manoeuvre. Yet initially Ofwat seemed to be operating like a watchdog with bite. Early reference was made to its 'growling at the rise in the number of disconnections and the lack of consumer friendliness among the water companies' (McRae 1992). Ofwat put pressure on companies to carry out investments prescribed for under the first determination and warned that water prices would be reduced if the companies failed to carry out their obligations (Pitcher 1990).

Ofwat appears to have remained independent of the water companies – immune to 'regulatory capture'. In fact, very frosty relationships have developed occasionally between the industry and the regulator, for example over the processes involved in the determination and setting of the second K, which even led some companies to refer Ofwat to the Monopolies and Mergers Commission. Despite this the industry generally regards the regulatory regime in a positive light. In the opinion of Haddon and Turner (1995), the second determination was 'tough but fair'.

There are concerns over Ofwat, however, which derive less from how resolutely its remit has been pursued and more from certain inherent features of the system, which will be explored in the following sections. For example, the 1989 settlement provided that modernisation would be largely self-financed. Whereas it is difficult enough to reconcile relevant interests, the effect of the 1989 solution was, apparently, to more overtly than before pit the interests of consumers and the environment against one another. As the price increases permitted under the first determination began to be imposed, complaints over Ofwat's narrow interpretation of its role were increasingly made. According to Vidal (1994: 2), the regulator was allowing companies to be 'socially inert and over-rewarded for their low-risk, secure work in a unique market where there is no competition'.

For the first quinquennium there is little evidence that Ofwat was a force that frightened companies into a highly efficient delivery of quality services for customers. Only during the drought year of 1995, when they became very unpopular, did Ofwat adopt a more assertive posture towards the companies.

Assessment

Demand management

Over the second half of the twentieth century the main issues facing the water industry have shifted. From concerns over insufficient supply capacity in the 1960s, attention moved on to administrative and water-quality problems in the 1970s and 1980s. In the 1990s resource sufficiency has once again re-emerged as a major theme. As noted previously, the deceleration in the growth of demand for water in the 1970s and 1980s led to supply matters being approached with some complacency. By 1994 it was anticipated that the increase in the demand for public supplies would be less than one per cent per annum over the following twenty years ('Water demand to stay flat', *WB*, 18 November 1994: 4). Flat trends in aggregate demand, however, concealed considerable sectoral and regional diversity. Between 1975 and 1990 metered water consumption (primarily industrial consumption) virtually stood still. Growth in water consumption has not ceased. Domestic water demand, in particular, has grown steadily and is expected to expand by a further twenty per cent over the next twenty years ('Water demand to stay flat', *WB*, 18 November 1994: 4). Moreover, regionally, the increase in demand has been greatest in the south of the country, which has relatively low rainfall, thus exacerbating the resource problem.

Among the reasons for the increase in domestic consumption are new and developing household needs for water. The ownership of automatic washing-machines, which reached eighty-five per cent of all households in England and Wales by 1991, was a contributing factor. The acquisition of showers, dishwashers and garden sprinklers has also increased, though in truth, these appliances make a relatively small impact on total household consumption. Toilet flushing remains the single major use of water, accounting for thirty-two per cent of total household consumption, followed by washing, bathing and showering (seventeen per cent together), and clothes washing (twelve per cent) (Gray 1994: 4). Car washing and garden watering only account for three per cent of total domestic consumption (Kinnersley 1994: 94).

The buoyancy of water demand in the south of England coincided with an above-average number of drier years. This led to the issue of resource sufficiency resurfacing. While not matching the droughts of 1976 and 1984, fairly severe conditions were experienced in parts of the country for prolonged periods after 1988. The years 1989, 1990 and 1991 were ones with substantially below-average rainfall in England and Wales. Shortages persisted into 1992, although 1992 and 1993 witnessed normal rainfalls. The year 1995, however, as discussed more fully in the postscript, experienced quite exceptional drought conditions.

Low rainfall and high demand were not the only factors placing the water environment under stress. Rivers were utilised very intensively for the reception and purification of liquid effluent, as well as for recreational and amenity purposes and, along with underground aquifers, were subjected to high levels of direct abstractions. These pressures led to reduced river flows and declining aquifer levels. They produced large-scale ecological changes in some regions, particularly the chalk valleys of the South-East, like that of the Hampshire Avon. From lush, wet places with water meadows, reed-beds and abundant wildlife, some valleys altered drastically and some rivers like the Kent Darent threatened to dry up completely. To counter the effects of drier weather and heavy abstractions, the NRA sought remedial measures. For example, trial pumping from underground sources in the Vale of York was undertaken with a view to replenishing the River Ouse. Such responses created their own set of problems, including falling water tables and disappearing farm ponds (Pearce 1992). To meet the expanding needs of fast-growing towns in Hampshire, Dorset and Wiltshire, the chalk aquifers of that region were subjected to heavy pumping (Clover 1992). In certain acute cases, like the Hampshire Avon, the NRA was able to co-ordinate special rescue programmes for the restoration of the river and its wildlife, and to combat pollution (Watts 1994). Such pressures were not confined to the chalk catchments of the South-East. Similar conditions prevailed in the Vale of York, where rivers like the Ure, heavily dependent on a high water table, was also in danger of drying up. The NRA (Kinnersley 1994: 97) identified twenty rivers across the country where flows were severely depleted and a further twenty under excessive strain.

These relatively novel threats demanded, however, a more strategic response than simply rescue schemes for individual rivers. The old solution of building large-scale, fixed-site reservoirs was resorted to for a while. Thames, South West Water and other companies began to plan large, new reservoirs during 1993. Momentarily, the NRA was drawn to an investigation of supply-side strategies, echoing the policies favoured by the WRB in the 1960s. Desalination and the towing of icebergs even got a mention in a NRA publication of 1992 (cited in Kinnersley 1994: 101). This appears to have been a temporary lapse and, by 1993, the NRA was promoting a more forward-looking strategy for 'sustainable' water development sensitive to biological and ecological impacts. Meanwhile, distribution was greatly improved with the completion in March 1994 of the fifty-mile London ring main. Based on gravitation rather than pumping, it enables huge savings in energy to be made. The demise of a supply-side orientation within the NRA became clear with the publication of its conclusion in 1994 that, due to the introduction of techniques to curb demand and reduce waste, no more plans for new reservoirs or major new transfer schemes would be required for at least twenty years ('No more reservoirs are needed, says NRA', WB, 8 April 1994: 3).

The evolving situation led to the recognition that even intensive recycling systems and well-managed river regulation schemes might not provide sufficient answers to future challenges. As Kinnersley (1994: 99) comments, capital spending and improvements on sewage treatment, leading to improved effluent quality, may well be 'a vital process for putting water back into rivers'. But he adds, taking 'less water out of catchments from the outset is an even better policy where the flow is so low that it becomes potentially harmful to people and the ecology of the river'. In pursuit of new approaches the NRA and other bodies have investigated methods of encouraging economy in water use. Among those under discussion are cutting down on leakages in supply and distribution, more in-firm recycling of water, and water-saving changes in production processes stimulated through the use of economic instruments. Towards the end of 1995 the NRA suggested it might increase its relatively low charges on water abstractions in order to send the correct signals and encourage efficiency in use.

These responses illustrate the instruments which may be employed in pursuit of water demand management. This concept, which was strongly supported by the NRA, amounts to more than just encouraging frugality, but seeks to achieve sustainability, in the use of water resources. It involves taking account of future needs, and requires the various costs and benefits associated with the different techniques to be balanced. Water demand management may have to accommodate the possibility of the effects of climate change. There is some resistance to the view that changes in British rainfall patterns are connected to global warming. Water industry sources tend to see in recent trends greater variability in rainfall rather than a movement towards a drier climate. The exceptional drought of 1995 was described by the Meteorological Office as a 'once in 500-year event'. However, the Intergovernmental Panel on Climate Change now accepts that evidence of global warming due to human activity does exist. It is claimed that, globally, the last decade has witnessed nine of the warmest years on record (Monbiot 1995). Some suggest that it is prudent to build into strategies for water management the assumption that the above-average number of very dry summers in recent years is not simply the result of chance but may represent the beginning of a longer-run trend.

Turning to specifics, the metering of domestic supplies is an important instrument of demand management. It has acquired special relevance, as the Water Industry Act of 1991 requires water companies to discontinue the use of rateable value as a basis for charging after 31 March 2000. As long ago as the mid-1970s (CWPU 1975: 7), empirical tests demonstrated that metering could lead to significant reductions in water consumption, possibly by as much as thirty to forty per cent. A major trial conducted from 1989 under the aegis of Ofwat confirmed that domestic metering could realise significant reductions in water demand. Metering is also a technical aid to leak detection and, furthermore, as noted above, it can facilitate the development of common carriage to permit competition among suppliers. While some consumer groups are concerned that domestic metering might cause social hardship and discourage the use of an essential public health aid, the results of the national metering trials and other surveys do suggest that customers generally accept the notion of payment by volume. The resistance of some companies and the government's lukewarm attitude is another problem. The

1991 Act does not require metering, only the phasing-out of rates-based charges. Anglia Water are pressing ahead with metering, but Northumbria, North West Water and Welsh Water have all emphasised that this is a route which they intend not to take (Garrett 1993). Kinnersley (1994: 110–12) regards metering, despite some difficult issues which it raises, as an essential reform, as part of an overall strategy to promote the use of water in a sustainable manner.

Water quality

An important objective of the 1989 settlement was the creation of a framework which would enable a substantial increase in investment and, thereby, a significant improvement in British water quality to be achieved. Has sufficient evidence accumulated to suggest that the new regime will deliver these gains? As Barty-King (1992: 182) noted, the legacy of under-investment could not be corrected overnight, and he thought that ten years would be needed to make the effluent discharged from 4,300 STWs meet NRA and EC requirements.

The RCEP (1992: 94), commenting on recent water-quality trends, noted that: 'In terms of pollution, the measures which have at last been initiated may be no more than a first step.' Confronted by fairly widespread criticisms of the water industry, writers close to it sought to clarify its performance since privatisation. Of the results of the latest NRA river survey, Carney (1992: 30) commented that they showed:

> very small deterioration in the period, related to the five years 1985 to 1990. They do not reflect the improvements which have already taken place since privatisation in September 1989, or those from current investment programmes. The general river quality picture does not justify ringing declarations about an urgent need for dramatic new clean-up programmes. The facts do not match the rhetoric.

It was a fair defence that critical assessments of river quality in the early 1990s were observing the effects of the pre-1989 system, not the impact of the new regime. Moreover, the more vigorous policies being pursued by the regulators were, perhaps, obscuring the inception of favourable new trends. The NRA's more active enforcement policy led to successful prosecutions against polluters to increase significantly after 1989. The DWI undertakes literally millions of drinking water samples, almost all of which have recently met the required standards. The number of 'determinations' contravening prescribed values (ranging from taste and colour to the presence of pesticides) actually increased from 1989 to 1993. This, however, was considered by the WSA (1994: 21) 'not … to be indicative of worsening water quality, but rather the product of a more focused monitoring strategy'.

The more vigorous enforcement regime appears to have led to attitudinal changes and to have encouraged polluters to take steps to internalise pollution costs. Faced with the threats of prosecution or adverse publicity, some industrial dischargers take steps to reduce or eliminate the release of toxic effluent. Elf Aquitaine, for example, which owns chemical plants that discharge into the Mersey, invested £7 million in 1991 to bring its operations up to EU standards. Whereas in 1989 about eleven per cent of the investment undertaken by ICI member companies was spent on environmental improvement, by November 1991 this had climbed to between twenty and twenty-five per cent (Carney 1992: 30). Kinnersley (1994: 154–5) has also noted changes in attitude among leading companies. Some increasingly do not regard pollution abatement as an extra cost but as an integral part of the production process. Once this concept is accepted companies search for the most efficient methods of pollution control, and thereby contribute to environmental improvement.

Threats of prosecution and fines likewise have an impact upon the WSCs which run the STWs. The NRA has initiated proceedings which has led to several major water companies being heavily fined (Jury 1993). Such pressures have stimulated the companies to take steps to improve their STWs and reduce the discharge of bad effluent. Thames Water, for example, which 'when in government control' had the worst record of all in the 1980s, reduced the number of STWs failing to comply with consent standards from eighty-six to forty-seven by December 1991 (Brown 1991). A culture of compliance now pervades the WSCs, who with pride report on the progress made in meeting required standards.

This has been possible because of a massive increase in capital expenditure since 1989. Investment being undertaken in the 1990s to improve water quality and modernise STWs is between two and three times greater in real terms than the expenditure that was undertaken in the 1980s.

As a result of these efforts there has been a deceleration and ultimately a reversal in the growth of the number of reported pollution incidents. Despite the NRA's vigorous enforcement policy the number of 'major' incidents fell by forty per cent between 1991 and 1992 (Kinnersley 1994: 142). The NRA reported a twenty-eight per cent drop in major pollution incidents and a thirty-one per cent fall in the total number of incidents between 1993 and 1994 ('Large reductions in pollution', *WB*, 4 August 1995: 4). Further, the percentage of tested STWs breaching their consents in England and Wales has progressively fallen – from twenty-one per cent in 1987 to five per cent by 1992 (WSA 1994: 30).

Turning to water quality *per se*, recent surveys suggest an improvement in rivers has occurred in the 1990s. For example, the NRA reported an overall twenty-six per cent improvement in river-water quality between 1990 and 1994, with more than ninety per cent of rivers monitored by the latter date graded as 'good' or 'fair' ('Rivers are getting cleaner', *WB*, 4 August 1995: 3). Some environmentalists may question the methodologies and interpretations employed in the publication of water quality statistics by the official agencies. In the light of the history of pollution prevention in Britain, it is certainly right to be vigilant. But since 1989 disappointing evidence has not been concealed by the Authorities and it seems highly improbable that an attempt is made to distort the picture of actual trends in water quality. That it has improved in England and Wales is evidenced by better compliance with EU water directives. Compliance with the bathing-water directives improved from seventy per cent in England and Wales in 1987 to seventy-nine per cent in 1993, regional compliance with the drinking-water directives improved from ninety-four per cent in 1991 to ninety-seven per cent in 1993, and STW compliance with discharge consent conditions improved from seventy-nine per cent in 1987 to ninety-five per cent in 1992 (WSA 1994). Of nearly 3.5 million samples of drinking water inspected, 99.3 per cent met exacting EU quality standards in 1994. A sharp drop between 1990 and 1994 in the number of service reservoirs and treatment works detecting coliforms (organisms which indicate the presence of harmful bacteria) represents further evidence of a significant improvement in drinking water sources (Turner 1995: 8).

The WSCs have also been anxious to develop and publicise their efforts in building upon the conservation and environmental renewal projects of the RWAs. Applying the extent to which the rehabilitation of the water environment led to the return of wildlife to habitats, as an additional measure of water quality improvement, not surprisingly, a mixed picture emerges. On the one hand, the renowned rare birds, plants and insects of the Norfolk Broads still showed signs of diminishing, in the face of intensive farming methods and the high use of fertilisers (Ghazi 1995a). On the other hand, and taking a broader canvas, naturalists would be encouraged by reports of a revival of wildlife in many parts of the water environment due to the effects of the clean-up measures: squid, octopus and sea trout were returning to the Mersey estuary, salmon to the Clyde, lamprey to the Humber. Surveys reveal a significant increase in otter distribution in a number of regions. Seals were benefiting from falling pollution levels along the north-east coast. Many other examples could be given, but especial note may be made of the revival of the Trent, once one of the most foul rivers in England. The reduction of sewage pollution and other changes led an ecologist to refer to 'a spectacular recovery' of this river, where now anglers were able to catch loach, salmon and brown trout (Leake 1995).

A massive national effort has been embarked upon to correct the consequences of past neglect and to improve the water environment, so that EU and wider public obligations can be fulfilled. There are clear signs that the trend of deterioration has been reversed. To sustain this progress the priority and resources given to river and coastal improvement must be maintained at the high level which was achieved in the early 1990s.

The regulatory system

There is a view that the regulatory arrangements established in 1989 represent a well-structured compromise. Barty-King (1992: 178) has referred to how it combined the principle of public supervision, necessary when a monopolist delivers a commodity as vital as water, with private ownership, which supplies the market dynamism necessary for the efficient production of goods and services.

Regulatory innovation was not confined to the creation of the NRA and Ofwat. In addition, the DWI was established to monitor tap-water quality, the first time a national, as opposed to local, body was established with such a remit. Standards are no longer, as in the past, defined with reference to terms like 'wholesome' supplies, but are based on up to fifty parameters, based on EU directives, which set limits for pesticides and other substances and criteria for drinking-water supplies. The DWI lays down compliance programmes which companies must carry out when its standards are not met. Also relevant is Her Majesty's Inspectorate of Pollution (HMIP). While the NRA set requirements for the quality of effluent discharged into a water channel, the HMIP set standards for the actual technologies and processes employed within industrial units and other plants which release discharges.

Arguably there has been an over-proliferation of regulatory bodies. Commonly, sources count three main regulators with responsibilities in the water sector, but Goldring (1993) was able to identify nine. The number of regulators is of less importance than the charge that the specification of their responsibilities, together with other characteristics of the 1989 settlement, may produce overlap, conflict and operational inefficiencies. The existing system appears to create winners and losers too crudely. Setting low Ks seems favourable to consumers but hard on environmental improvement; setting Ks higher appears tough on consumers, potentially good for environmental targets, but soft on the companies. Such paradoxes are inherent in the regulatory model that has been adopted, and in particular arises from the decision to place the burden of financing the industry's modernisation upon internal sources. In some business situations the aversion to debt and a reliance on self-finance may represent sound practice. Hutton (1994) observes, however, that it makes less sense for the water industry today, the modernising of its aged infrastructure being a massive national undertaking. Hutton notes that under private ownership internally-generated funds are not free, but are owned by shareholders who, in the current market situation, may expect paybacks on their investments over a very short period. The industry, however, is now undertaking projects with time horizons of up to fifty years. In such a situation a greater use of external debt to finance improvements would be reasonable.

This issue is linked to the tensions which have developed between Ofwat and the NRA. For Barty-King (1992: 178) the two agencies pulled beneficially in opposite directions, the one championing the environment, the other the customer. But Helm and Rajah (1994) claim convincingly that the separation of environmental and economic regulation between the two is an unsatisfactory arrangement. This is especially the case because Ofwat, in its price-determination role, directly influences investment levels and, thereby, the tempo of environmental improvement, which is the concern of the NRA. Ofwat's tendency to comment on environmental policy led to public clashes between the regulators' two leaders, Crickhowell and Byatt. From 1993 Byatt suggested persistently that the raising of environmental standards to comply with EU requirements was becoming an unacceptable burden on consumers, on account of the higher bills they have to pay, and was probably unwarranted in cost-benefit terms. Byatt's advocacy of a lowering of EU standards infuriated Crickhowell. He denied that there was 'some mindless march towards an environmental Utopia, regardless of costs', maintaining that rising expenditure was the result of the long overdue drive to clean up the rivers, and claimed that EU directives were, in fact, 'urgently needed' (quoted in Brown 1993: 7; Vidal 1994: 3). Differences between the two continued to be publicly aired in 1995, although now Crickhowell seemed to be straying into Ofwat's sphere when he recommended that a greater part of the 'huge' water company profits should be devoted to cleaning up dirty rivers (Ghazi 1995b). It was virtually inherent in the arrangements constructed in 1989 that there would be tension between the two main water regulators and that they would find it difficult to stick to their remits: the NRA to set environmental standards and Ofwat, in particular, to confine itself to getting the water companies to achieve the least-cost solutions to the meeting of these standards.

The privatisation of water undertakings has certainly not, contrary to expectations, eliminated political interference from the water industry. There have been signs since 1993 that the Major government has been less anxious than the last Thatcher administration to display green credentials. It appeared to be sympathetic to Byatt's position over the need for a renegotiation of EU standards. In 1994 the Secretary of State for the Environment indicated that it would be appropriate for water companies to drop the requirement to exceed EU obligations, which would have the effect of significantly reducing the previously agreed programmes of investment down to the year 2000 (Helm and Rajah 1994). Further, the NRA was embarrassed by the Environment Secretary's decision to refuse to fund more than half of its bid to clean up 3,000 miles of badly polluted rivers (Vidal 1994). This undermined long-established targets for the reduction of river pollution and involved the rejection of 131 schemes put forward by the NRA for STW modernisation in England and Wales. The rationale for such action was that the NRA plans were simply too expensive.

For some years the government has been developing proposals for integrated pollution control (IPC). This approach recognises the existence of interlinkages in the natural environment and the possibility of the transfer of pollution from one medium to another. IPC offers a way of addressing any confusion of purpose which the regulatory system gives rise to, and creates an opportunity for extending the current strong approach to water pollution control to other media. The government also, however, links its interest in IPC to rather more traditional preoccupations, if presented in modern terms, namely the principle of BATNEEC ('best available technology not entailing excessive cost' – see Kinnersley 1994: 156–7).

To progress IPC, HMIP began to be formed as an executive unit from as early as 1987. The Environmental Protection Act of 1990 was a further step forward, providing for a multimedia approach to pollution control, covering air, water, land and substances prescribed by HMIP or local government inspectorates. In 1991 the government published proposals for an Environmental Protection Agency (EPA), so as to convert interest in IPC into concrete policies. Under the proposals responsibility for pollution control, currently dispersed across a number of agencies, would be centralised in an EPA. Initially there appeared a danger that integrated management would be undermined by the reform if the river-basin and environmental responsibilities of the NRA were divided between two bodies. The NRA lobbied vigorously against this, and won its case up to a point: it was not to be dismantled but to be transferred in its entirety to the EPA, where its structures would constitute, in staffing terms, easily the largest components.

The government published more refined proposals in a draft Environmental Protection Bill in October 1994. There were many misgivings about these plans, the details of which led many to question the government's environmental convictions. For example, whereas the NRA's duty was to 'further conserve and enhance the environment', the new agency merely had to 'have regard to the desirability of preserving the environment' (Brown 1993). In the NRA's view the government's draft guidelines placed too much stress on protecting industry from the potential impact of pollution controls, rather than protecting the environment, and it claimed that the need to justify every environmental protection move in detailed cost-benefit terms was biased in favour of industry ('EA guidelines attacked', *WB*, 11 August 1995: 4). Despite strong opposition the Bill received Royal Assent in the summer of 1995. The legislation provided for the transfer to the Environmental Agency of all the functions of HMIP, the NRA and the waste-regulation authorities, the agency assuming responsibility for IPC, provided for in the Environmental Protection Act of 1990, and commencing its duties from April 1996.

Thus, at the time of writing the entire UK environmental protection system was once again in a state of flux. From a water industry perspective, there may have been some merit in desisting from further regulatory reorganisations until more time had elapsed to take stock of the reforms introduced between 1989 and 1991. If changes were needed, it is arguable that some attention to the difficulties created by the separation of environmental and economic regulation was a more urgent need than establishing an EPA. On economic regulation, the water industry and other utility regulators have been subject to increasing scrutiny, and a view is emerging that for water, for example, the RPI+K model makes it difficult to achieve a reconciliation of consumer, water company, investor and environmental interests in a sufficiently flexible manner. During 1995 the government appeared to agree that there was a case for investigating the effectiveness of the current regulatory model for the privatised utilities.

Conclusion

Since 1989

An evaluation of the development of the water industry over the last five or six years, including an assessment of the privatisation reforms, must necessarily be tentative in nature at a moment so close to the events.

Whatever the shortcomings of the settlement of 1989, in a number of respects it was an ingenious reform, given the ideological parameters which defined the objectives of the responsible government. Relative to the previous situation, it established mechanisms whereby capital expenditure for major improvements in water quality would be funded much more adequately. An early assessment by McRae (1992) of the work of the regulators was favourable. He judged that they were already doing 'what Westminster failed to do when these industries were under public ownership: impose higher standards of service'. The new regulatory bodies represented an important, but very new-style, element of public-sector involvement, and were designed to promote business efficiency and environmental improvements. As the postscript will indicate, however, the patterns of commercial success and environmental investment which have occurred in the water industry since 1989 have proved very controversial. It is not evident that the new system creates benefits and costs which are fairly distributed among all interested groups.

On some matters more definite conclusions can be offered. For example, it is difficult to exaggerate the influence of EU environmental directives upon the development of water management and environmental protection systems in the UK. It significantly influenced the arrangements established in 1989, notably the creation of the NRA, as EU rules do not permit private companies to discharge regulatory duties. The separation of the operational business of running water services from regulatory and environmental protection functions was also a positive achievement. Events have emphasised the importance of ensuring the autonomy of the regulators.

Although the new arrangements were relatively rigorous, the 1989 settlement has proved fairly popular with the water industry. This suggests that it has provided the managerial freedoms and delivery from financial constraints anticipated by the exponents of privatisation. Of the K and AMP assessing functions of Ofwat, Brindley (1993: 80) has observed: 'This is such an important plank in the UK regulatory process that we must do all we can to make it work successfully . . . . This is not a stultifying cost-plus or rate-of-return model; we need the stimulus of the opportunities to retain the fruits of innovative thinking and effective management.' Satisfaction with the operation of the existing regulatory model is also registered by the stock market's valuation of water company shares, which have consistently outperformed indicators such as the FTSE 100 share index, which rose by twenty-two per cent between October 1989 and July 1993, while the shares in the leading WSCs increased by between eighty-five per cent and 135 per cent over this period (Kinnersley 1994: 179).

This evidence supports the impression that the industry has been operating within a fairly broad comfort zone and raises doubts as to how sharp the teeth of the regulatory watchdogs truly were. The WSCs appear content with their ability to handle relationships with the regulators. For example, as Kinnersley (1994: 172–3) observes, there appear to be limits to the extent to which Ofwat can pressurise the companies to move on with replacing the rates-based charging system with metering.

While the 1989 settlement did provide the water companies with a secure monopoly, their core business was regulated, but another dimension was the new opportunities for diversification. Initially, there was almost a flight of enterprise overseas to escape the constraints of the regulated domestic market. A number of the WSCs took leading positions in consortia for the provision of water and waste-water services throughout the world, for example in Malaysia, Thailand and Australia. Operating in relatively unfamiliar areas, however, has not proved as easy or as profitable as the companies had envisaged. It has been said of the industry that it 'has not exactly covered itself with glory, particularly when it has diversified outside its core regulated water and sewage business'. Many companies admit that non-core business takes up a disproportionate amount of management time, and produces losses or only small profits (Bannister 1995). This contrasts with the French franchising model, which contributed to the emergence of utility companies capable of demonstrating exceptional technological and commercial expertise at an international level (Hassan *et al.* 1996).

Kinnersley (1994: xv–xvi) outlines with great clarity current issues facing water industry professionals and policy-makers, for example on the need to introduce charges for water services based on sound economic principles. He is guardedly optimistic that the reforms and systems introduced since 1989 involve a greater dependence on market disciplines, and are contributing to a 'long, slow process of adaption to repair' the effects of market failure, which have become 'irreversible'. This writer, however, feels that an opportunity to inject greater competitive disciplines into the water sector was lost when the government decided that water privatisation should leave the managerial structures inherited from the RWA era virtually intact. Changes in ownership were a salient feature of the reform but do not, of themselves, promote competition or efficiency.

Turning to environmental protection, there is a large literature about the value of economic instruments for environmental policy. Although a preliminary step was made when the NRA started charging for consents in 1991, in general the market characteristics of UK environmental policy have been very weak. That the water companies strive to obtain a substitute for market information by carrying out numerous customer surveys only underlines the minimal impact of market signals upon corporate decision-making. Helm (1993) has gone so far as to describe the UK pollution prevention system as a 'chain of command', from the pinnacle of EU directives, down through various levels including NRA standards, with costs finally being dumped on consumers, not polluters, in the shape of higher prices permitted by Ofwat. There is no market role in this process, claims Helm, it is all intervention – in fact a command-and-control exercise. While this may be an overstatement, it is true that at the time of writing the influence exercised by competition upon managerial decision-making, or by economic instruments upon water users, is minimal.

To compensate for the lack of competitive disciplines in the product market, it was necessary for safeguards to be incorporated into the 1989 privatisation model. The regulator endeavours to inject some element of surrogate competition through the AMP-scrutiny and K-determination procedures. However, first, there remains doubt as to whether these processes do meaningfully reproduce competitive disciplines among suppliers. Second, they are complex and costly. Ofwat has considerable powers to investigate and to intervene in water company affairs. Kinnersley describes (1994: 170) this 'elaborate' system of supervision as 'heavyweight regulation indeed'. Contact between Ofwat and the companies are continual, the latter employing significant numbers of highly-qualified staff in regulatory departments to respond to Ofwat moves and to supply cost and operational information as required. Yet, for all the apparent regulatory rigour, companies remain confident in their market power.

Another observation provoked by recent experience is that the expectation that the transfer of water assets out of the public sector would help to inhibit political interference in the water industry has proved a little pious. In the past political failure, as much as market failure, has been the hallmark of the development of UK environmental protection policies. As has been seen, since 1993 water has again become a political hot potato, and some might feel that the government's recent interventions have not been especially creative.

Nevertheless, the final words on the post-1989 period should not be negative, as important gains have certainly been achieved during this short period. This may be better appreciated by placing the events of these years in a broader, long-run perspective.

General conclusion

This book covers the period from the industrial revolution to the end of the twentieth century. Over these years, water ceased to be treated virtually as a free gift from the heavens, and gradually came to be recognised as a resource which required careful management if it were to adequately perform its essential role in supporting human activity. Water does not deplete globally, but it does shift from one physical state or region to another. As Gray (1994: 43) notes: 'The total volume of water in the world remains constant. What changes is its quality and availability.' This process of change is the water cycle. Water, a renewable rather than a continuing resource, requires careful management if it is to be made available for indefinite exploitation. This is especially true in a small, densely populated island such as Britain, where small river basins receive relatively much greater pollution loads then those discharged from large conurbations in continental Europe or North America (Kinnersley 1988: 73). Degradation of sources and transfer pollution can cause long-term damage to the aquatic environment, creating difficulties for attempts at recycled usage. The history of water in England and Wales for the period in question is largely the history of how public policy and industrial structures have been slowly reformed in ways which take account of these imperatives. In the process water has been 'commodified' and provision de-municipalised, no longer a sudsidised public health service but the responsibility of commercial organisations (Parker and Sewell 1988: 766–7; Newson 1992a: 266). Latterly, however, the involvement of the State has, if anything, increased with the creation of powerful regulators.

Over the last two centuries water use has increased enormously, the use of the water environment for removing and purifying human-created wastes on a large scale during the early Victorian period being an especially important addition to the more obvious uses of water. As domestic and industrial consumption continued to grow it was necessary to establish the development and distribution of water on a more formal basis. Supply-side challenges were overcome through a decentralised, largely municipal approach to water management; this proved effective in harnessing the energy of civic and local interest, which was instrumental in enabling the expanding urban demand for water to be effectively met up to the inter-war years. Meanwhile, science aided municipal initiative in making significant progress in the treatment of potable water. Outside the more obvious public health dimension, the organisation of water and wastewater services on the municipal model, determined by local government interests and hydrologically inappropriate boundaries, proved much less successful in responding to the externalities of water use. Sewage treatment and pollution prevention remained very low-priority issues until recently. Also, other than for fisheries, it was only in the very recent past that the interests of amenity, nature conservation and recreational use of the water environment received greater consideration.

Among the reasons for the historical indifference towards water is that it displays many public good characteristics offering, also, many opportunities for free-riders. Further, public policy for much of the period was based on the premise that the public interest is enhanced by the maximisation of private interests. Also, propertied and industrial interests often opposed reforms, such as stricter anti-pollution legislation, which would limit their ability to externalise the pollution and other costs caused by their use of water resources. Through appealing to threats to the rights of property or threats to economic health, this lobbying often exercised a significant influence upon parliamentarians and policy-makers. Consequently, until the post-1945 period – arguably until 1973 – water reform tended to follow a piecemeal and partial pattern. Moves to introduce radical solutions were invariably postponed to a later date. Only when conditions came to be viewed as quite unacceptable for a modern society illustrated, for example, by Michael Heseltine's reaction to the condition of the Mersey in the early 1970s, did government come to accept that the results of past political and market failures in this field could no longer be ignored. Public perception of intolerability was manifested in the 'greening' of politics from the 1960s. Legislative and institutional means to combat water pollution were introduced in the 1950s and 1960s; effective action began to be taken from the late 1960s and, following a subsequent hiatus, from the late 1980s. Meanwhile, as it was recognised that pressures arising from the rapid increase in water demand formed part of a wider water-management problem, steps began to be taken to merge supply-side and resource conservation functions; important progress towards achieving a more integrated management of the water cycle was made with reforms in 1963 and 1973.

Thus water management has been thoroughly reformed over the last forty years. Integrated river-basin management was achieved with the establishment of the RWAs in 1973. Many remaining problems of environmental regulation were overcome with the formation of the NRA in 1989 and refinements to pollution prevention legislation enacted about that time. As a result the water industry is now better equipped to respond to society's requirements – from supplying tap water of invariably the highest quality, to meeting the needs of recreational users of the water environment. In a sense supporting the role of the regulators as watchdogs of the water industry and government are the environmental pressure groups, a more environmentally aware public (even organised into action groups vigilantly tracking the water companies for signs of mismanagement), and EU environmental law. As a result of these influences the long-term decline in the quality of English and Welsh waters was decisively reversed from the late 1980s. Environmental groups quite rightly waging a constant campaign on the government and industry for a further raising of standards, most probably would not agree with the optimistic conclusions offered here, and yet, by helping to maintain awareness of the issues, contribute to an improvement of water quality.

An economic and environmental history of water must take account of the complex interplay of political forces – of sectional interests and lobbies, and party-political or governmental forces pursuing their different agendas on water. The great challenge has been to reconcile and balance so many different interests, while achieving forward momentum on water reform. This writer is not absolutely convinced that the undoubted regulatory and water quality improvements of recent years are irreversible. Events over the period studied do not necessarily support the conclusion that the historical pattern of change in water management inevitably points onwards and upwards. Ultimately the gains which were made will become cumulative, only as long as the protection of the natural environment continues to command the general interest and support it has

Table 6.2   *Consumer satisfaction with water industry services, 1989–95 (%)* (respondents to MORI opinion polls expressing satisfaction with services)

	1989	July 1995
Overall service	85	74
Value for money	25	4
Drinking-water quality	75	59
Beach quality	47	59

Source: Haddon 1995.

attracted in recent decades; in other words, continuing environmental progress will be made only as long as the legislative body and political parties believe there are votes in water.

Postscript – 1995

Performance and public relations

It is unrealistic to try to incorporate the significance of near-contemporary events into a historical study. But those of 1995 seemed so calamitous for the water industry that neither could they be ignored entirely. Reactions to the industry's handling of its difficulties were very hostile, and were linked to other aspects of its 'performance' which had been receiving critical comment for some time.

Well before the full effects of the dry conditions of 1995 imposed themselves, the water industry had not enjoyed great popularity. Kinnersley (1994: 204) noted that the water utilities seemed isolated from effective dialogue with their customers, despite sophisticated but remote systems of enquiry or complaint. The number of complaints received by the water companies' consumer service committees increased from 4,613 in 1990/1 to 14,302 in 1993/4 (WSA 1994).

According to the results of MORI opinion polls summarised in Table 6.2, the only area where public satisfaction with the quality of the service supplied by the companies recently improved was with respect to bathing-beach waters. A telling indicator of consumer unease was booming sales of bottled water, growing at thirty per cent per annum by 1994 (Gray 1994). These negative consumer responses were a paradox because they occurred at a time when, as shown above, the quality of the water supplied by the companies, according to objective criteria, was in most respects improving.

Such contradictory trends may be attributable to growing dissatisfaction with the means of funding the industry's expansion and rewarding those who managed it. Consumer and environmental groups questioned whether the companies were achieving their economic miracle of buoyant profits and soaring share prices fairly (Vidal 1994). On the one side, note could be made of the fact that cost reductions were being made by laying off staff, with the total number of jobs lost between privatisation and 1995 being between 4,000 and 7,500, in ways that did not necessarily improve the quality of some services customers were receiving; even more negatively, water bills had increased substantially, by an average of seventy-seven per cent between October 1989 and July 1994, and by up to twenty-five per cent in any one year; disconnections, because of the non-payment of bills, were rising; and, allegedly, the unemployed and low-paid were being crippled by the weight of the water charges, the exaggerated claim even being made that 'Some pensioners are spending up to twenty-five per cent of their income on water' (Harrison 1994). On the other side, the following observation was made (Harrison 1994):

> The astronomical rise in consumers' water bills since privatisation has been matched by a spectacular increase in water companies' profits, salaries and dividends. The figures are an investor's dream: water companies' operating profits up on average 20 per cent each year … ; profit margins up from 28.7 per cent to 35.6 per cent; the industry's total share value up to £13 billion from £5.2 billion; and dividends are up by 58 per cent since 1989.

Indignation at the methods of financing the industry's modernisation, and of distributing the fruits of its financial success, intensified as attention shifted to the directorial rewards, which senior managements of the privatised utilities were able to secure for themselves. The row erupted over the seventy-five per cent pay increase, announced in 1995, to the Chief Executive of British Gas. The same issue arose in the water industry. It was alleged, for example, that the salary of one WSC chairperson in 1989 was £54,825, and increased by 1995 to £163,000 (Wilkinson and Cook 1995). What also caused comment was the use of the device of share options to bolster the rewards of top management in the utilities to very generous proportions. Also, these revelations were being reported at the very time that water company staff were being dismissed to improve 'efficiency', that charges were being increased and the industry was unable to handle the drought. Bonuses and share options were commonplace in the competitive private sector, but observers were unable to fathom how senior managers in the monopoly utilities, faced with little or no risk, had merited such generous rewards, which were frequently many times greater than those they had earned for doing the same work before privatisation. It was alleged that forty-four directors in the water industry enjoyed share options and benefits worth over £10 million by May 1995 (Nelson and Calvert 1995).

The water companies came under fierce attack on these issues. Also caught in the crossfire was Ofwat, not entirely out of sympathy with such assaults upon the companies, but also under criticism for the manner in which it was controlling the industry. Not surprisingly, the industry's tarnished image deteriorated further during 1995, when the companies, because of erratic rainfall, were unable to

execute their statutory duty of guaranteeing regular supplies of water to households. Nevertheless, some in the industry seemed genuinely puzzled at its falling
popularity ratings; a conference was organised in December 1995 to probe such
questions as (Economist Intelligence Unit): 'Is the industry the caring environmental custodian it would have us believe? Why is the industry's image so far
removed from the public view? Have managers simply failed to get the message
across or does the problem lie in the message itself?'

The drought

The drought of 1995 was one of the worst ever experienced in England and Wales.
The summer was one of the hottest, driest and sunniest since records began in
1727, and it is probable that the year overall was the warmest in the country for 340
years. The year did start wet, which led to groundwater levels being fairly well
charged; it was the regions that relied heavily on surface reservoirs which experienced the greatest difficulties later in the year.

Despite the great difficulties which the drought caused the water companies,
in the wake of the adverse publicity over other matters reaction to their handling
of the crisis was intense. The companies' unpopularity was so great that their staff
were even liable to violent assault when attempting to turn off vandalised fire
hydrants (Burdett 1995). Among the measures countenanced by the companies as
they endeavoured to balance supply and demand were the following: investigating
the possibility of pumping water from abandoned tin mines in Cornwall, negotiating with a soft-drinks company for the bottling of tap water so as to create a
crisis reserve for at-risk groups like invalids, abstracting more water from rivers
thereby threatening their ecological balance, and cutting off supplies to households
on a rota basis. Perhaps the most dramatic example of the crisis measures which
were taken was the non-stop shuttle of 1,000 road tankers, which transported water
from the abundant supplies in Kielder reservoir to West Yorkshire. By August,
twenty-two per cent of the population was under a hosepipe ban.

The water industry had to weather a storm of criticism. An unflattering contrast was made between the handling of the droughts in Yorkshire by local water
undertakings in 1959 and by the regional company in 1995. If the former were run
by 'often duds', they were chosen and liable to dismissal by the electorate, while
the performance by privatised company in 1995 had allegedly been inept
(Wainwright 1995). It was claimed that this company had told the wool industry,
which employs 25,000 in West Yorkshire, that it was imposing a fee to cover the
cost of treating water tainted by the industry, provoking the latter to threaten to
refuse bill payment; later, during the height of the drought the water company had
suggested firms should consider relocating to reduce water demand (Wilkinson
and Cook 1995). The unpopularity of this company, persistently hounded by the
pressure group Yorkshire Water Watch, was demonstrated in the unusual fact that
despite the firm's appeals for economies, demand for water did not alter greatly. A

report of its management of the crisis commissioned by the company appeared to support some the criticisms made of it during the drought, including a high leakage rate, bad forward planning and poor customer relationships. By November, it had imposed rota cuts in selected areas. Yorkshire was perhaps the region the most severely affected by the drought, with its reservoirs at only 17.4 per cent of capacity in November. However, other regions were also badly hit, including the North-West and the South-West, with reservoirs at 36.3 per cent and 33.2 per cent of capacity respectively (Editorial, *WB*, 17 November 1995: 3).

Critical evaluations of the water companies' handling of the drought led to their performance being scrutinised in the area of supply and conservation measures, particularly leak detection. Water demand management had been a concept more debated than acted upon in recent years. Allegedly some twenty per cent of supplies throughout the country, and up to thirty-seven per cent in Yorkshire, were lost through leaks, and very little had been done to introduce metering to assist leak detection. These criticisms were not managed very well. At first, exaggerated claims were made that billions had been invested in combating leaks and upgrading mains, for it to be later admitted that only £60 million per annum had been devoted to repairing leaks since 1989 (Calvert and Nelson 1995). Clearly a failure to act on the small, but important area of leak detection had occurred. Ofwat criticised the companies for failing to achieve agreed leakage targets: 'In many cases reductions planned, and paid for, in the price limits set in 1989 have not been achieved' (quoted in Bannister *et al*.1995).

Indignation increased with record profits and directorial rewards being announced as reports of management's mishandling of the water shortage were published. As one article was incautiously headlined, '"Obscene" profit fuels water anger' (Bannister and Wainwright 1995). The water companies' response to such public anger included the concession of cash rebates to customers, but this did little to placate opinion. In commenting on North West Water's payback in Spring 1995, Ian Byatt said that he did not think 'the special dividend for shareholders would have been acceptable without the pay-outs to customers' (quoted in Fagan 1995).

The drought drew Ofwat into adopting a more assertive posture towards the water companies. Its criticism of the failure to achieve leak reduction targets has been noted. During the summer, Ofwat demanded that the companies make refunds to customers where there were shortfalls in performance, and engaged the NRA and DWI to report back on companies that failed to achieve quality standards allowed for in the price limits set the preceding year. In November 1995, Ofwat appeared to accuse a number of companies of failing to meet targets over a wide range of activities, despite charging customers for the investment specified in these areas. The companies were required to report back with plans to remedy the claimed deficiencies (Barrie 1995). Subsequently, Ofwat prepared plans to impose penalties on companies which failed to meet leakage targets.

One can only speculate about the long-term significance of the 1995 drought. There is clear evidence that the companies are accelerating the introduction of water demand management. The drought may lead to some refinements to the regulatory system. Already Ofwat has toughened up its mode of relating to the companies. There are even hints that the government, normally quite positive about the performance of this privatised industry, might be adjusting its position. Ian Lang, the Trade and Industry Secretary, while defending the regulatory regime, did come close to conceding that it might require modification; it was still in an evolutionary phase, adding, 'As a system evolves it will build upon a record of sound achievement' (quoted in Bannister *et al.* 1995).

There has been considerable public discussion over the incentives built into existing arrangements for senior management to unduly favour performance as expressed in profitability and dividend pay-outs. Even Byatt observed that 'Meeting shareholders' wishes for ever-higher dividends could be inconsistent with the longer-term investment needs of the industry' (Fagan 1995). The industry – and its profitability – since 1989 benefited from low inflation and a slump in construction costs. But there was a feeling that customers had to shoulder too much of the burden of financing quality improvements. The consumer magazine, *Which ?*, complained that much of the £15 billion invested since 1989 has come from the higher prices customers have had to pay. In reply, the companies maintain that they are 'accelerating' their external borrowing, and that between two-thirds and seventy per cent of their profits are reinvested (Vidal 1994; Bright 1994). Such responses do not, however, constitute a denial that most capital expenditure has been internally financed since 1989. These recent events underline the tensions present in the existing institutional model, and emphasise the heavy burden that is placed upon the regulators to discharge their complex functions effectively.

References

Primary sources

BA (1848), AB 25/1/1, Records of the Bolton Waterworks Department, committee minutes, volume I.

BA (1854), ABPP/6/9, Bolton Improvement Act, briefs in support of bill.

BA (1864), ABPP/8/8, Bolton Improvement Act, briefs in support of bill.

BA (1871), ZAH/13/1A, Ainsworth Papers, brief re. opposition to South Lancashire Waterworks Bill.

BRL (1885a), Minutes of proceedings of the SC of the HL on the Bury Improvement Bill, 8 July.

BRL (1885b), Minutes of speech to the SC of the HL on the Bury Improvement Bill, 15 July.

BRL (1889a), Minutes of proceedings taken before the SC of the HL on the Bury Corporation Bill, 24 May.

BRL (1889b), Minutes of proceedings taken before the SC of the HL on the Bury Corporation Bill, 27 May.

BRL (1889c), Minutes of proceedings taken before the SC of the HL on the Bury Corporation Bill, 30 May.

BRL (1900), Bury, County Borough of, Report of the case for the corporation in the action brought by the Mersey and Irwell Joint Committee.

BRO (1845–1940), 40619/A/2/b–c, Bristol Water plc Records, Annual Reports.

LRO, PHM (County public health and housing committee minute books) (1902–60), 2–21.

LRO, PWM (County water and sewage sub-committee minute books) (1931–64), 1–2.

PRO (1923), HLG/50/81, minutes of the first meeting of the ACW, 18 January.

PRO (1925), HLG/50/108, South West Lancashire Water committee, September.

PRO (1927a), HLG/50/22, Notes by the Clerk, County Office, Preston, 21 January.

PRO (1927b), HLG/50/25, Warner, L. to Mersey Harbour Board, 28 January.

PRO (1929a), HLG/50/78, ACW, Second report of the legislation sub-committee, 22 April.

PRO (1929b), HLG/50/78, Report on waterworks clauses, 25 July.

PRO (1930), HLG/50/25, City of Liverpool, Report re discharge of crude sewage into the River Mersey.

PRO (1931), HLG/50/80, Annual Report of the ACW, year to 1 May.

PRO (1933a), HLG/50/36, Central Council for Rivers Protection, memorandum, 20 November.

PRO (1933b), HLG/50/110, Cox, R., paper on the National Water Grid, 20 November.

PRO (1934), HLG/50/108, Regional Committees, 2 March.

PRO (1936), HLG/50/81, minutes of meeting of ACW, 14 February.

PRO (1937), HLG/50/83, Wood, K., memorandum, 23 March.

PRO (1938), HLG/50/108, Report of a technical sub-committee, March.

PRO (1943a), HLG/50/2243, Memorandum of regional water committees, 8 April.

PRO (1943b), CAB/117/118, Committee on Water, Report, 30 July.

PRO (1944), HLG/50/1884, Restler, Col. J. to Milne, A., 28 March.

PRO (1948a), HLG/50/2274, Labour Party, Water supplies as a public service, September.
PRO (1948b), HLG/50/2265, minutes of first meeting, Committee on the causes of the increase in water consumption (water increase Committee), 10 December.
PRO (1949a), HLG/50/2265, minutes of interim report, water increase Committee.
PRO (1949b), HLG/50/2265, South Staffordshire Water Company, letter to MHLG, 17 January.
PRO (1949c), HLG/50/2265, minutes of fourth meeting, water increase Committee, 25 February.
PRO (1949d), HLG/50/2098, Fenwick, A. to Farner, I., 30 June.
PRO (1950a), CAB/124/234, Nationalisation of public water supply, 10 March.
PRO (1950b), CAB/124/234, memorandum by Lord Privy Seal, A National Water Scheme, 11 May.
PRO (1951a), HLG/50/2075, Pearce, C. J. to Holmes, H.
PRO (1951b), CAB/124/234, Pimlott, J. A. R., Water, 14 February.
PRO (1951c), HLG/50/2100, Mills, L. to Dalton, H., 24 February.
PRO (1951d), HLG/50/2100, Hutchinson, H. to Dalton, H., 28 March.
PRO (1951e), HLG/68/104, secretaries of the three associations to Symon, H., 12 July.
PRO (1953), HLG/127/102, Jenkins, A. M., The Water Act, 1945, 17 December.
PRO (1954), HLG/127/102, Hutchinson, Sir G. to Macmillan, H., 2 March.
PRO (1955a), HLG/50/2075, report on Rivers Act 1951: extension to tidal water, 12 January.
PRO (1955b), HLG/127/102, WCA, Reorganisation of the water supply industry, April.
PRO (1955c), HLG/50/2542, Tyneside sewage disposal, April.
PRO (1957a), HLG/50/2850, Coventry and District Anglers' Association, telegram, 5 June.
PRO (1957b), HLG/50/2850, Notes on river pollution, November.
PRO (1958), HLG/127/63, CACW, sub-committee on growing demand for water, First Report.
PRO (1959), HLG/127/67, draft cabinet paper of Home Affairs Committee, Water supplies, November.
WRO, RB (West Riding of Yorkshire River Board Records).
WRO, RB (1930), Central Council for River Protection: deputation to Christopher Addison on Land Drainage Bill.
WRO, WA (Wakefield & Ardsley Joint Sewerage Committee minute book, 1897–99).

Parliamentary papers

Royal Commission on the Sewage of Towns, *Preliminary Report* (1857–58) [2372], XXXII.
Royal Commission on Water Supply to the Metropolis and Large Towns (1867–69), XXXIII.
Royal Commission on Rivers Pollution, *First report* (Mersey and Ribble), vol. I (1870) [c.37], XL.1.
Royal Commission on rivers pollution, *Sixth report* (Domestic water supply of G.B.) (1874) [c.1112], XXXIII. 311
Report from the Joint Select Committee on the water supplies (Protection) Bill [H. L.], together with the *Proceedings of the Committee* (1910) (226), vi. 563.
Return of water undertakings (1914), LXXXIX (395).
Royal Commission on Sewage Disposal, Fourth Report (1904) [Cd.1883; Cd.1886-II]; *Final report of the Commissioners, General summary of conclusions and recommendations* (1915) [Cd.7821].
Board of Trade (1920), *Second interim report of the water power resources committee* [Cd.776], xxv. 483.
Report of the Royal Commission on Land Drainage in England and Wales (1927) [Cd.2993].
Joint Committee on water resources and supplies (1934–35), vol. II, minutes of evidence, appendix (121), vi. 503.
Report from the Joint Committee on water resources and supplies, Proceedings of the Committee (1935–36), minutes of evidence and appendix (159), vi. 983.
Report by the Joint Committee of the House of Lords and the House of Commons appointed to consider the Water Undertakings Bill [H. L.], *Proceedings of the Committee and minutes* (1938–39) (130), viii. 513.
Ministry of Health (1942–43), *Third report of the Central Advisory Committee* [Cd.6465], vi. 707.
Ministry of Health (1943–44), *A National Water Policy* [Cd.6515] ,viii. 717.

HM Government (1960), *Public investment in Great Britain* [Cd.1203], London, HMSO.

Ministry of Housing and Local Government (1961), *Pollution of the tidal Thames*, London, HMSO.

(Proudman report), Central Advisory Water Committee, Sub-committee on growing demand for water (1962), *Final report*.

Ministry of Housing and Local Government (1963), *Conference on water resources in the North-West*, London, HMSO.

Ministry of Housing and Local Government (1958–71):
> *Report for 1957* [Cd.419];
> *Report for 1965–66* [Cd.3282];
> *Report for 1969–70* [Cd.4753].

(Jeger Report), Ministry of Housing and Local Government, Welsh Office (1970), *Taken for Granted: Report of the working party on sewage disposal*, London, HMSO.

Department of the Environment (1971), *The future management of water in England and Wales: A report by the Central Advisory Committee*, London, HMSO.

Royal Commission on Environmental Pollution (1972), *Third report: pollution in some British estuaries and coastal waters* [Cd.5054], London, HMSO.

Department of the Environment, Welsh Office (1973), *A background to water reorganisation in England and Wales*, London, HMSO.

Department of the Environment (1973), *Out of Sight, Out of Mind: report of the working party on sludge disposal in Liverpool Bay*, vol. 3, London, HMSO.

Department of the Environment, Welsh Office, Ministry of Agriculture and Fisheries (1976), *Review of the water industry in England and Wales*, London, HMSO.

Department of the Environment (1982a), *Abolition of the Water Council*, London, HMSO.

Department of the Environment (1982b), *Cleaning up the Mersey*, London, HMSO.

Department of the Environment, Welsh Office (1986), *The Water Environment, The Next Step. The Government's consultative proposals for environmental protection under a privatized water industry*, London, HMSO.

HM Government (1990), *This Common Inheritance: Britain's environmental strategy*, London, HMSO.

HM Treasury (1990), *Economic briefing*, no. 1, London, HMSO.

Royal Commission on Environmental Pollution (1992), *Sixteenth report: Freshwater quality*, [Cd.1966], London, HMSO.

Hansard, Parliamentary Debates, House of Commons.

Other sources

Addyman, O. T. (1979), 'The utilization of research results in catchment control', in G. E. Hollis (ed.), *Man's Impact on the Hydrological Cycle*, Norwich, Geo Abstracts, 243–50.

Allen, E. (1976), *Wash and Brush Up*, London, A. & C. Black.

Ashmend, F. (1879), 'Report presented to the Committee of the Sanitary Authority on the disposal of the sewage of Bristol, Committee of the Sanitary Authority, Bristol, 22 May.

Baker, K. (1990), 'Why privatisation has paid off for the public', *Observer*, 14 October, 5.

Bannister, N. (1994), 'Water price rules take heat off consumers', *Guardian*, 29 July, 2.

Bannister, N., Smithers, R., and Hunter, T. (1995), 'Ofwat attacks leaks failure', *Guardian*, 1 December, 23.

Bannister, N., and Wainwright, M. (1995), '"Obscene" profits fuels water anger, *The Guardian*, 30 November, 2.

Barber, B. (1982), 'Municipal government in Leeds, 1835–1914', in Fraser, D. (ed.), *Municipal Reform and the Industrial City*, Leicester, Leicester University Press, 61–110.

Barber, L. (1983), 'Water: time running out', *Sunday Times Business News*, 30 January, 57.

Barrie, C. (1995), 'Watchdog renews water attack', *Guardian*, 14 November, 19.

Bartrip, P. (1985), 'Food for the body and food for the mind: the regulation of freshwater fisheries in the 1870s', *Victorian Studies*, **28**, 285–304.

Barty-King, H. (1992), *Water The Book: An Illustrated History of Water Supply and Wastewater in the United Kingdom*, London, Quiller Press Ltd.

Beavis, S. (1994), 'Consumer groups say ruling is step in right direction', *Guardian*, 29 July, 2.

Bellak, J. (1988), 'The customers' benefits from privatisation', *WB*, 14 October, 330, 9–11.

Bidwell, R. (1992), 'Meeting standards effectively', in Gilland, T. (ed.), *The Changing Water Business*, London, CRI, 17–26.

Biggs, A. (1949), 'A Geographical Study of Water Resources in England and Wales', unpublished M.Sc. thesis, University of London.

Bilsky, L. J. (ed.) (1980), *Historical Ecology: Essays on Environmental and Social Change*, Port Washington, NY, National University Publications.

Binnie, G. M. (1981), *Early Victorian Water Engineers*, London, Thomas Telford.

Bolton, County Borough of (1947), *A Record of the Development of the Bolton Corporation Waterworks Undertaking During the Past Hundred Years 1847–1947*, Bolton, County Borough.

Bolton Chronicle.

Bolton Free Press.

'Bolton's sanitary crusade' (1902), *The Municipal Journal*, 21 February, 11: (473), 151–152.

Bowden, S., and Offer, A. (1994), 'Household appliances and the use of time: The United States and Britain since the 1920s', *Economic History Review*, 47: (4), 725–48.

Bowler, P. J. (1993), 'Science and the environment: new agenda for the history of science', in Shortland, M. (ed.), *Science and Nature: Essays in the History of the Environmental Sciences*, Oxford, Alden Press for the British Society for the History of Science, 1–22.

Bright, M. (1994), 'A very costly clean-up', *Guardian: Educational Supplement*, 19 April, 11.

Brindley, J. (1993), 'Capital efficiency, asset management plans and output monitoring', in Gilland, T. (ed.), *Efficiency and Effectiveness in the Modern Water Business*, London, CRI, 73–84.

Bristol, Corporation of (1898), *Main Drainage: Report*, Bristol, Sanitary Committee of the Corporation.

BWA (1950), *Organization of the Water supply Industry: Report to the Executive Committee*, October.

Broome, R. J. (1971), 'Pollution and the development of water resources', unpublished M.Sc. thesis, Victoria University of Manchester.

Brown, P. (1991), 'NRA to force clean-up of "sewer" rivers', *Guardian*, 12 December, 5.

Brown, P. (1993), 'Quangos clash over standards of water quality and rising bills', *Guardian*, 7 April, 7.

Brown, P., Wolf, J., and White, M. (1992), 'Britain guilty of breaching drinking water standards', *Guardian*, 26 November, 3.

Burdett, J. (1995), 'Terror of the cool-off mobs', *Manchester Evening News*, 11 August, 1.

Calvert, J., and Nelson, D. (1995), 'Water leaks are low priority', *Observer*, 27 August, 1.

Carney, M. (1992), 'The cost of compliance with ever higher quality standards', in Gilland, T. (ed.), *The Changing Water Business*, London, CRI, 27–50.

CSO (1964/74–1988), *National Income and Expenditure*, London, HMSO.

CWPU (1975), *Household Use of Water*, Technical note 7, CWPU, Reading.

CWPU (1978a), *The Impact of Social and Economic Factors on Consumption*, Technical note 29, CWPU, Reading.

CWPU (1978b), *Long-term Trends in Per Capita Consumption of Water*, Technical note 34. CWPU, Reading.

Chattock, H. E. (1926), 'Bristol and its water supply', *The Engineer*, 27 August, 231–2.

Chevalier, L. (1973), *Labouring Classes and the Dangerous Classes in Paris in the First Part of the Nineteenth Century*, London, Routledge.

Clapp, B. W. (1994), *An Environmental History of Britain since the Industrial Revolution*, London, Longman.

Clifford, F. (1887), *A History of Private Bill Legislation*, vol. II, London, Butterworths.

Clover, C. (1992), 'River of no return?', *Daily Telegraph*, 3 May, 6.

Coleman, D. (1994), 'A sewage celebration', *WB*, 16 December, 635, 14.

Cooper, J. A., and Smith, L. G. (1960), 'The utilisation of water in the chemical industry', *Proceedings of the Institute of Civil Engineers*, **17**, 1–14.

Cowan, R. S. (1983), *More Work for Mother: The Ironies of Household Technology from the Open Hearth to the Microwave*, New York, Basic Books, Inc.

Cowe, R. (1991), 'Chemical producers battle to turn tide on Britain's rivers of death', *Guardian*, 2 May, 13.

Craine, L. E. (1969), *Water Management Innovations in England and Wales*, Washington, DC, John Hopkins Press for Resources for the Future.

'Croydon leads the way' (1995), *WB*, 23 June, **659**, 5.

Davies, G. (1992), 'Catchment management planning', in Gilland, T. (ed.), *The Changing Water Business*, London, CRI, 1–16.

Davies, P. (1989), *Troughs and Drinking Fountains*, London, Chatto & Windus.

DoE (1985), 'Water privatisation: a discussion paper', in Terry, F. (ed.), *Privatisation in the Water Industry*, London, Public Finance Foundation, 67–81.

De Rance, C. E. (1897), 'Hydro-geology and hygiene – Law and Legislature, *TWE*, **1**, 53–73.

Dickinson, H. W. (1954), *Water Supply of Greater London*, Leamington Spa and London, printed for the Newcomen Society at the Courier Press.

Dimock, M. E. (1933), *British Public Utilities and National Development*, London, George Allen & Unwin Ltd.

Dingle, A. E. (1982), '"The monster nuisance of All": landowners, alkali manufacturers and air pollution, 1828–1864', *The Economic History Review*, **2**(35), 529–48.

'Discussion on the "The Water Supplies Protection Bill, 1910"' (1910), *TWE*, **15**, 22–38, 220–33.

Dixon, F. J. (1920), Presidential Address, *TWE*, **25**, 6–22.

Dupuy, G. (1982), 'Types of urbanisation and sewage techniques', in Laconte, P., and Haines, Y. Y. (eds), *Water Resources and Land-use Planning: A Systems Approach*, The Hague, M. Nijhoff, 243–54.

'EA guidelines attacked' (1995), *WB*, 11 August, **666**, 4.

Economist Intelligence Unit (1995), The Water Industry: The Slings and Arrows – conference registration details, *The Economist*, 1 December.

Editorial (1995), 'Resourcewatch', *WB*, 17 November, **680**, 3.

Editorial (1902), *The Municipal Journal*, 12 December, **11**(473), 1015.

Elliott, A. (1982), 'Municipal government in Bradford in the mid-nineteenth century', in Fraser, D. (ed.), *Municipal Reform and the Iindustrial City*, Leicester, Leicester University Press, 111–62.

Ellis, J. B. (1979), 'The nature and sources of urban sediments and their relation to water quality', in Hollis, G. E. (ed.), *Man's Impact on the Hydrological Cycle*, Norwich, Geo Abstracts, 199–216.

Elsdon, G. D. (1941), 'Sanitation and water purification', *Reports of the Progress of Applied Chemistry*, **26**, 470–87.

'The Epping epidemic and the East London water supply (1932), *WWE*, **34**, 340–20.

Escritt, L. B., and Rich, S. F. (1949), *The Work of the Sanitary Engineer: A Textbook on Water Supply, Sewerage and the Sanitation of Buildings*, London, MacDonald & Evans Ltd.

Fabry, J. (1991), *Water Reflections*, Cambridge, Granta Editions for Lyonnaise des Eaux.

Fagan, M. (1995), 'Ofwat warning as North West announces payout', *Independent*, 31 March, 41.

Falkus, M. (1977), 'The development of municipal trading in the nineteenth century', *Business History*, **19**, 134–61.

Flick, C. (1980), 'The movement for smoke abatement in 19th-century Britain', *Technology and Culture*, **21**, 29–50.

Foreman-Peck, J., and Millward, R. (1995), *Public and Private Ownership of British Industry 1820–1920*, Oxford, Oxford University Press.

Fowler, Sir H. (1900), 'Municipal finance and municipal enterprise', *Journal of the Royal Statistical Society*, **63**, 383–409.

Gardiner, J. L., and Cole, L. (1992), 'Catchment planning: the way forward for river protection in the

UK', in Boon, P. J., Callow, P., and Petts, G. E. (eds), *River Conservation and Management*, Chichester, J. Wiley, and Sons.

Garner, J. H. (1933), 'Sanitation and water purification', *Reports of the Progress of Applied Chemistry*, **18**, 679–710.

Garrett (1993), 'Metering: the jury's out', *WB*, 17 September, **574**, 8–9.

Ghazi, P. (1995a), 'Norfolk Broads wildlife faces toxic overload', *Observer*, 27 August, 2.

Ghazi, P. (1995b), 'Use profits for clean-up, bosses told', *Observer*, 16 April, 3.

Gill, L. (1953), 'The river pollution prevention officer: an inquirer and coordinator', paper presented to *The Institute of Sewage Purification Annual Conference*, 23 June.

Glick, T. F. (1980), 'Science, technology and the urban environment: The Great Stink of 1858', in Bilsky, L. J. (ed.), *Historical Ecology: Essays on Environment and Social Change*, Port Washington, NY, National University Publications, 122–39.

Goddard, N. (1995), 'The urban pactolus: reflections on the "sewage question" in Victorian Britain', paper presented to the Annual Environmental History Association Conference, University of Cambridge, May.

Goldring, M. (1993), *Water* (television production written and presented by Mary Goldring), A Juniper Production, Channel Four, February.

Goubert, J. (1986), *The Conquest of Water*, Cambridge, Polity Press.

Gourley, H. J. F. (1935), Presidential Address, *TWE*, **40**, 12–23.

Gray, B. M. J. (1986), 'Bristol's sewage and the birdlife of the tidal River Avon', *Proceedings of the Bristol Naturalists Society*, **46**, 19–24.

Gray, N. F. (1994), *Drinking Water Quality: Problems and Solutions*, Chichester, J. Wiley & Sons.

Green, J. (1848), 'Account of the recent improvement in the drainage and sewerage of Bristol', Excerpt minutes of proceedings of the Institute of Civil Engineers, London.

Guruswamy, D., Papps, I., and Storey, D. J. (1983), 'The development and impact of an EEC directive: the control of discharges of mercury into the aquatic environment', *Journal of Common Market Studies*, **22**(1), 71–100.

Gustard, A., Cole, G., Marshall, D., and Bayliss, A. (1987), *A Study of Compensation Flows in the UK*, Institute of Hydrology, Report no. 99, November.

Haddon, M. (1994), 'Barking up the right tree', *WB*, 1 July, **612**, 10–11.

Haddon, M. (1995), 'Fact and friction', *WB*, 7 July, **661**, 8.

Haddon, M. and Turner, A. (1995), 'Efficiency rules OK', *WB*, 7 April, **647**, 8–9.

Hall, J. (1949), 'Peril in the bath tub', *Daily Mail*, 13 May.

Halsall, M. (1989), 'A row that just won't dry up', *Guardian*, 8 August, 11.

Hamlin, C. (1982), 'Edward Frankland's early career as London's official water analyst, 1865–1876: the context of "previous sewage contamination"', *Bulletin of the History of Medicine*, **56**, 56–76.

Hamlin, C. (1985a), 'Providence and putrefaction: Victorian sanitarians and the natural theology of health and disease', *Victorian Studies*, **28**(3), 381–411.

Hamlin, C. (1985b), 'William Dibdin and the idea of biological sewage treatment', *Technology and Culture*, **29**, 189–218.

Hamlin. C. (1987), *What Becomes of Pollution? Adversary Science and the Controversy on the Self-Purification of Rivers in Britain, 1850–900*, New York and London, Garland Publishing.

Hamlin, C. (1988), 'Muddling in Bumbledon: on the enormity of large sanitary improvements in four British towns, 1855–1885', *Victorian Studies*, **32**(1), 55–83.

Hamlin, C. (1990), *A Science of Impurity: Water Analysis in Nineteenth-Century Britain*, Berkeley and Los Angeles, University of California Press.

Hamlin, C. (1994), 'Environmental sensibility in Edinburgh, 1839–1840: the "fetid irrigation" controversy', *Journal of Urban History*, **20**: (3), 311–39.

Hardy, A. (1984), 'Water and the search for public health in London in the eighteenth and nineteenth centuries', *Medical History*, **28**, 250–82.

Hardy, A. (1993), *The Epidemic Streets: Infectious Disease and the Rise of Preventive Medicine, 1850–1900*, Oxford, Clarendon Press.

Harper, B. (1992), 'Business excellence everyone wins', in Gilland, T. (ed.), *The Changing Water Business*, London, CRI, 97–118.

Harrison, D. (1994), 'Water economics just won't wash', *Observer*, 24 July, 11.

Hassan, J. (1984), 'The impact and development of the water supply in Manchester, 1568–1882', *Transactions of the Historic Society of Lancashire and Cheshire*, 133, 25–45.

Hassan, J. (1985), 'The growth and impact of the British water industry in the nineteenth century', *Economic History Review*, 2(38), 531–47.

Hassan, J. (1995), 'The water industry 1900–51: a failure of public policy?', in Millward, R., and Singleton, J. (eds), *The Political Economy of Nationalisation in Britain 1920–1950*, Cambridge, Cambridge University Press, 189–211.

Hassan, J., Nunn, P., Tomkins, J., and Fraser, I. (1996), *The European Water Environment in a Period of Transformation*, Manchester, Manchester University Press.

Hassan, J., and Taylor, P. (1996), 'The politics of water in early and mid Victorian Britain, Manchester Metropolitan University, Department of Economics Discussion Paper no. 96–01.

Hassan, J., and Wilson, E. R. (1979), 'The Longdendale water scheme 1848–1884', *Industrial Archaeology*, 14(2), 102–21.

Helm, D. (1993), 'Market mechanisms and the water environment-are they practical?', in Gilland, T. (ed.), *Efficiency and Effectiveness in the Modern Water Business*, London, CRI, 21–34.

Helm, D., and Rajah, N. (1994), 'Water regulation: the periodic review', *Fiscal Studies*, 15(2), 74–94.

HM Government (1990), *This Common Inheritance: Britain's environmental strategy*, London, HMSO.

Hibbert, F. (1948), 'A description of the Liverpool water undertaking, 1847–1947', *WWE*, May, 51, 202–11.

Hobbs, A. T. (1950), *Manual of British Water Supply Practice*, Cambridge, W. Heffer, & Sons Ltd for The Institution of Water Engineers.

Hodgson, A. (1991), *The Story of the Bristol Waterworks Company 1939–1991*, Bristol, Bristol Waterworks Company.

Houston, A. C. (1913), *Studies in Water Supply*, London, Macmillan.

Houston, A. C. (1917), *Rivers as Sources of Water Supply*, London, John Bale, Sons & Danielsson Ltd.

Howarth, W. (1992), 'New strategies for water directives', *European Environmental Law Review*, 1(4), 117–21.

Hoyle, N. (1987), *Reservoirs from Rivington to Rossendale: A Short History*, Warrington, NWWA.

Hutton, W. (1994), 'Water profiteers should have been made to borrow', *Guardian*, 29 July, 12.

Institution of Water Engineers and Scientists Handbook 1985–86, London, The Institute.

Jackson, A. A. (1973), *Semi-Detached London*, London, George Allen & Unwin.

Johnson, P. (1986), 'Operational developments and regulatory functions', in Institution of Water Engineers and Scientists, *Symposium on Regulatory Aspects of Water Services*, London, IWES, 4(2), 1–5.

Johnston, P. A., Stringer, R. L., and French, M. C. (1991), 'Pollution of UK estuaries: historical and current problems', *The Science of the Total Environment*, 106, 55–70.

Jones, E. L. (1979), 'The environment and the economy', in Burke, P. (ed.), *The New Cambridge Modern History, XIII, Companion Volume*, Cambridge, Cambridge University Press, 15–42.

Jones, F. C. (1946), *Bristol Water Supply and its Story 1847–1946*, Bristol, St Stephens Press.

Jones, G. (1985), 'A management view of the privatisation possibilities', in Terry, F. (ed.), *Privatisation in the Water Industry*, London, Public Finance Foundation, 47–62.

Jordan, A. G., Richardson, J. J., and Kimber, R. H. (1977), 'The origins of the Water Act of 1973', *Public Administration*, 55, 317–34.

Jury, L. (1993), 'Muddying the waters', *Guardian*, 16 July, 13.

Kay, J. A., and Thompson, D. J. (1986), 'Privatisation: a policy in search of a rationale', *The Economic Journal*, 96, 18–32.

Kearns, G. (1991a), 'Biology, class and the urban penalty', in Kearns, G., and Withers, C. W. J. (eds), *Urbanising Britain: Essays on Class and Community in the Nineteenth Century*, Cambridge, Cambridge University Press, 12–30.

Kearns, G. (1991b), 'Cholera, nuisances and environmental management in Islington, 1830–55', *Medical History*, Supplement no. 11, 94–125.

Kinnersley, D. (1985), 'The regulatory framework: essential safeguards or a constraint on enterprise', in Terry, F. (ed.), *Privatisation in the Water Industry*, London, Public Finance Foundation, 3–14.

Kinnersley, D. (1988), *Troubled Water: Rivers, Politics and Pollution*, London, Hilary Shipman.

Kinnersley, D. (1994), *Coming Clean: The Politics of Water and the Environment*, Harmondsworth, Penguin.

Kirby, C. (1984), *Water in Great Britain*, Harmondsworth, Penguin.

Kneese, A. V., and Bower, B. T. (1968), *Managing Water Quality: Economics, Technology, Institutions*, Baltimore, MD, John Hopkins Press for Resources for the Future.

Kuchenrither, R. D., and Gay, S. D. (1994), 'Sludge – a common problem', in Eden, G., and Haigh, M. (eds), *Water and Environmental Management in Europe and North America*, Chichester, Ellis Horwood, 371–8.

Lambert, A. (1988), 'Regulation of the River Dee', *Regulated Rivers: Research and Management*, **2**, 293–308.

Lanz, K. (1995), *The Greenpeace Book of Water*, Newton Abbot, David and Charles for Cameron Books and Greenpeace Publications.

'Large reductions in pollution' (1995), *WB*, 28 July, **664**, 4.

Lawson, J. D. (1986), 'Conservation of the environment', in Institution of Water Engineers and Scientists, *Symposium on Regulatory Aspects of Water Services*, London, IWES, 2(1), 1–5.

Leake, J. (1995), 'Wildlife returns to cleaned-up rivers', *Sunday Times*, 13 August, 6.

Lean, G., and Pearce, F. (1989), 'Your tap water: pure or poisoned', *Observer Magazine*, 6 August, 16–24.

Lee, C. H. (1991), 'Regional inequalities in infant mortality in Britain, 1861–1971: patterns and hypotheses', *Population Studies*, **45**, 55–65.

Lees, E. A. (1914), 'Birmingham's water supply', *Municipal Journal*, 24 April, **23**, 501.

Liverpool, City of (1903), *Handbook Compiled for the Congress of the Royal Institute of Public Health*, Local Executive Committee, Liverpool.

Lloyd, J. G. (1978), 'Underground dereliction in the North West', *Royal Society Seminar*, 1 February.

Lockyer, A. G. (1957), 'A study of water supply in Derbyshire', *East Midlands Geographer*, 32–44.

Lowe, P. D. (1983), 'Values and institutions in the history of British nature conservation', in Warren, A., and Goldsmith, F. B. (eds), *Conservation in Perspective*, Chichester, J. Wiley, and Sons, 329–52.

Lucas, A. F. (1937), *Industrial Reconstruction and the Control of Competition: The British Experience*, London and New York, Longmans.

Luckin, B. (1986), *Pollution and Control: A Social History of the Thames in the Nineteenth Century*, Bristol, Adam Hilger.

Luckin, B. (1990), *Questions of Power: Electricity and Environment in Inter-War Britain*, Manchester, Manchester University Press.

Lynk, E. L. (1993), 'Privatisation, joint production and the comparative efficiencies of private and public ownership: the UK water industry', Casec, *Fiscal Studies*, **14**(2), 98–116.

McFadzean, A. (1987), *Wythburn Mine and the Lead Miners of Helvellyn*, Ulverston, Red Earth Publications.

Macgregor, D. (1930), 'Problems of rationalisation', *The Economic Journal*, **40**(159), September, 351–68.

Maclean, M. (1991), *French Enterprise and the Challenge of the British Water Industry: Water Without Frontiers*, Avebury, Gower Publishing Co.

Macleod, R. M. (1967), 'Government and resource conservation: the Salmon Acts Administration, 1860–1886', *Journal of British Studies*, **7**, 114–50.

McRae, H. (1992), 'A new robustness in regulation', *The Independent*, 11 June, 29.

Maddison, A. (1982), *Phases of Capitalist Development*, Oxford, Oxford University Press.

Massa, I. (1993), 'The paradox of insignificant change: perspectives on environmental history'. *Environmental History Newsletter*, 5, 3–14.

Manchester Corporation (1974), *Water for Millions 1920–1974*, Manchester, The Corporation.

Maund, R. (1982), 'The Greater Manchester adventure: an exercise in strategic environmental improvement', *Environmental Education and Information*, 2(2), 79–96.

'Memorandum on the Final Report of the Water Power Resources Committee' (1922), *WWE*, 20 July, 24, 241–45.

'Memorandum to the Report on National Water Policy' (1935), reprinted in *TWE*, 40, 7–16.

Mersey and Weaver River Authority (1965/66–1972/73), *Annual Reports*, Warrington, River Authority.

Millward, R. (1989), 'Privatisation in Historical perspective: the UK water industry', in Cobham, D., Harrington, R., and Zis, G. (eds.), *Money, Trade and Payments: Essays in Honour of D. J. Coppock*, Manchester, Manchester University Press, 188–209.

Mitchell, B. (1971), 'Water in England and Wales: supply transfer and management', Department of Geography, University of Liverpool, Research paper 9.

Mnobiot, G. (1995), 'Last warning on earth', *Guardian*, 14 December, 19.

MYB (*The Municipal Yearbook*), London, The Municipal Journal Ltd.

NEDO (1986), *The nation's infrastructure: water*, London, NEDO.

NRA (1993), *The Quality of the Humber Estuary 1980–1990*, Bristol, NRA.

NRA (1995), *The Mersey Estuary: A Report on Environmental Quality*, Bristol, NRA.

NWC (1974/75–1978/79), *Annual Reports and Accounts*, London, NWC.

NWC (1978), *Water Industry Review 1978*, London, NWC.

NWC (1982), *Water Industry Review 1982: Supporting Analysis*, London, NWC.

Nelson, D., and Calvert, J. (1995), 'Share greed', *Observer*, 14 May, 12–13.

Netbuoy, A. (1968), *The Atlantic Salmon*, London, Faber & Faber.

Newcastle upon Tyne, City and Council of (1958), *Report to be Presented for Consideration at the Council Meeting*, Newcastle Town Improvement and Street Committee, 28 July.

Newson, M. (1992a), *Land, Water and Development: River Basin Systems and Their Sustainable Management*, London, Routledge.

Newson, M. (1992b), 'River conservation and catchment: a UK perspective', in Boon, P. J., Callow, P., and Petts, G. E. (eds), *River Conservation and Management*, Chichester, J. Wiley and Sons, 385–96.

'No more reservoirs are needed, says NRA' (1994), *WB*, 8 April, 600, 3.

NWWA (1974/75–1988/89), *Annual Reports and Accounts*, Warrington, NWWA.

NWWA (1983), *Improving Rivers, Estuaries and Coastal Waters*, Warrington, NWWA.

NWWA (1984), *Long Term Improvement Programme For Sewers and Sewage Treatment*, Warrington, NWWA.

O'Brien, T. H. (1937), *British Experiments in Public Ownership and Control*, London, George Allen & Unwin Ltd.

Parker, D. J., and Derrick Sewell, W. R. (1988), 'Evolving water institutions in England and Wales: an assessment of two decades of experience', *Natural Resources Journal*, 28(4), 751–85.

Parker, D. J., and Penning-Rowsell, E. C. (1980), *Water Planning in Britain*, London, George Allen & Unwin Ltd.

Parker, P. (1913), *The Control of Water as Applied to Irrigation, Power and Town Water Supply Purposes*, London, Routledge.

Pearce, F. (1992), 'The great drain robbery', *Guardian*, 30 October, 23.

Pepper, D. (1984), *The Roots of Modern Environmentalism*, London, Croom Helm.

Petts, G. E., and Lewin, J. (1979), 'Physical effects of reservoirs on river systems', in Hollis, G. E. (ed.), *Man's Impact on the Hydrological Cycle*, Norwich, Geo Abstracts, 79–92.

Pitcher, G. (1990), 'Water watchdog warns nine on capital spend', *Observer*, 7 October, 58.

Pitkethly, A. S. (1990), 'Integrated water management in England', in B. Mitchell (ed.), *Integrated Water Management: International Experiences and Perspectives*, London, Bellhaven Press.

Pooley, M. E., and Pooley, C. G. (1984), 'Health, society and environment in Victorian Manchester', in Woods, R., and Woodward, J. (eds), *Urban Disease and Mortality in Nineteenth-Century England*, London, Batsford, 148–75.

Porter, E. (1978), *Water Management in England and Wales*, Cambridge, Cambridge University Press.

Prentice, R. (1981), '"Welsh Water" and the effectiveness of the Water Charges Equalisation Act 1977', *Water Supply and Management*, 5(3), 283–93.

Priestly, C. H. (1905), 'Municipal ownership of water undertakings', *TWE*, **10**, 114–26.

Ravetz, A. (1968), 'The Victorian coal kitchen and its reformers', *Victorian Studies*, 11(4), 435–60.

Read, G. (1979), 'Manchester's main drainage system past and present', Report to the Highways Committee of Manchester City Council, 24 July.

'Regulatory aspects of water services' (1987), *European Water and Sewage*, January, **91**(1091), 30–4.

Reid, K. (1995), 'Neighbourly advice', *WB*, 2 June, **656**, 8–9.

Rennison, R. W. (1979), *Water to Tyneside: A History of the Newcastle and Gateshead Water Company*, Newcastle-upon-Tyne, Newcastle and Gateshead Water Company.

Renton, J. (1989), 'Water: quantity vs quality', *Observer*, 30 July, 55.

'Report of the Joint Conference of the Institution of Water Engineers, the British Waterworks Association, and the Water Companies Association on National Water Policy' (1935), appendix to *TWE*, **40**, 1–6.

'Report of the water areas and statistics Committee on the "Water Supplies Protection Bill"' (1910), *TWE*, **15**, 213–33.

Reynolds, R. (1943), *Cleanliness and Godliness: Or the Further Metamorphosis*, London, George Allen & Unwin Ltd.

Richards, T. (1982), 'River Pollution in Industrial Lancashire', unpublished Ph.D. thesis, Lancaster University.

Richardson, J. J., Jordan, A. G., and Kimber, R. H. (1978), 'Lobbying, administrative reform and policy styles: the case of land drainage', *Political Studies*, **26**, 47–64.

'Rivers are getting cleaner' (1995), *WB*, 4 August, **665**, 3.

Robson, B. T. (1971), *Urban Analysis: A Study of City Structure*, Cambridge University Press, Cambridge.

Rofe, B. H. (1994), 'The impact of reservoirs on the environment', in Eden, G. E., and Haigh, M. (eds), *Water and Environmental Management in Europe and North America: A Comparison of Methods and Practices*, Chichester, Ellis Horwood, 119–30.

Rose, C. (1991), *The Dirty Man of Europe: The Great British Pollution Scandal*, London, Simon & Schuster.

Russell, C. (1983), *Science and Social Change 1700–1914*, London, Macmillan.

Rydz, B. (1974), 'Water needs and resources', in Funnell, B. M., and Hey, R. D. (eds), *The Management of Water Resources in England and Wales*, Farnborough, Saxon House, 1–35.

'Sewage disposal' (1920/21), *MYB for 1920/21*, 510–15.

Sheail, J. (1981), *Rural Conservation in Inter-War Britain*, Oxford University Press, New York.

Sheail, J. (1982), 'Underground water abstraction: indirect effects of urbanisation upon the country-side', *Journal of Historical Geography*, 8(4), 395–408.

Sheail, J. (1983), 'Planning, water supplies and ministerial power in inter-war Britain', *Public Administration*, **61**, 386–95 .

Sheail, J. (1986a), 'An historical perspective on the development of a marine resource: the Whinstable oyster fishery', *Marine Environment Research*, **19**, 279–93.

Sheail, J. (1986b), 'Government and the perception of reservoir development in Britain: an historical perspective', *Planning Perspectives*, **1**, 45–60.

Sheail, J. (1987), 'Historical development of setting compensation flows', appendix A1 in Gustard, A., Cole, G., Marshall, D., and Bayliss, A., *A Study of Compensation Flows in the UK*, Institute of Hydrology, report 99, November, 1–28.

Sheail, J. (1993a), 'Pollution and the protection of inland fisheries in inter-war Britain', in Shortland,

M. (ed.), *Science and Nature: Essays in the History of the environmental Sciences*, Oxford, Alden Press for the British Society for the History of Sciences, 41–57.

Sheail, J. (1993b), 'Public interest and self-interest: the disposal of trade effluent in inter-war England', *Twentieth Century British History*, 4(2), 149–70.

Sheail, J. (1993c), 'Sewering the English suburbs: an inter-war perspective', *Journal of Historical Geography*, 19(2), 433–47.

Sheail, J. (1993d), '"Taken for granted" – the inter-war West Middlesex Drainage Scheme', *London Journal*, 18(2), 143–56.

Sheail, J. (1996), 'Town wastes, agricultural sustainability and Victorian sewage', *Urban History*, 23(2), 189–210.

Sidwick, J. M., and Murray, J. E. (1976), 'A Brief History of Sewage Treatment', *Effluent and Water Treatment Journal*, February, I, 65–71; April, II, 193–9; June, III, 295–303; August, IV, 403–9; October, V, 515–20; December, VI, 609–16.

Simon, O. (1986), 'Investing in the Infrastructure', *National Westminster Quarterly Review*, May, 2–16.

Sleeman, J. P. (1953), *British Public Utilities*, London, Sir Isaac Pitman & Sons.

Smith, C. T. (1969), 'The drainage basin as an historical basis for human activity', in Chorley, R. J. (ed.), *Water, Earth, and Man: A Synthesis of Hydrology, Geomorphology and Socio-Economic Geography*, London, Methuen, 101–10.

Smith, F. B. (1979), *The People's Health 1830–1919*, London, Croom Helm.

Smith, K. (1972), *Water in Britain: A Study in Applied Hydrology and Resource Geography*, London, Macmillan.

Speight, G. (1986), 'Planning the infrastructure', *Water Services: The Journal for Water, Sewage and Industrial Effluent*, 90(1083), May, 195–6.

Spencer, F. H. (1911), *Municipal Origins*, London, Constable.

Steinberg, T. L. (1990), 'Dam-breaking in the 19th-century Merrimack Valley: water, social conflict and the Waltham-Lovell mills', *Journal of Social History*, 24(1), 25–46.

Stephenson, T. (1989), *Forbidden Land: The Struggle for Access to Moorland and Mountain*, Manchester, Manchester University Press.

Stilgoe, H. E. (1930), Presidential Address, *TWE*, 35, 10–18.

Styles, P. W., and Robinson, G. K. (1984), 'Planning and implementing a sewerage strategy', paper A1, *Conference on the Planning, Construction, Maintenance and Operation of Sewerage Systems*, Cranfield, BHRA, 1–10.

Surrey, M. (1982), 'United Kingdom', in A. Boltho (ed.), *The European Economy: Growth and Crisis*, Oxford, Oxford University Press, 528–53.

Szreter, S. (1992), 'Mortality and public health, 1815–1914', *Recent Findings in Economic and Social History*, Spring, 14, 1–4.

Taylor, G. (1946), Presidential Address, *TWE*, 51, 22–32.

Taylor, I. C. (1976), '"Black spot on the Mersey": a study of environment and society in eighteenth and nineteenth century Liverpool', unpublished Ph.D. thesis, University of Liverpool.

Taylor, S. M. (1986), 'Bristol's water supply – history and environmental aspects', *Proceedings of the Bristol Naturalists Society*, 46, 11–18.

Thompson, J. T. (1935), 'Sewage disposal', *MYB for 1935*, 1249–55.

Tomkins, J. (1996), 'Instruments for water quality management', in Hassan, J. *et al.*, *The European Water Environment in a Period of Transformation*, Manchester, Manchester University Press, 38–64.

Tomkins, J., and Wharton, A. (1996), 'The water resource: economic characteristics, industrial structure and management', in Hassan, J. *et al.*, *The European Water Environment in a Period of Transformation*, Manchester, Manchester University Press, 18–37.

Turing, H. D. (1947), *Second Series of Reports on Pollution Affecting Rivers in England and Wales*, prepared for British Field Sports Society.

Turing, H. D. (1952), *River Pollution*, London, Edward Arnold.

Turner, A. (1995), 'World class wate', *WB*, 7 July, 661, 8.

Twort, A. C. (1963), *A Textbook of Water Supply*, London, Edward Arnold.

Tyneside Joint Sewerage Board (1974), *Tyneside Joint Sewerage Board 1966–1974: the polluted Tyne*, Newcastle, Sewerage Board.

Veal, T. H. P. (1950), *The Supply of Water*, London, Chapman & Hall Ltd.

Vidal, J. (1994), 'A twist of the tap', *Guardian: Supplement*, 28 July, 2–3.

Wainwright, J. (1995), 'The dry and the mighty', *Guardian: Supplement*, 14 November, 2–3.

Walklett, H. J. (1993), 'The pollution of the rivers of Lancashire by industrial waste between *c.* 1860 and *c.* 1900', unpublished Ph.D thesis, Lancaster University.

Wall, D. (1994), *Green History: A Reader in Environmental Literature, Philosophy and Politics*, London, Routledge.

Walters, R. C. S. (1936), *The Nation's Water Supply*, London, Ivor Nicholson & Watson Ltd.

Warren, A., and Goldsmith, F. B. (1983), 'An introduction to nature conservation', in Warren, A., and Goldsmith, F. B. (eds), *Conservation in Perspective*, Chichester, J. Wiley and Sons, 2–15.

WB (*Water Bulletin: Weekly Journal of the Water Industry*), London, WSA.

'The water enterprises of some of our larger towns' (1898), *British Medical Journal*, 29 October, 1351.

'Water demand to stay flat' (1994), *WB*, 18 November, **631**, 5.

'Water pollution: survey of the River Tees' (1932), *WWE*, **34**, 497–500.

WRB (1964/65–1973/74), *Annual reports*, London, HMSO.

WRB (1973), *Water resources in England and Wales*, vol. I, *Report*, London, HMSO.

WSA (1992), *Waterfacts 1992*, London, WSA.

WSA (1994), *Waterfacts 1994*, London, WSA.

'Water supply matters' (1922), *Municipal Journal*, 493.

'Water supply: obligations of Water Authorities' (1932), *WWE*, 20 July, 34, 343–5.

Watts, S. (1994), 'Hampshire Avon granted £15 million to fight pollution', *The Independent*, 4 August, 7.

Weale, A. (1992), *The New Politics of Pollution*, Manchester, Manchester University Press.

Webb, S. and Webb, A. (1922), *Statutory Authorities for Special Purposes*, London, Longmans.

Wegmann, E. C. E. (1918), *Conveyance and Distribution of Water for Water Supply*, New York, D. Van Nostrand Company.

Wilkie, J. S. (1986), 'Submerged sensuality: technology and perceptions of bathing', *Journal of Social History*, **19**(4), 649–64.

Wilkinson, P., and Cook, L. (1995), 'Chairman's exit at Yorkshire Water may start a flood', *The Times*, 26 December, 2.

Winpenny, J. (1994), *Managing Water as an Economic Resource*, London, Routledge.

Wohl, A. S. (1983), *Endangered Lives: Public Health in Victorian Britain*, London, Methuen.

Wood, L. B. (1982), *The Restoration of the Tidal Thames*, Bristol, Adam Hilger.

Wright, J. (1992), 'Economic regulation in the water industry', in Gilland, T. (ed.), *The Changing Water Business*, London, CRI, 73–96.

Wright, L. (1960), *Clean and Decent: The History of the Bathroom and the W.C.*, London, Routledge & Kegan Paul.

Yarwood, D. (1981), *The British Kitchen: Housewifery since Roman Times*, London, Batsford.

YWA (1974–1988), *Annual Reports and Accounts*, Wakefield, YWA.

Index